STREETWISE FRANCHISING

STREETWISE FRANCHISING

Everything You Need to Know About Taking
Up and Running a Successful Franchise

Danielle Baillieu

Century · London

To James

First published in the United Kingdom in 1988 by Hutchinson Business

This edition published in the United Kingdom by
Century Limited
Random House, 20 Vauxhall Bridge Road, London SW1V 2SA

Random House Australia (Pty) Ltd
20 Alfred Street, Milsons Point
Sydney, NSW 2061, Australia

Random House New Zealand Ltd
18 Poland Road, Glenfield
Auckland 10, New Zealand

Random House South Africa (Pty) Ltd
PO Box 337, Bergvlei, South Africa

Random House UK Limited Reg. No. 954009

ISBN 0 7126 6129 8

Set in Times by SX Composing Ltd, Rayleigh, Essex
Printed and bound in Great Britain by Clay's Ltd, St Ives plc

Contents

How To Use This Book

This book will not make you a 'franchise expert' overnight. But it will help you make the right decision. By carrying out the DIY research outlined you will automatically ensure that you only consider the opportunities that offer you a good return on your investment.

The following method of working through this book will prove the most beneficial:

* Read the book quickly to get a general idea of what franchising is all about.

* In your second reading concentrate on and digest the following chapters:

    Chapter 3 – Raising Finance
    Chapter 4 – Organizations to consult
    Chapter 11 – Other sources of information

* Go through the franchise listing at the back of the book to see if anything interests you. Also read the franchise magazines listed on page 233 and my newspaper column in the *Evening Standard* (Mondays in the Business pages) to keep informed of new developments.

* If you are interested in a particular franchise then obtain as much information about the business including a copy of the contract and then read the following again:

Chapter 5 – Preliminary enquiries. Work through the questions and record the answers in writing.
Chapter 6 – Research a franchise. Actively carry out the research procedure outlined.
Chapter 7 – The franchise contract. Understand the implication of the clauses in general, bearing in mind that franchise contracts differ.

If the franchise opportunity of your choice survives the close scrutiny outlined in this book then get a second opinion (from a franchise consultant or franchise solicitor) before signing on the dotted line.

Making a large monetary investment will be one of the biggest decisions of your life. Don't leave it to chance. And remember no matter how much research you carry out business always carries risk – although with a franchise that risk is considerably reduced.

Acknowledgements

I would like particularly to thank Professor John Adams for his kind assistance and constant support over the last several years. Much has happened since the first edition of this book. I would like also to take this opportunity to thank all those who were involved in making the first edition a success and those who have assisted in updating the book: William Baillieu, Professor Martin Mendelsohn, Mansoor Ishani, Steven Kenton, Brian Smart of the BFA, Michael Power, Peter Stern of the National Westminster Bank, Robert Valentine and PizzaExpress.

My family and friends have been a source of constant support, patience and encouragement and I'd like to thank Sheila Baillieu, William Baillieu, James Baillieu and Ernie Perry.

Foreword to the Second Edition

by Margaret Stone, Editor, *Enterprise Money Mail*

Running one's own business is everybody's daydream at some time or another. The redundancies which stemmed from the harsh recession of the early 90s coupled with dramatic technological changes in the workplace mean that many have no option but to set up in business for themselves.

It's an exhilarating and liberating choice, but it can be dangerous too. Of the 400,000 small firms which are set up every year, one in three will cease trading. But the good news is that few of those are franchisees.

Franchising is a superb half-way house for entrepreneurs who have the personal and psychological characteristics for 'doing their own thing' combined with the strategic marketing advantages that a large corporation can bring.

Since its launch in 1990, *Enterprise Money Mail*, the small business section of the *Daily Mail*, has regularly covered franchising as a major small business topic. I have been consistently impressed by the enthusiasm of franchisees for their new career, and by their success.

Franchisees believe in the enterprise culture; they believe in hard work; they know they can create jobs for others; and they all look forward to taking on their next franchise.

There are about 400 franchise operations in the UK with an estimated turnover of £5 billion a year – and over 85 per cent of them are trading profitably. But the fact that franchising is so successful is also a tribute to the bankers, accountancy firms and business consultancies which advise the hundreds of men and women who are ready to take the plunge into franchising.

High on the list of those who give invaluable advice is Danielle Baillieu, who has been one of the most prolific writers on this topic, even at a time when it was less fashionable than it is now. She draws on her experience both as a lawyer and an ex-franchisee to give her readers the hard facts of franchising: the do's and don't's, what to look for from the franchisor and what questions you should ask yourself before signing up.

The sound and solid principles of *Streetwise Franchising* provide a practical route to becoming a successful franchisee.

Preface

Does franchising work? And if so, why does it sometimes go wrong and how can problems be avoided?

Franchising is big business. Witness household names that are part of the franchise success story: McDonald's, Burger King, Kentucky Fried Chicken, PizzaExpress, Servicemaster, Kall Kwik and Dyno Rod. The list is very long and ever-increasing.

The franchise industry currently consists of about 400 franchise systems which have an overall turnover of about £5 billion. Statistics show that franchising has survived the onslaught of the recession and fared far better than traditional business start-ups.

Inevitably there have been casualties. Headline stories of 'people losing their life savings' have been few and far between but there have been a number of unexpected collapses of well-known names. So, how do you choose the right franchise business?

The keys to success are:

Information
Good advice
Being in the right place at the right time with the right idea
Hard work
A lot of luck
And remembering there is no such thing as zero risk

While professional advice is essential initial DIY research will cut down your costs. In this book franchise problems are highlighted so you will know what to look out for. There are many good franchises – they sell themselves. They do not rely on artificial hype and un-realistic earnings projections.

As a business person you must be au fait with basic accounting principles. This book gives you the basics of what you need to know.

A franchise relationship is unique. There are many areas of law involved, some of them quite complex. The franchise contract is dealt with 'clause by clause' allowing you to grasp the spirit behind the contract and enabling you to appreciate the implications of various clauses and the need for professional advice before signing on the dotted line.

This book has been written to give you an overall picture of franchising – warts and all. If you're an existing franchisee with a problem this book will show you how to handle your situation and objectively outline the options open to you. It explains everything from the role of consultants to what to do if the worst happens – and you have to close down.

There is no better teacher than adversity. My first lesson in franchising way back in the eighties was an eye opening experience that was to be the foundation of not only the first edition of this book but years of franchise consultancy and journalism.

How could a 'blue chip' franchise that was a member of the British Franchise Association and a household name suddenly go bust leaving franchisees (many of whom, like myself, had only been trading for a few months) high and dry without an investment? That franchise was The Youngs Group which consisted of Pronuptia bridal wear, La Mama maternity wear and Youngs formal wear hire.

Because of the franchisors collapse I found myself in the unenviable position of having premises in an excellent location – but with inadequate, unsaleable stock. Luckily property prices were still commanding high premiums and I was able to sell my retail premises and recoup some losses.

Determined to recover my initial franchise investment I found lady luck once again on my side; the franchisor had gone into liquidation but the business had been sold on.

Having graduated in business law I felt sure that I had a legal claim. So, my next step was to commence discussions with the new franchisor. These eventually led to an out of court settlement. I had to sign a 'secrecy undertaking' so as not to divulge any details.

The consequences of the Youngs fiasco were a disaster for most of my fellow franchisees. Some lost their homes – others their marriage. It was impossible not to feel incredible anger against the franchisor who disappeared as a tax exile to Spain.

Back in the eighties the downside of franchising was a well-kept secret. My mission in writing the first edition of *Streetwise Franchising* was to highlight the problems and thereby ensure that every potential franchisee invested wisely.

The response to the book has been phenomenal. Not only have I been contacted by numerous potential franchisees for advice but also by existing franchisees experiencing problems. Over the last several years I have been able to use 'amicable negotiating skills' to successfully resolve franchise disputes out of court.

In most cases I have negotiated cash settlements for franchisee clients. It doesn't work in every case but I reckon it works in 95 per cent of the cases I handle. Problems are not confined to small franchisors. Most of the cases I deal with are big high street names.

Problems are an inevitable part of business life but good franchisors resolve them effectively and quickly. The franchise horror stories we read about always involve irresponsible franchisors – who often know nothing about ethical franchising.

The aim of this book is to shed light on the realities of franchising as a commercial business practice. So often, franchisees are referred to as 'soft entrepreneurs'. It is my intention to ensure that they are well-informed soft entrepreneurs.

This book is a realistic down to earth approach to franchising. It may not be welcomed by everyone in the industry but it certainly has the support of many professionals who have given unlimited time and support in the preparation of this work.

The book will go a long way to ensuring that franchisees – potential and existing – are well-informed in all aspects of franchising – an essential ingredient for ethical franchising.

1

Franchising as a legal concept

DEFINITION OF FRANCHISING

Franchising is not easily defined. The term is sometimes applied loosely and even inaccurately to distribution and licensing arrangements, for example petrol distribution and manufacturing licensing. You may come across the terms 'first generation' and 'second generation' franchising; these tend to be used by the US Department of Commerce. First generation franchises are the petrol service station and soft drink bottler types where there is a franchised dealer concentrating on one company's product line. The second generation franchise is the one with which you will be primarily concerned – i.e. business format franchising.

Business format franchising involves the franchising company (franchisor) granting a licence to its franchisees for a predetermined financial return (usually an initial franchise fee with or without future royalty payments). The franchisee is then entitled to a complete business package whereby the franchisor makes available to the franchisee:

1) Expertise and market research.
2) Financial planning based on their expert experience.
3) Training.
4) Support.
5) The use of the corporate name.

In theory the above should enable the franchisees to operate their own businesses to exactly the same standards and format as all the other units in the franchised chain.

1

For those of you who want to delve deeper into the franchising realm the British Franchising Association defines a franchise as:

A concentrated licence granted by one person (the franchisor) to another (the franchisee) which:
a) permits or requires the franchisee to carry on, during the period of the franchise, a particular business under or using a specific name belonging to or associated with the franchisor; and
b) entitles the franchisor to exercise continuing control during the period of the franchise over the manner in which the franchisee carries on the business which is the subject of the franchise; and
c) obliges the franchisor to provide the franchisee with assistance in carrying on the business which is the subject of the franchise (in relation to the organization of the franchisee's business, the training of staff, merchandising, management or otherwise); and
d) requires the franchisee periodically, during the period of the franchise, to pay the franchisor sums of money in consideration for the franchise, or for goods or services provided by the franchisor to the franchisee; and
e) which is not a transaction between a holding company and its subsidiary (as defined in section 154 of the Companies Act 1948) or between subsidiaries of the same holding company, or between an individual and a company controlled by him.

This definition may be compared with that of the International Franchise Association:

A franchise operation is a contractual relationship between the franchisor and franchisee in which the franchisor offers or is obliged to maintain a continuing interest in the business of the franchisee in such areas as know-how and training; wherein the franchisee operates under a common trade name, format or procedure owned or controlled by the franchisor, and in which the franchisee has or will make a substantial capital investment in his business from his own resources.

Comparing and contrasting the above two definitions show that:

1) A franchise is a *contractual relationship* under which the franchisor grants a *licence* to the franchisee to carry on business under a name etc., owned or associated with the franchisor.
2) The *franchisor controls* the way in which the franchisee carries on the business.
3) The franchisor provides the franchisee with *support*.

4) The *franchisee* provides and *risks his own capital*.

In many cases a franchisee is given a specific territory within which to operate and this will be stated in the franchise contract.

The franchise relationship has both advantages and disadvantages. Everyone considering a franchise must be aware of these and should weigh them up carefully and assess them in relation to their own experience and personality to ensure that they are suitable candidates for a franchise. All too often we hear that a franchise has failed because the wrong type of franchisee was running it. True, this can happen but it should be the exception rather than the rule. Make sure it is not you. Where it does actually happen – rare and isolated cases – the blame can be apportioned equally to the franchisee for not assessing his own suitability correctly and to the franchisor who should be an expert in everything relating to his franchise including vigorous recruitment procedures. This reasoning has been put forward in many cases where large chains of franchises are experiencing difficulties. When considering such franchises the reader should be wary of a franchisor who habitually 'chooses the wrong franchisees'.

ADVANTAGES TO THE FRANCHISOR

Many franchisors, whether they are established corporations or successful entrepreneurs, want to franchise because:

1) They can expand more quickly.
2) They are not using their own capital – it is the franchisee's money that is at risk.
3) They benefit from the economics of scale of bulk buying.
4) As they can build a chain of units quickly they are in a better position to get contracts than an individual.
5) Management is easier because franchisees tend to be highly motivated (it is their capital at risk after all!) and are even prepared to work anti-social hours in order to achieve success. It is not unknown for franchisees to work all the hours God sends for no salary when the business first starts up or until they are in a profit situation. Remember this could be you. You must be prepared for it, and if a salary is necessary it will have to be allowed for in the business plan (see Chapter 3) and will affect any borrowings you may need.

ADVANTAGES TO THE FRANCHISEE

1) The biggest advantage to the franchisee is that they can set up a business at a lower risk than with traditional methods. However, the statistic usually quoted – a 10 per cent failure rate in franchising, as opposed to a 90 per cent failure rate in ordinary businesses – is a fallacy. The risk is lower because the concept is proven and accepted by consumers, but it is not that low. Franchises can and do fail and the reader should always bear that in mind.
2) The franchisee benefits from the market research, support and training that the franchisor provides. This is ideal for those people who themselves lack ideas and technical knowledge in the field of the franchise of their choice. Indeed many franchisors will only recruit franchisees who have no experience in that field on the basis that they haven't picked up any bad habits.
3) Franchisees will be given assistance in setting up the business – everything from finding a site, fitting it out and then continuing day to day assistance.
4) Franchisees will benefit from bulk buying.
5) They also benefit from advertising as a group.
6) One of the biggest advantages to the franchisee is the use of the franchisor's 'name' or 'brand', e.g. Wimpy.
7) The franchisee will also get preferential treatment from banks. For example, National Westminster, who have a specialized franchising unit (as indeed do many banks now), will lend up to 75 per cent of the investment. Banks rarely do this otherwise.

You should consider carefully the above advantages and weigh them against the following disadvantages.

DISADVANTAGES TO THE FRANCHISEE

Even though a franchisee owns his franchise business he is not his own boss. A franchisee is often referred to as a 'soft entrepreneur'. Under the franchise contract a franchisee forgoes a considerable amount of independence. If you don't like being told what to do and you often have bright ideas – which may mean your unit being different from the other franchises in the chain – a franchise is not for you! The concept of franchising dictates the necessity for maintaining a uniform image. Your fantastic idea may be just what your customers want and a real money spinner but if your contract does not allow you to do it you won't be allowed to use your entrepreneurial skills – even when it could mean the difference between making losses and breaking even. If you go ahead regardless you may find yourself being sued for breach of contract.

Most franchises require the franchisee to make continuing payments – called royalty payments – to the franchisor. After a period of time some franchisees feel that the payments they have to make are not a correct representation of the support and assistance they receive from their franchisor. In some cases the royalty payment will make the difference between the business making a loss or a profit. Some franchises may operate a two-tier royalty fee structure in which the more profitable franchises pay the higher royalty fee. This can lead to dissatisfaction between franchisees who feel that the system is unfair.

A franchisee may be restricted in the disposal of his business and normally has to seek the franchisor's approval. A franchisee may also experience difficulty in the renewal of his agreement (most of which run for five to ten years). There has been a case where the franchisor insisted that the franchisee modernize and revamp the premises before renewal – and after the franchisee had gone to considerable expense to do just that the franchisor still refused to renew the franchise contract.

In some cases the franchisor has decided that he no longer wishes to operate a franchise. The franchisee is left out of pocket, having paid a franchisee fee, and with no franchise – his only recourse being to go through the courts which is a very expensive and time consuming business.

There is also a possibility that the original franchisor may assign the franchise to another franchisor. At present, this can be done without the franchisees' consent and could have dire results on the success of the franchisees' business. For example, the original franchisor could have had a staff of eight-five to support the franchisees (and this is what the franchisees expected when they took out the contract). However, the franchisor they assign to may only have a staff support system of three people! In such a situation franchisees may find that their business undergoes a rapid decline as they no longer have sufficient support to sustain the standards they have achieved to date.

A franchisee may find that the franchisor does not provide sufficient services, adequate stock or even enough advertising. At worst, his sales may be nowhere near the figures projected in the business plan and he may make hefty losses.

A franchisee's business may also suffer from mistakes, bad commercial decisions, misrepresentations or fraud by the franchisor. If the latter is true the franchisee may be in a position where his business fails and there is always the risk of liquidation or bankruptcy. In some cases franchisees have had to sell businesses and have still owed money to the bank. In most cases personal guarantees had to be given at the outset with the bank taking a second mortgage over the matrimonial home. In many cases the home has had to be sold in order to repay the bank. Thus, even though banks are willing to lend up to 75 per cent of the investment, it can be argued that this may not be such a good idea.

If possible, it is better to avoid personal guarantees, in particular such guarantees as a second mortgage on your home. Remember that the more under-capitalized you are (i.e. the higher your borrowings) the greater the chance that you will fail. For those readers who are now not so keen on the idea of franchising, let me hasten to add that providing you are well informed, realistic in your approach at all times, and careful in your research of the franchise it can be an excellent way of doing business, especially when it succeeds. A certain element of risk will of course always be present.

For those readers who think franchising is the ideal method of doing business, let me caution you to tread carefully and send off for the franchise packs which the franchises you are interested in will be only too happy to provide.

2

Entering into the franchise relationship

FRANCHISE PACKS AND GLOSSY BROCHURES

Always remember that the franchisor is basically a salesman. He is trying to sell you a franchise. In order to do this he has to convince you that:

1) His product/services are excellent.
2) He has carried out market research which shows that there is a real demand for the product/services.
3) He has a successful pilot operation.
4) Turnover and profits are good. He should show you a specimen profit projections and business plan for a three to five year period.
5) The success of the product is due to his management expertise in that field and that you too could enjoy his success if he helped you with the business. Basically he is justifying the payment of the initial franchise fee.
6) If a royalty fee is payable that fee is worth the support and services he provides you with and that the business can bear the burden of the royalty fee and still make profits. If no royalty fee is payable and he merely provides a product then he will assure you that his mark-ups on that product are the minimum.

Many verbal assurances will be given. He will be making all the right noises to reassure you. You have decided to go into a franchise because of the many benefits and support a genuine and ethical franchisor will provide. Those franchisors who are not ethical – and they do exist – not to mention 'cowboys' will take advantage of that and will make empty promises. It is no more than hard sell. Do not be taken in. The people you will be dealing with are trained to be re-assuring, well presented, well dressed, well spoken and to appear professional. Be wary of smooth tongues and the gift of the gab. All salesmen have them! Absorb what you are told and what you read – but do not believe a word until everything has been checked and re-checked and professional advice obtained.

A professional and ethical franchisor will welcome this cautious approach and all the questions that must be asked.

It is worth remembering that sometimes a franchisor may not just make positive statements. He may *omit* to tell you some crucial facts. The ball is in your court and you have to anticipate where it is going to land and how you are going to make the return. At this stage it is vital that you keep an open mind until all research is carried out.

Many potential franchisees begrudge spending money on research and advice. However, it is crucial. Better to spend, say £100 on find-ing out that a franchise is not worth going into than losing thousands at the end of the day. No matter how small or large your investment it is *your* money and you obviously do not want to lose it. Even if you spend money researching several franchises it is still worth it and is certainly better than losing all your capital, being in debt, losing a year or so of your life in misery and trauma, and ending up on tran-quillizers and involved in a court case!

Having read the glossy brochures the next step will be your appointment with the company. If you are particularly interested in a franchise you will go through several meetings with the franchisor.

THE INITIAL MEETING

This will be an introductory meeting to give you the feel of the fran-chise and general details. There will be no financial commitment at this stage. If you are interested in a particular territory this may not be secured until you have paid the initial franchise fee. Do not let the franchisor hurry you. If you are very interested in the franchise then go ahead and carry out research on everything represented (see Chapters 5 and 6) *before* you pay the initial franchise fee and before your next meeting.

This is a good time to start writing down a checklist for yourself on the following points:

Yourself and your attitude to the franchise

Assess your desire, interest and capability to run the franchise of your choice. Do you have family support? If unsociable hours of work are necessary can you and your family cope?

Professional assessment of a particular franchise

Put this into motion. See Chapter 4 for details.

Examine the franchise yourself

It is very important that you meet other franchisees of that franchise. The franchisor should be happy to assist you in giving names and addresses of franchisees *but* make sure you speak to whom you want and to as many franchisees as possible. Ask them:

1) How long have they traded?
2) Are they content with the franchise generally?
3) Are they getting the support and services from the franchisor that they were led to expect and are the franchisors as experienced as they say they are?
4) Did the franchise cost what it should have?
5) Is the product as good as the franchisor states?
6) Are they breaking even?　⎫　Are the projections that the
7) Are they making a profit?　⎬　franchisor anticipated being
　　　　　　　　　　　　　　⎭　achieved realistically?
8) Is the royalty a burden or can the business easily support it?
9) Is the advertising that the franchisor carries out both sufficient and what he undertook to carry out?
10) Is there a franchise association? If not, why not? Would the franchisor object to one being set up?

You cannot ask enough questions, and it's always a good idea to ask the franchisor for a specimen franchise contract.

At this stage it would be wise to have an initial meeting with several banks. From your preliminary enquiries, you will already have a rough idea of how much finance will be necessary and how much you will require from the bank. The bank will give you some indication of their approach and how much they will be prepared to lend. Of course you will have to finalize matters when you can put a proper business plan to them for consideration.

When you have done all the above it would be wise to consider professional advice before entering into any financial commitment.

3

Raising Finance

THE BANKS' ATTITUDE

Even if you have sufficient savings and do not need to borrow to invest in a franchise opportunity, you should still undertake the same investigation as someone who has to convince a bank to lend him the money.

The criteria for lending money are now far more strict than in the free-wheeling 1980s when credit was plentiful and relatively easy to get. The banks have lost vast sums lending to small businesses which have been hit hardest by the recession.

Any bank will first assess the viability of your business proposition, and whether the cash-flow generated by the business can pay off any business loans. The bank will also want to see whether you have enough collateral to cover the bank borrowings should anything go wrong. In the gloomy 1990s the banks will look for the maximum security to support their loans, including taking a second charge over your home. If you need to borrow you will have little choice but to agree to their terms.

Traditionally the banks tend to take a more positive approach to lending money for a franchise than other business opportunities, and rightly so, because franchisees will be backed by expertise from the franchisor in a business that has supposedly already proved to be a success. However, any prospective franchisee should be very prudent as to how much of their total investment they borrow. It is essential to analyze carefully the franchise opportunity, methodically prepare a business plan with financial projections and then approach your bank manager to see what they can offer.

The banks have a wealth of experience lending to franchised businesses, and whilst they have suffered in the recession with bad debts and franchise failures, National Westminster Bank and The Royal Bank of Scotland particularly remain very committed to franchising. The main clearing banks in the UK (with the exception of Barclays) continue to have central franchise units and provide helpful information packs on franchising which are available free. With their experience lending to franchises and their specialist and local knowledge, even if you do not have to borrow to invest in a franchise, you should still discuss with your own bank and any other bank that has a specialist franchise unit your plans to see what additional information or guidance they may be able to provide.

National Westminster Bank have been hard hit by the recession. In the 1980s their specialist Central Franchise Unit claimed to be the biggest lender to the Franchise Industry. The bank established a dedicated Franchise Section by appointing a Franchise Manager. The bank is still very committed to franchising, and continues to sponsor a number of franchise exhibitions. In association with the British Franchise Association they also sponsor the annual franchise survey.

The Franchise Unit works by providing essential back-up information on any franchise to the local branch manager who is approached by a prospective franchisee. This gives the prospective franchisee the benefit of both specialist and local advice. The bank provides a specialist 'franchisee finance scheme' for established and proven franchises: as much as two-thirds of the total investment cost can be lent to prospective franchisees under the scheme.

The bank provides a useful information pack which all prospective franchisees should read – it contains useful information on franchising and gives helpful guidelines on how to represent your case to your local branch manager.

As NatWest has been involved in franchising since 1981 they have collated a wealth of information on franchisors and available franchises. You would be well advised to bear this in mind and to heed carefully any comments the bank is prepared to make about a specific franchise.

The Royal Bank of Scotland has a franchise department consisting of three Franchise Units nationwide. The department has existed for several years and is committed to franchising. Their franchise specialists highlight early pitfalls and give useful insight into the pros and cons of different types of operations.

Barclays Bank closed their Central Franchise Unit in 1993 as part of their restructuring. They claim to be still committed to the franchising scene, with the franchisor and franchisee receiving better customer service from developing a relationship with a local manager through their branch network rather than dealing with someone at a specialist head office department.

Those franchisors who previously maintained a relationship with the Central Franchise Unit are now looked after by local managers. A list of contacts is published within the bank so that any UK branch can easily locate the Barclays Bank Manager responsible for any particular franchise.

Midland Bank produce a useful Franchise Guide which should be read together with their *Guide to starting a Small Business*. Loan applications are left to each branch manager who can provide a tailor-made finance package to suit your financial needs. The bank is prepared to consider loans up to two-thirds of the total cost of the franchise (including any working capital), but they will usually ask for security.

Lloyds Bank has a specialist small Franchise Unit based in Bristol. The bank also provides a free promotional and franchise information pack. A telephone help-line is also available on 0272-433089.

The franchise unit services the Lloyds business centres around the country and also can deal with enquiries direct from the public. The business centres have dedicated small-business advisers who have access to a PC database linked to Franchise World to provide a directory of franchises, and the bank has developed its own database providing additional information.

Individual lending decisions are made by the local branch manager, who can liaise with their central franchise unit for guidance. Ordinary Business Development loans and overdraft facilities are available, and the bank are generally prepared to lend more for the more established and successful franchises. Like other banks, Lloyds have stopped joint promotions with franchisors, but the bank continues to exhibit at the main franchising exhibitions.

INDEPENDENT INVESTORS

3i – Investors in Industry are the world's largest Development Capital provider, investing in established companies and business start-ups.

Basically their function is to provide medium and long-term loan and equity capital to all types and sizes of viable businesses in return for a shareholding. They are an independent investor, and they will consider investing in franchised businesses, usually in the franchisor and not individual franchisee units.

The Development Capital industry in the UK has had some unfortunate experiences investing in franchised businesses, and has suffered losses in some of the bigger collapses. Unless a large investment is required, it is unlikely that a franchisee will want to raise finance from 3i, simply because it will mean giving away a slice of the business.

GENERAL CONSIDERATIONS

The banks' attitude to lending has changed considerably since the credit boom of the free-wheeling 1980s. The recession has cost them dear and their exposure to the small business sector has meant that they are very much more conservative in their lending approach. This is no bad thing, because in the past they sometimes encouraged businesses to borrow too much money, and then when it could not be repaid pushed those businesses into bankruptcy. It was common to see banks lending up to 75 per cent (and in some cases even 100 per cent) of the funds required to invest in a franchise. I have always advocated that ideally you should borrow no more than 50 per cent of the total investment required, and that includes working capital.

In the recession-hit 1990s, the banks want to see that any borrowings can be serviced from the cash-flow of the business, and they also want to have security for their loans, often in the form of a second mortgage on your home. The lending criteria of all the banks is now very much more prudent. Politicians are not the only ones who have gone back to basics! The old tried and tested fundamental financial and banking principles have been rediscovered. So, if you find that a bank refuses to lend to you because it considers the franchise too risky or perhaps because you are borrowing too much, they may be doing you a favour!

It may be that the franchisor's own bank has special arrangements and will be able to offer franchisees more favourable terms than other banks. After you have approached your own bank, it can still be worth discussing your proposal with other high street banks to see what advice and funding they can offer.

Do not be frightened to ask the banks:

1) Questions about the franchisor company. What do they know about the company?
2) If you qualify for a Business Development loan or fixed term loan, what capital repayment holidays can they offer?
3) What vetting procedures have they subjected the franchisor to?
4) Their advice on whether there is a demand for that type of franchise business in a particular area. Remember, the local branch manager is in an ideal position to make such comments as he will be aware of how local trade is performing. He may also be assisted with back-up information from a specialist franchise unit within the bank.

But a word of warning – do not rely on what the banks say as gospel. They will deny liability if things go wrong. There is no substitute for your own research and you are responsible for taking independent professional advice. Remember the bank is in business to make a profit from you, and they also want to see their money back! Banks are profit-making institutions, and there has been plenty of adverse publicity and criticism condemning the behaviour of the banks when they demand repayment from small businesses, regardless of what difficulties they are experiencing. Whether your business succeeds or fails, they want their money back. If they have security for their loans (e.g. like a mortgage over your home), they can and will call in that security and repossess your house. Given the choice, they would like everyone to do well – but unfortunately businesses fail and it makes commercial sense for the banks to protect themselves. The information packs they produce on franchising should be read carefully and any advice or comments they make should be taken seriously.

Bank managers are not supposed to recommend investing in particular franchises, and in this economic climate rarely do so. Where they are reluctant to lend, or appear concerned about a particular franchise of your choice, think twice before proceeding further! They may know something you don't!

THE BUSINESS PLAN

Whenever you go into business as a franchisee you should always prepare a business plan with the help of the franchisor and an independent accountant who should test the financial projections to see if they are realistic and achievable. This plan will set out your business objectives, and the financial projections will identify the total investment you require to finance the franchise opportunity.

Let us assume you have already approached your own bank with your plans and have a rough idea how much finance you require. The bank may or may not have agreed *in principle* to provide a borrowing facility. Either way you need to go back to them with a detailed business plan which the franchisor should help you to prepare based on his own expertise in that particular business. Some franchisors will only assist you with a detailed business plan *after* you have paid them an initial franchise fee. It is better to insist that they provide the assistance *before* you commit yourself financially.

You will most probably have seen a hypothetical business plan for a unit within the franchise network at one of your earlier meetings. The research you should have carried out by now will give you a realistic indication as to whether the franchisor is doing as well as he says he is and whether the financial projections are realistic.

In many cases where franchisees have lost money, it has transpired that the projected figures they were shown by the franchisor were not just optimistic but sometimes fanciful to the point of being fraudulent. Remember, any projected figures you are shown or you discuss with your franchisor are nothing more than projected figures based on certain assumptions. They are not a forecast of what will happen or what figures the business will achieve. It is absolutely essential that you seek the advice of an independent professional adviser like an accountant or experienced franchise consultant to review the projections. Any ethical franchisor won't mind.

If the franchisor is only starting to franchise, or where it is a foreign franchise starting up in the UK, it is essential to ascertain what market research has been carried out in the UK and also in your particular area, and whether there is a successful pilot operation here. Remember to obtain all answers from the franchisor *in writing*.

Preparation of a Business Plan

Never hurry over this. All too often franchisors are optimistic with their projections, over-stating the sales you are likely to achieve and under-stating the costs – this will not help you in the slightest.

If you have carried out the research recommended in this book and your potential franchisor has survived the scrutiny, you may at this stage be prepared to have some confidence in him. The franchisor's experience in the field of your choice will be invaluable and you should be able to rely on him heavily for guidance. Make sure that all aspects of the business are covered by the business plan and the financial projections include financing costs.

Trading from shop premises – The Leasehold Minefield

In recession-hit British high streets lease premiums (the capital sum of money paid to purchase a lease in addition to the rent) are rare.

Where payable, lease premiums vary. They can be substantial and will usually be payable where the current rent under the lease is below the current market rent. The difference will be 'capitalized' and will be reflected in the size of the premium the purchaser will have to pay.

Premiums are never included in the cost of the franchise, so if you do have to trade from a shop where a lease premium is necessary, remember to budget for the additional cost.

In the current desperate economic climate landlords anxious to attract 'big name' businesses often offer 'Reverse Premiums' i.e. the landlord or existing tenant will pay you a capital sum to induce you to buy the lease. Be careful. Being paid to buy a lease may seem attractive, but you could be taking on very onerous obligations under the lease.

Under our archaic property law anyone who takes on a lease is responsible for the rent and all the other obligations of the lease until that lease expires. So, if you stop trading and are unable to sell the lease, you will still be responsible for the rent. The landlord won't care that you have ceased trading. Even where the lease is assigned to someone else, the landlord can pursue you if the subsequent lessee fails to pay the rent.

There have been several well-publicized cases where small businessmen have retired and sold their shop leases, only to find that years later they are being pursued by the landlord for arrears of rent owed by the new lessee. This is very unfair, but under the Law of Property it is perfectly legal. So if you are buying or selling a shop lease, it is essential to obtain the advice of a solicitor experienced in conveyancing and commercial property.

Remember that everything is negotiable in business. Even landlords stuck with empty properties are keen to negotiate the terms of a lease. You will need the professional advice of a solicitor or chartered surveyor (your average estate agent will not have sufficient experience), and varying the terms of a lease could save you thousands.

What should be included in your Business Plan, and what do the banks want to see?

1) Start your business plan with a profile of yourself (and partners), setting out your working experience and how it applies to your plans for being a franchisee.
2) Profile the franchise opportunity you are interested in and why, giving details of the territory and catchment area you are interested in. Describe the product(s) and the market.
3) From information obtained from the franchisor and your own research give details of:
   (a) pilot operations and existing franchisees of the franchise.
   (b) the market research carried out by the franchisor.
   (c) a profile of the competition, particularly in the area you have chosen.
4) State the total funding you will require. Break it down to the cost of the franchise, the working capital required, and what savings you can invest in the franchise. Remember to include a contingency reserve in case you do not meet the projected figures.
5) If you need to trade from shop premises, describe the size and location of the premises, the cost of fitting them out and the principal terms of the lease.
6) Give financial projections, both Trading Profit and Loss figures and cash-flow projections and the assumptions on which the figures are based. These should be prepared with the assistance of the franchisor and an independent accountant.

The financial projections are not just a numerical or accounting exercise. They will give you a clear picture of what you have to achieve to create a profitable business, and what total funding you will require. In addition to a projected Trading Profit and Loss account, a simple cash-flow projection should be provided, for example:

	Jan	Feb	Mar	April	May	June	July	Aug
Sources								
Capital introduced								
Sales								
Interest received								
Other income								
TOTAL RECEIPTS								

<u>Expenditure</u>
Capital equipment
Start-up expenses
Rent & rates ⎫
Heating/lighting ⎪
Stock ⎪
Wages/NI/PAYE ⎪
Drawings ⎬ Overheads
Advertising ⎪
Insurance ⎪
Sundries ⎪
Motor/Travelling ⎪
Telephone/Fax ⎭
HP/Leasing
Bank interest and charges
Credit cards
TOTAL EXPENSES

CASH BALANCE

When carrying out your research (see Chapter 6) you will have calculated the gross profit, the gross profit margin, the net profit and the break-even figures:

Gross profit = Projected Sales − Direct Costs (Purchases + Carriage)

$$\text{Gross Profit margin} = \frac{\text{Gross Profit}}{\text{Sales}} \times 100$$

Net Profit = Gross Profit − Overheads and Financing Costs

$$\text{Break-even} = \frac{\text{Overheads}}{\text{Gross Profit margin}} \times 100$$

Overheads comprise all the indirect expenses of the business. They include:

Salaries and wages + NIC
Rent and Rates
Light/heating
Telephone/Fax
Postage

Stationery
Advertising
Insurance
Repairs
Travelling
Professional charges
Sundries
Depreciation on fixed assets
Credit card commissions
Bank interest and charges/HP

This is not a definitive list, but gives you an idea of the range of expenditure that any business will incur.

Note from the author: I have never seen a set of financial projections that were actually achieved in every detail. Projections, and the business plan, should be regularly up-dated in light of actual trading performance. With good judgement and good luck you may do even better!

7) The latest available financial information on the franchisor, including the last set of audited accounts of the franchisor company. If none are available ask the franchisor for up-to-date management accounts.
8) If there are any special features of your proposal, or your solicitor or accountant have specific recommendations, include these in your plan.

SMALL FIRMS LOAN GUARANTEE SCHEME

Raising finance for a new business can be very difficult especially where a large part of the finance is from bank borrowings. Where there is a viable business proposal and a conventional bank loan has been refused, either because of the lack of security or the limited business track record, you may be able to raise finance under the Small Firms Loan Guarantee Scheme.

This scheme is a joint venture between the Department of Trade and Industry (the DTI) and the banks. By providing a government guarantee to the lending bank in the event that the borrower defaults on the loan, the scheme enables the high street banks and other institutions to lend between £5,000 and £100,000 to new businesses. Up to 70 per cent of the total loan (85 per cent for firms in the Inner City Task Force and City Challenge areas) is guaranteed by the DTI.

The cost to you the borrower for this guarantee is an annual premium payment of 1.5 per cent of the total loan for variable rate lending and a 0.5 per cent premium payment for fixed rate lending. For firms within the Inner City Task Force and City Challenge areas the premium payment is 0.5 per cent a year on the whole loan whether fixed or variable rate.

If the loan is for £30,000 or less, the lender can grant the application themselves without first referring to the DTI.

You will need a detailed business plan and financial forecasts to show the viability of your franchise and to establish your finance requirements. The scheme only applies where a lender would have offered a conventional loan but for the lack of security.

The advantage of this scheme is that a borrower can raise loan finance when, without the DTI guarantee, a lender would refuse to provide a conventional loan. But there is a cost involved with the annual premium of the total loan, and remember, if your business fails and you lose everything, although there is a guarantee for part of your borrowings, you are still liable to pay the full outstanding loan back to the lender.

Details of this scheme are available from your bank or direct from the DTI.

4

Franchise consultants & organizations to consult

FRANCHISE CONSULTANTS

These usually fall into two categories: 1) Those advising potential franchisors on how to set up their business using franchising as a distribution option, and 2) Franchisee consultants who advise potential franchisees as to whether or not they should invest in a particular franchised business.

A good franchise consultant should be able to advise on both aspects because they are inextricably linked. Ensure the consultant you are dealing with is reputable. Fortunately, franchising is a close knit industry and while professional jealousy always exists it is relatively easy to find out if a consultant is genuine.

Always request the following from a consultant:

A CV. Are they qualified (academically) and do they have the relevant work experience to give good franchise advice?

A list of some of the cases they have handled and the outcome.

Their fee structure and a copy of their 'Terms & Conditions'.

Free advice
Free advice is worth what you pay for it – nothing! Not surprisingly a number of individuals (who have set themselves up as franchise experts overnight) have grasped people's reluctance to part with money as a means of making a living for themselves.

The carrot of 'free advice' is usually a way of introducing you to franchise opportunities that they hope you will invest in. Such consultants are unable to give you independent advice because they make their living from monies received from the franchisors that they are directly or indirectly promoting. Usually they receive an introduction fee or 'commission' or simply money for promoting the franchisor. Be wary. There's no such thing as a free lunch. By all means see what franchisors they are promoting – but always carry out the DIY procedure outlined and then have a final check carried out by a genuine franchise consultant or solicitor.

THE FRANCHISE SHOP LTD

This works rather like an estate agency, bringing together franchisor and franchisee. For a nominal fee (currently £5.88) they will register details of your franchise requirements on their database for a twelve-month period. If there is a business opportunity on their books which fits with your specifications they will inform you.

Contact Ray Childs on 0962 855530 for further information.

THE BRITISH FRANCHISE ASSOCIATION (BFA)

This is the trade association for franchisors. It was formed in December 1977 by eight well-established companies engaged in the distribution of goods and services through independent outlets under franchise and licence agreements. These were

Budget Rent-a-Car	
Holiday Inns	
Kentucky Fried Chicken	Of American origin
Service Master	
Ziebart	
Dyno Rod	
Wimpy	Of British origin
Prontaprint	

The BFA aims to promote ethical franchising. Because it does not have legislative powers, at the end of the day it is essentially a watchdog without teeth. However, in the absence of franchise legislation it is useful to have some sort of an industry watchdog.

Franchisors can choose whether or not to become a member of the BFA. While many well-known franchisors are members it is worth bearing in mind that some of the leading franchisors are not members.

Because the BFA have a 'vetting' procedure for members, membership is a useful criterion to look out for.

BFA Memberships

Full Members
Franchisors must show that they use an ethically constructed contract, offer documents that present a fair picture and have proven their franchise concept over time in a number of franchised outlets.

Cost to franchisor: £1,550 per annum + VAT for prompt payment or £1,700 per annum + VAT for late payment.

Associate Members
Same standards as full members but franchisor has not been established for the same length of time.

Cost to franchisor: £1,450 per annum + VAT for prompt payment or £1,600 per annum + VAT for late payment

Provisional Listing
For companies new to franchising.

Cost to franchisor: £1,000 per annum + VAT for prompt payment or £1,100 per annum + VAT for late payment.

Obviously there is much more risk attached to a 'provisional member' than a full member simply because the former is new to franchising. Also bear in mind that franchisors pay to become members and as such some see it as 'buying themselves credibility' because they are then associated with the BFA.

BFA franchisor members are not immune to failure. Use membership only as a guidance and remember that at the time of writing there are many successful franchisors (like the Body Shop) who choose not to be BFA members.

BFA Code Of Ethics
The BFA's Code Of Ethics (written by Professor Martin Mendelsohn) is highly commendable.

Paragraph 9 states 'Fairness shall characterise all dealings between a franchisor and its franchisees. A franchisor shall give notice to its franchisees of any contractual breach and grant reasonable time to remedy fault.'

The only problem with this noble sentiment is that people's perception of what is fair varies. The Code examines specific problem areas:

Renewal of the Contract

Most franchise contracts are renewable. It would appear reasonable that contracts should be renewable on the terms of the then used franchise agreement and that a franchisee should rectify any breaches.

However, over the last several years many franchisors have tried to use 'renewal' as a means of imposing wider and more onerous conditions on the franchisee.

A 'revamp' clause could mean that a franchisee has to completely refit his shop. The costs involved can be enormous – sometimes even more than the franchisee's original set-up costs. The franchisee may not be able to afford the changes or be concerned that the changes will not be cost effective.

There is clearly a conflict of interest between the franchisee and franchisor. The latter will want to keep his business competitive and up-to-date – at whatever cost. Because enforcement of such revamp clauses can be unfair, the BFA have laid down guidelines for members:

* The revamp should be tested by the franchisor who must be able to demonstrate actual financial benefits at specified pilot operations.
* The testing must take place in a sufficient number of representative operational units.
* The franchisor should assist the franchisees in making arrangements with their banks for financing or refinancing.
* Revamps should not be required so often that franchisees cannot recover their investment or make an increase in profit over a reasonable period.

A 'relocation' clause may make it a condition of renewal that a franchisee must relocate to a new site (of the franchisor's choosing). This is, of course, very risky and expensive for the franchisee who in effect has to set up a completely new business from scratch.

The franchisor may be right that a fresh approach is necessary. An example is Wimpy who have now introduced 'counter service' restaurants to run alongside their 'table service' restaurants.

In such cases the BFA recommends that the following considerations should be taken into account:

* Whether the franchisee can afford to relocate.
* Whether the 'old' and 'new' concepts can live alongside each other.
* Can the franchisor prove (using pilot operations) that relocation will be cost effective for the franchisee?
* Is the franchisor prepared to assist the franchisee in raising finance?
* Is the franchisor using 'relocation' for ridding himself of the franchisee unfairly or is his motive genuine, i.e. to enhance and promote the franchise system?

New Technology

The franchisor may wish to introduce new technology. The most common area is the introduction of computerized tills that link with the head office computer and which can provide franchisees with monthly profit and loss accounts and stock order lists.

Such technology is often welcomed by franchisees when part of their original package but if introduced at a later stage franchisees are justly concerned about the costs involved.

The BFA is concerned that this can cause unfairness and recommends:

* That the franchisor can show the cost effectiveness of the new changes and
* That the cost of the new service should not be significantly more than the franchisee would expect to pay to someone else for a similar service.

If a franchisor thinks that they may introduce new technology at a later stage the best solution is probably to put a clause in the contract indicating a 'ceiling' for the additional costs.

Advertising Contributions

Many franchisees are concerned that advertising contributions are not spent properly. The BFA recommends that franchisors should provide annual audited accounts to show franchisees that contributions have been spent for the intended purpose.

Sale of Products
If franchisees have to buy products from the franchisor they may be subject to unfair price increases.

If the franchisor also sells to 'non-franchisees' the BFA recommends that the prices can be compared to the prices paid by franchisees and used as a benchmark.

If the franchisor only supplies to franchisees then there should be some protection in the contract to ensure that the franchisor cannot increase margins unfairly.

Minimum Franchise Fee
The BFA have always indicated a dislike of minimum franchise fees. A set fee can be hard on a franchisee in the early stages because he is trying to build up his business. However, once the business has established itself, the franchisee will be better off.

The franchisor, however, does not benefit from the network becoming more successful and therefore has no motivation to assist franchisees.

Product Tied Franchise Agreements
Franchisees should avoid minimum purchase requirements by the franchisor because they are just another form of minimum franchise fees.

Sale of the business by the franchisee
In some cases, where a franchisee wishes to sell his business, the franchisor is unfair in vetting the new applicant the franchisee has put forward. The same criteria should be applied whether an applicant applies directly to the franchisor or through the existing franchisee.

Usually contracts allow the franchisor to have a 'first option' to purchase the franchised business. In such cases the franchisor must make a decision within a reasonable time otherwise the franchisee may lose a prospective purchaser. The option should not allow the franchisor to buy the business for less than it is worth on the open market as a going concern.

Franchisors should be able to charge a reasonable fee for dealing with an application.

Death of a franchisee or principal shareholder

The BFA take the view that in such a case the franchisor should not be allowed to just terminate the agreement but should give the franchisee's dependants an opportunity to qualify as franchisees or to sell the business to an approved purchaser.

Breaches by the franchisee

The Code of Ethics provides that the franchisor must give the franchisee notice of any breach and a reasonable time to remedy it. What is a 'reasonable time'? This is not stipulated because it will depend on the nature of the breach.

Resolution of disputes

Paragraph 10 of the BFA's Code Of Ethics provides: 'A franchisor should make every effort to resolve complaints, grievances and disputes with its franchisees with good faith and goodwill through fair and reasonable direct communication and negotiation.'

If only franchisors did this! Over the last several years I have carried out an enormous amount of 'dispute resolution' on an independent consultancy basis. Getting the parties to talk and appreciate each other's situation was what got results.

In a very few cases the franchisor refused to discuss anything. Those cases ended up in litigation and in many cases the franchisor's network went bust.

In contrast to my informal negotiations, the BFA have a formal Arbitration Scheme. Franchisees can apply to use the Scheme as an alternative to court action. The problem is that once you have started using the Scheme you cannot start again with court action because awards under the Scheme are final and binding on all the parties.

The franchisors' agreement to arbitration is necessary. The BFA only has the power to encourage the franchisor to agree. If the franchisor refuses the franchisee's only remedy will be through the courts.

I have not had favourable feedback about the Scheme and feel that it is in the interests of franchisees to pursue their grievances through the courts if amicable negotiations break down.

For completeness, details of how the Scheme works follow:

The BFA Arbitration Scheme

The Scheme is administered by The Chartered Institute Of Arbitrators. When there is a dispute the franchisee contacts the BFA and obtains a Request for Arbitration form which he must complete and return to the BFA with a deposit of £150. The form is sent to the franchisor via the BFA and if the franchisor agrees to arbitration he simply signs the form and also pays a deposit of £150.

The BFA sends the form to the Institute. An arbitrator is appointed and the franchisee has twenty-eight days to submit written evidence in support of his argument. The franchisor has a further twenty-eight days to respond. Written evidence should be sufficient. However, the franchisee or arbitrator can request an oral hearing. The arbitrator may request further evidence from one or both parties. A typical case should take four to six months to resolve. If the franchisee loses he will only have to pay one third of the costs. If the franchisor loses he has to pay all the costs.

The Scheme is open to non-BFA members – but it is highly unlikely that they will agree to use it.

More information about the scheme can be obtained from the BFA booklet 'The Ethics of Franchising'.

THE BFA ARBITRATION SCHEME

Request for Arbitration Form (from BFA)
+ £150
↓
BFA
↓
RAF sent to franchisor
signs + £150
↓
BFA
↓
RAF sent to Institute
↓
Appointment of arbitrator

4/6 months	Franchisee has 28 days to submit written evidence	Franchisor has 28 days to reply

Request for further evidence
if necessary
↓
Oral hearing if required
↓
Final decision

The Chartered Institute of Arbitrators/ BFA Arbitration Scheme
Application for Arbitration

To: The Chartered Institute of Arbitrators, International Arbitration Centre, 75 Cannon Street, London EC4N 5BH. Tel. 071-236 8761.
(To be submitted through the British Franchise Association.)

1. (Franchisee) ....
   of ....
   .... Tel. ....

   and

   (Franchisor) ....
   of ....
   .... Tel. ....

Hereby apply to the Chartered Institute of Arbitrators for the following dispute to be referred to arbitration to the Rules of the BFA Arbitration Scheme for the time being in force for determination by an arbitrator appointed for that purpose by the Institute.

2. The dispute has arisen in connection with the following:
   ....
   ....
   ....
   ....
   ....

Note: only an outline is required here to enable the dispute to be identified by the parties. The Franchisee will be asked to submit his specific claim in detail as soon as the arbitration request has been accepted by the Institute.

3. We, the parties to this application, are each in possession of the current (1987) Rules of the Scheme. We agree to be bound by these Rules (or any amendment thereof for the time being in force that may be notified to us) and by the award of the Arbitrator appointed to determine the dispute.

4. A cheque for the sum of *£150 in respect of the Franchisee's deposit, and a cheque for the same amount in respect of the Franchisor's deposit are enclosed.

We agree to the disposal of these deposits in accordance with the Rules of the Scheme.

Signed (Franchisee) .... Date ....

Signed (Franchisor) .... Date ....

*Cheques should be in favour of: The Chartered Institute of Arbitrators.

The Chartered Institute of Arbitrators British Franchise Association Arbitration Scheme Rules

(1987 Edition)

These Rules provide an inexpensive and informal method of resolving disputes between franchisors and franchisees which the parties cannot resolve amicably between themselves. The Rules will apply to arbitrations commenced under the Scheme after 1 May 1987.

INTRODUCTION
1. In these Rules:
    - (i) 'the Institute' shall mean the Chartered Institute of Arbitrators of 75 Cannon Street, London EC4N 5BH.
    - (ii) 'the BFA' shall mean the British Franchise Association of 74a Bell Street, Henley on Thames, Oxon RG9 2BD.
    - (iii) 'the Arbitrator' shall mean a sole and independent arbitrator appointed by the President or Vice-President of the Institute in an arbitration under this Scheme.
    - (iv) 'the Franchisor' shall mean a company firm or person who is the franchisor in respect of any agreement under which a dispute arises and is referred to arbitration under this Scheme.
    - (v) 'the Franchisee' shall mean a company firm or person who is the franchisee in respect of any agreement under which a dispute arises and is referred to arbitration under this Scheme.
    - (vi) 'the costs of the arbitration' shall mean the total of the Arbitrator's fees and expenses, the Institute's administrative costs, and the cost of any independent examination under Rule 8(iv).
    - (vii) 'costs in the reference' shall mean legal or other costs incurred by a party in connection with an arbitration under this Scheme.
2. The Franchisee may apply for arbitration under this Scheme as an alternative to court action. He must decide at the outset whether to use this Scheme or to seek his remedy through the Courts. If he uses this Scheme he will not be able to start again with court action, because awards made under the Scheme are final and binding on the parties.
3. (i) Application for arbitration must be made on the prescribed application form which may be obtained from the BFA.
    - (ii) A deposit of £150 is payable by each party when an application for arbitration is submitted. These deposits may be refunded or may be applied in whole or part towards defraying the costs of the arbitration, at the discretion of the Arbitrator.

4. (i) The application form should be completed by the Franchisee and returned to the BFA with the Franchisee's deposit.

(ii) The BFA will then refer the application form to the Franchisor, to be completed and returned to the BFA with the Franchisor's deposit.

(iii) The Franchisor's agreement to arbitration is necessary for the application to proceed. The BFA will encourage the Franchisor to agree, but he is not obliged to do so. If the Franchisor does not agree to arbitration, he is required to inform the BFA accordingly. The Franchisee's deposit will be returned and he may seek his remedy through the Courts.

INSTITUTION OF ARBITRATION PROCEEDINGS

5. Provided the application form has been signed by both parties and is accompanied by the appropriate deposits, it will be forwarded to the Institute by the BFA with the deposits.

6. The arbitration commences for the purposes of these Rules when the Institute despatches to the parties written notice of acceptance of the application. The notice sent to the party making the claim will be accompanied by a claim form.

PROCEDURE

7. *General*

Subject to any directions issued by the Arbitrator the procedure will be as follows:-

(i) The Franchisee is required, within 28 days of receipt of the claim form, to send the completed form, together with any supporting documents in duplicate, to the Institute. The Franchisee is also required to notify the Institute at this stage if he requests an attended hearing. (The Franchisee may not, without the consent of the Institute, claim an amount greater than specified on the application for arbitration.)

(ii) A copy of the claim documents will be sent by the Institute to the Franchisor, who is required, within 28 days of receipt of the documents, to send to the Institute his written defence to the claim together with any supporting documents in duplicate. (The Franchisor may include with his defence a counterclaim in respect of any balance of payment alleged to be due on the contract between the parties, or in respect of any other matter notified to the Franchisee before the Franchisee applied for arbitration.)

(iii) A copy of the defence documents will be sent by the Institute to the Franchisee, who is entitled to send to the Institute any written comments which he wishes to make on the defence documents within 14 days of their receipt. Such comments should be in dupli-cate. They must be restricted to points arising from the Franchisor's defence, and may not introduce any new matters or points of claim.

(iv) The President or a Vice-President of the Institute, at such stage of the proceedings as the Institute considers appropriate, will appoint the Arbitrator, taking into account the nature of the dispute and the location of the Franchisee's trading premises. The Institute will notify the parties of the Arbitrator's appointment.

(v) The Arbitrator may in his discretion call the parties to an attended hearing, and shall do so if the Franchisee has so requested in accordance with Rule 7(i). Subject to that, the Arbitrator will make his award with reference to the documents submitted by the parties.

(vi) The Arbitrator will send his award to the Institute for publication. Unless the parties otherwise agree the arbitrator's reasons will be set out or referred to in his award.

(vii) The Institute will notify the parties when it received the award from the Arbitrator, and will also notify the Franchisor of any costs of the arbitration payable under Rule 11. On payment of such costs, the Institute will publish the award by sending copies to each of the parties. In normal circumstances the Institute will also send a copy to the BFA.

(viii) After publication of the award the Institute will return the Franchisee's deposit in whole or in part if so directed by the Arbitrator.

(ix) Unless directed otherwise in the award, within 21 days of despatch by the Institute to the parties of the copy award, payment shall be made of any monies directed by the award to be paid by one party to the other. Such payment shall be made by the party liable direct to the party entitled, and not through the Institute.

(x) If either party has sent original documents in support of its case to the Institute that party may within six weeks of publication of the award request the return of those documents. Subject to that, case papers will be retained by the Institute and may in due course be disposed of in accordance with the Institute's policies from time to time.

8. *Supplementary*

(i) Attended hearings shall be conducted in private at a place to be notified to the parties by the Institute on behalf of the Arbitrator, who shall use his best endeavours to take into account the convenience of the parties. The parties may attend a hearing in person or be represented by an employee (but not a person employed to give legal advice) unless the Arbitrator agrees they may be legally represented.

(ii) The Arbitrator may, through the Institute, request the provision of any further documents/information which he considers would assist him in his decision. If the documents/information are not supplied to the Institute within such time as it prescribes, the Arbitrator will proceed with the reference on the basis of the documents already before him.

(iii) Where in the opinion of the Arbitrator it is desirable, he may make an examination of the subject matter of the dispute without holding an attended hearing. The parties shall afford the Arbitrator all necessary assistance and facilities for the conduct of this examination.

(iv) Where, in the opinion of the Arbitrator, it is desirable that independent examination of the subject matter of the dispute be made, an independent examiner will be appointed by the Institute to make such examination and a written report thereon. The parties shall afford the examiner all necessary assistance and facilities for the conduct of this examination and copies of his report shall be sent by the Institute to the parties who will then be given 14 days in which to comment thereon.

(v) If the Franchisee does not furnish his claim within the time allowed and does not remedy his default within 14 days after despatch to him by the Institute of notice of that default, he will be treated as having abandoned his claim. The arbitration will not proceed and the Franchisee's deposit will be returned less the Institute's administrative costs to date. The Franchisor's deposit will be returned in full.

(vi) If the Franchisor does not furnish his defence within the time allowed and does not remedy his default within 14 days after despatch to him by the Institute of notice of that default, the Arbitrator will be appointed and subject to any directions he may give the dispute may be decided by him by reference to the documents submitted by the Franchisee.

(vii) If a party fails to attend or be represented at an attended hearing the Arbitrator shall either make an award ex parte, or, if he so decides, adjourn the hearing for such time as he considers reasonable and serve notice on the party failing to attend that the matter will be dealt with ex parte at the adjourned hearing.

COSTS

9. The Franchisor shall be responsible for the costs of the arbitration less any amount which the Arbitrator may order the Franchisee to pay but the Franchisor shall in any event be responsible for not less than two-thirds of the costs of the arbitration. Where the arbitration is conducted on the basis of documents only, the Arbitrator will not order the Franchisee to pay a contribution to the costs of the arbitration in excess of £150 unless he considers the application by the Franchisee to have been frivolous or vexatious. In the case of an attended hearing, if the

costs of the arbitration exceed £300, the Arbitrator may order the Franchisee to pay part of such excess in addition to the sum of £150 (or more if he considers the application frivolous or vexatious).

10. The Arbitrator may order the Franchisor to pay some or all of the Franchisee's costs in the reference, and may order the Franchisee to pay up to one-third of the Franchisor's costs in the reference.

11. The Franchisor agrees to pay to the Institute within 14 days of notice from the Institute of receipt of the Award and of the amount of the costs of the arbitration, a total sum equal to the costs of the arbitration less the amount of any deposits ordered to be utilised towards payment of the fees and expenses. This is without prejudice to any right which the Franchisor may have to recover from the Franchisee a contribution to the costs of the arbitration or the Franchisor's costs in the reference, ordered in the Arbitrator's award to be paid by the Franchisee.

MISCELLANEOUS

12. The arbitration shall be conducted in accordance with the law of England.

13. The Institute reserves the right to appoint a substitute Arbitrator if the Arbitrator originally appointed dies or is incapacitated or is for any reason unable to deal expeditiously with the dispute. The parties shall be notified of any substitution.

14. Awards made under the Scheme are final and binding on the parties. Subject to the right of a party to request the Institute to draw the Arbitrator's attention to any accidental slip or omission which he has power to correct, neither the Institute nor the Arbitrator can enter into correspondence regarding awards made under the Scheme.

15. Rights of application or appeal (if any) to the Courts are as under the relevant Arbitration Acts provided that the special costs provisions of the Scheme shall not apply to any such application or appeal.

16. Neither the Institute nor the Arbitrator shall be liable to any party for any act or omission in connection with any arbitration conducted under these Rules save that the Arbitrator (but not the Institute) shall be liable for any conscious or deliberate wrongdoing on his own part.

The Chartered Institute of Arbitrators
International Arbitration Centre
75 Cannon Street
London EC4N 5BH
Telephone: 071-236 8761
Telex: 893466 CIARB G

OTHER TRADE ORGANIZATIONS

At the time of writing the BFA is considering setting up a Franchisee Association. The mechanics of how such an organization will be funded and how it could maintain its independence is a matter of much debate.

COMMERCIAL SOLICITORS AND ACCOUNTANTS

It's very important to get professional advice. But ask yourself whether you'd go to your local GP for major heart surgery. Of course not. So many people go wrong when they seek advice from their local solicitor – who is usually concerned with domestic and property matters.

Franchising is all about commercial law and intellectual property rights. So, go to a commercial solicitor who has preferably handled franchise cases before.

If you have an accountant to look at projected figures for a franchise opportunity, make sure he or she is familiar with franchise set-ups and the fact that you will probably be paying royalties on turnover.

5

Preliminary Enquiries

Once you know which franchise or franchises interest you, you should start making preliminary enquiries. You should ask:

yourself
the franchisor
other franchisees
the banks
and the BFA

the following crucial questions, which will greatly assist in the analysis of the franchise opportunity.

QUESTIONS TO ASK YOURSELF

1) Do you have the *desire, interest* and *capability* to run the franchise of your choice?
2) Do you have the family support?
3) If unsociable hours of work are necessary, can you and your family cope?
4) No business is risk free. Should the business not work for any reason, can you and your family cope with the pressure?
5) What capital monies do you have available?
6) For the franchise of your choice how much will you have to borrow?
7) Will you have to have a second mortgage on your home – if yes, and the business fails, how are you going to pay it off?

QUESTIONS TO ASK THE FRANCHISOR

You can never ask enough questions. The following is a long list but you would be well advised to work through it methodically and to record each answer. Set up a file on the franchise you are researching. By the time you have answered all these questions and worked through all the research necessary you will have a sound foundation for making future decisions:

1) Note the address of the principal place of business.
2) Is the franchisor resident in the UK. If not, where?
3) Are the trading and company names different? If so, what are they?
4) Does the franchisor have a parent or holding company?
5) Is the franchisor a member of the BFA? If yes, look at the questions to ask the BFA as well.
6) Has the franchisor made full disclosure to the BFA of the franchise contract and accounts for at least five years?
7) How long has the franchisor been franchising?
8) How many franchised businesses are they running at the moment?
9) What are the addresses of these franchises?
10) Can you interview other franchisees of your own choice? Look at the questions to ask other franchisees.
11) How many company-owned outlets are there?
12) Ask to see the accounts of the pilots for the period they were run before franchising. Ask to see all the market research carried out.
13) What does the office organization consist of? Who are the directors?
14) Obtain CVs of all key personnel and directors.
15) Who will be dealing with you in the day-to-day running of the franchise?
16) How often will you see them?
17) Can they provide sufficient services, especially back-up services in the case of emergencies?
18) Have any of the key personnel/directors operated any other franchise business? If yes, give details.
19) Have any employees/key personnel/directors been convicted of any offence?

20) Have any employees/key personnel/directors ever been declared bankrupt?
21) Have any employees/key personnel/directors ever been party to a civil action for fraud or misrepresentation?
22) Have any of the above parties been involved in any other business that has become insolvent?
23) Which personnel/directors have been involved in preparing the projections.
24) If it is subsequently proved that any material misrepresentations or omissions have been made by the franchisor in terms of information and advice given to the franchisee, will the persons actually responsible for the misrepresentations or omissions hold themselves personally liable to the franchisee for loss, damage and expense? If not, why not?
25) Has the franchisor been convicted of any offence?
26) Has the franchisor been a party to a civil action involving fraud or misrepresentation?
27) Has the franchisor been, or is he, involved in litigation with a present or former franchisee?
28) Who are the franchisor's bankers?
29) Can you take up a bank reference for them?
30) Can they give any other references?
31) Does the franchisor have a special relationship with any bank in relation to loans for its franchisees? If yes:
32) Has that bank/other banks seen the franchise contract that the franchisor is offering?
33) Has that bank/other banks seen the franchisor's projections?
34) What finance is that bank prepared to lend?
35) Which of their franchise shops have had a turnover of people running them? How often? And for what reasons?
36) How many shops have failed? Where and why?
37) Has the franchisor bought back any franchises?
38) How much does the franchise cost? What does this consist of? Obtain a complete breakdown, i.e. initial fee, deposit etc.
39) What additional costs may be incurred, for example, a lease premium?
40) How much working capital is necessary?
41) Under what conditions are the initial fee and deposit returnable?
42) What recurring payments (of any kind) will the franchisee have to make?

Projections

43) What information are the projections based upon? – pilot operations or
44) company shops, and what period do they cover? What size shop, which area?
45) Can you see the accounts that support the projections?
46) Are the projections based on a mature business or do they take into account start-up and development time?
47) How accurate have the projections been in the past?
48) Have any franchisees had to put in additional monies?
49) What was the discrepancy between the projected and actual cost figures in these cases?
50) Are franchisees attaining the turnover projected? If not, why not?
51) What delay period is there in attaining the projected figures?
52) Is the business seasonal – if so, what turnover can the franchisee expect in the different seasons?
53) When is the best time to open the business?

CAUTION

Obtain professional advice. Interpret all the projected figures yourself, and with your accountant.

54) Is there any franchised or company shop which is trading unprofitably?
55) Ask to see a set of the latest audited accounts. Carry out the research on these figures stated in the book. Have there been any material changes since these accounts were prepared? What amount is spent on advertising existing franchises?
56) What amount, if any, is spent on advertising for new franchisees?

The franchise

57) Can you have details of the historical development of the business?
58) Details of the way the business runs presently.
59) What market research has been carried out? Ask for full details of what the research consisted of.
60) What pilot operations were opened before franchising – what size shops were they and where were they? Were they company-owned? Ask to see audited accounts for all of them.
61) Will franchisees need to purchase any services from the franchisor or any other person affiliated to the franchisor? If yes, give details.

62) Is specialist equipment required? If yes, give full details of acquisition and methods of payment.
63) Is there any other equipment/machinery that the franchisee is required to buy/lease/rent from any other supplier? If yes, give details.
64) Are any such suppliers in any way connected with the franchisor?
65) Does the franchisor obtain any commission/'kick-backs' from introducing the franchisee to these suppliers? If yes, how much?

Advertising
66) Is there an advertising fund? If yes, what contribution will the franchisee have to make to it? How is the money spent? Give details.
67) How much, if any, of the royalty payments are spent on advertising with regard to a) advertising the franchise and b) advertising for new franchisees?
68) If a territory is allocated, is a franchisee confined to advertising within the territory?

The Property
69) From where will the franchised business operate?
70) Will freehold/leasehold rented property have to be acquired?
71) Is any such property acquired from the franchisor?
72) If obtaining property from the franchisor, will the lease expire on termination of the franchise agreement?
73) How long is the lease?
74) What will be the permitted use of any lease?
75) Will you have to obtain permission for change of usage?
76) What are the provisions relating to rent review?
77) What rent will have to be paid?
78) Is a premium payable? If yes, how much?

Fitting out the premises
79) How much do the fixtures and fittings cost (including adapting the premises)?
80) The franchisee should be given plans of how their shop is to be fitted out. Who supervises the fittings?
81) Who pays for the plans? If the franchisee, how much do they cost?
82) Does the franchisor recommend builders/contractors?
83) Who oversees that the work is done correctly?

84) If the franchisor recommends that a firm of architects are employed to supervise the works, who pays for it and what does it cost?
85) In the past, what overrun in costs have been incurred?
86) How long should the work take?

Training
87) What training is given to the franchisee before commencing business?
88) How long does it take?
89) Where does it take place?
90) Who pays for it? If the franchisee, how much will it cost?
91) What additional training is given during the term of the franchise agreement? Who pays for it?

Restrictions
92) What restrictions will be placed on the franchisee in relation to the goods/services they provide?
93) If they can obtain goods from other sources, is consent necessary; oral/written? Is there quality control? Which other, if any, franchisees do it and why?
94) Are there restrictions on a franchise supplying goods/services too?
95) Are there restrictions as to the geographic area in which the franchisee can sell such goods/services?
96) Is there a territory allocation? If yes, how large is it and how was it calculated?
97) Are there restrictions on advertising outside a given 'territory' or area?
98) Are there any restrictions on whom the franchisee can employ?
99) What restrictions, if any, are there on what the franchisee/ employees wear on the franchised premises, e.g. is there a uniform?

Competition and territory
100) How is the franchisee protected from other businesses operating under the same name?
101) What protection against competition is given to the franchisee from other businesses connected with or affiliated to or controlled by the franchisor?
102) What territorial protection, if any, is given to franchisee?

103) Is territory allocation, if any, stipulated on a map? If not, why not?
104) What policy does the franchisor adopt if the franchisee obtains orders from outside his territory?
105) Can the franchisee advertise outside his territory? If yes, is consent required?
106) How are territorial disputes between franchisees resolved?
107) Can the franchisor unilaterally reduce the territory granted to the franchisee, if yes, in what circumstances can he exercise that right? Has he exercised it in the past? If yes, for what reasons?
108) If the franchisor can reduce the territory what, if any, right does the franchisee have?
109) In such cases does the franchisee whose territory is reduced have a right of first refusal to start another business in that same territory?
110) Where a territory has been reduced what effect has it had on that franchisee's turnover?
111) If an exclusive territory is not granted, how many franchises are permitted in a given area and how has the franchisor calculated this, i.e. what market research has he done?

Day to day running of the business
112) Will the franchisee have to run the business or can a manager/manageress be employed?
113) How many employees will be necessary?
114) What will their wages be, approximately?
115) Will uniforms have to be worn?
116) What are the usual hours of business necessary to achieve the projections the franchisor has put forward?
117) Will the franchisee ever have to work longer hours?
118) Is Sunday trading included in the projections? If yes, then will the franchisor accept liability if the franchisee is prosecuted for trading on a Sunday?

Goods to be supplied
119) How frequent are deliveries?
120) Who pays delivery/freight charges?
121) What quality control is undertaken?
122) If goods are faulty, how soon must they be returned to the franchisor?

Read in conjunction with Chapter 7 on the franchise contract

The franchise agreement
123) What is the duration of the agreement?

Renewable option
124) Is the contract renewable? If yes, for what period and under what conditions? If not, why not?
125) Can the franchisor refuse to renew? If yes, under what circumstances?
126) Has the franchisor ever refused to renew. If yes, for what reason?

Termination
127) Can the franchisor vary or terminate the contract unilaterally?
128) Under what circumstances can the franchisee terminate the agreement?
129) How many, if any, agreements has the franchisor terminated and why?

Sale
130) Can the franchisor assign the franchise unilaterally? If yes, what safeguards are there to ensure that the new franchisor offers the same standard of services that the franchisee originally contracted for?
131) Are there any limitations on sale/assignment of the franchise business?
132) Does the franchisee have to give the franchisor the right of first refusal? If yes, then is the open market value to be used?
133) Where the franchisee sells/assigns to a third party does the franchisor have to give his consent? If yes, what criteria does the franchisor apply?
134) Can the franchisor withhold consent unreasonably?

Death/incapacity
135) In case of death/incapacity of the franchisee, what steps will the franchisor take to assist?
136) What rights will accrue to the franchisee's next of kin?
137) What assistance will the franchisor give if the next of kin wish to take over the business/sell the business?

Restraint of trade

138) Will the franchisee be restrained from carrying on any similar business after the termination of the agreement? If yes, what are the conditions of such a restraint of trade?

Association

139) Is there a franchisee association? If not, why not, and would the franchisor mind if one was set up?
140) Does the franchisor hold regular franchise meetings? How often do they take place and where?
141) What system does the franchisor have for keeping in touch with franchisees?
142) Does the franchisor have a newsletter and/or hold seminars?

Company outlets?

143) Where are all the company-owned outlets?
144) How do they operate, e.g. do they contribute to advertising; how do they pay for stock?
145) Do company shops provide the same goods/services as franchised shops?

Refurbishment

146) How often does the franchisee have to refurbish the premises?
147) Does the franchisor share some of the cost?
148) Does the franchisee have an option whether to refurbish or not?
149) Can refurbishment be made a prerequisite for renewal of the contract or an excuse to terminate the contract?

Franchise services

150) What assistance does the franchisor provide for its franchisees to ensure that high standards are maintained?

The operating manual

151) Who compiles it and how often is it updated?
152) Can you see a copy of the operating manual before you sign the contract? If not, why not?
153) Does it adequately cover all aspects of the franchise business including accountancy and bookkeeping practices?
154) What is the VAT number of the franchisor? Are there any payments to be made to the franchisor which are subject to VAT?

155) Has the franchisor submitted a copy of the franchise agreement to the Office of Fair Trading?
156) If the business does not perform as projected for whatever reason what, if any, steps will the franchisor take to find out why the business is performing poorly? Will the franchisor give additional assistance in the form of management help on the franchise premises?
157) In cases of emergency/franchise holidays can the franchisor provide management back-up services?

Specialist staff

158) If the business relies on specialist staff, e.g. computer salesmen, does the franchisor assist in recruitment?
159) How expensive is the recruitment process? E.g. 'head-hunting' for a computer salesman is very expensive and can cost significant sums.
160) What turnover rate can one expect in such specialist staff?

Accounts and insurance

161) Is the franchisee obliged to have stipulated auditors for the franchise or can they choose their own?
162) If auditors are stipulated, who are they? Are they chartered accountants? What do they charge?
163) Does the franchisor have employers' public liability insurance?
164) Will the franchisee have to take out employers' and public liability insurance? If yes, are they obliged to use a particular insurance company? If yes, which one and how much does it cost?
165) In what way is the franchisee covered against claims by third parties against the franchisor?

Credit

166) Will the franchisor have to offer credit to customers? If so, does the franchisor have a special relationship with any of the finance houses?

Future growth

167) What is the growth rate the franchisor is planning over the next five years? Does the franchisor have the resources to cope with the additional growth – do they intend to increase their staff?

CAUTION

Obtain the answers to *all* the above questions and go through them together with all of your other research with a commercial solicitor and chartered accountant.

QUESTIONS TO ASK OTHER FRANCHISEES ALREADY TRADING OR EX-FRANCHISEES

1) How long have they traded?
2) Are they content with the franchisor generally?
3) Are they getting the support and services from the franchisor that they were led to expect, and are the franchisors as experienced as they say they are?
4) What did the franchise cost to set up and was this comparable with the franchisor's projection?
5) Is the product/service as good as the franchisor states?
6) Are they breaking even?   Are the projections that the franchisor anticipated
7) Are they making a profit?   realistically being achieved?
8) Is the royalty a burden or can the business easily support it?
9) Is the advertising that the franchisor carries out sufficient and in accordance with what he represented he would do?
10) What are supplies like – prompt/slow delivery?
11) Is there a franchisee association? If not, why not? Would the franchisor object to one being set up?
12) How good is the operating manual? Does it deal with all aspects of the franchise business adequately? If not, in which areas is it lacking?
13) Was training good/bad or adequate?
14) Is the contract fair? Was legal advice obtained before entering into the contract? Were variations requested? Were they successful?

QUESTIONS TO ASK THE BANK

About the franchisor
1) Ask them what they know about the franchisor.
2) How long has the franchisor banked with them?

About the finance
3) What vetting procedure have they subjected the franchise to?
4) What security will the bank require?
5) How much are they prepared to lend?
6) What capital repayment holiday can they offer?
7) What will the bank charges be?

QUESTIONS TO ASK THE BFA

1) When did the franchisor gain member/other status?
2) Was the criteria for membership fulfilled?
3) Was the franchise piloted successfully for the correct period?
4) Were the correct documents disclosed?
   i.e. disclosure document ⎤
        franchise agreement ⎥
        prospectus   ⎬ request photocopies
        accounts   ⎦
5) Have there been any complaints against the franchise? If so, by whom and what was the outcome?
6) Has any franchisee used or wanted to use the BFA Arbitration Scheme in relation to the franchisor? If yes, did the franchisor agree to it or not?

6

Researching a franchise

There are essentially two stages to researching a franchise:
Stage 1 – Researching the franchise opportunity and the franchisor company.
Stage 2 – Researching the franchise contract and the implications of all its clauses.

The first of these two stages will be discussed in this chapter. Stage two will be dealt with in Chapter 7.

THE RESEARCH BUDGET

Many people think that research is a waste of time and they cannot be bothered with it. They often end up losing large amounts of money simply because they are not cautious. Make sure this does not happen to you. Anyone who believes everything they are told in business will never succeed. You need to check everything yourself and you need to obtain independent advice.

Research is cheap if you want to find a good business and you want to stay in business. When you have found a franchise you are really interested in it is advisable to allocate about 1 per cent of the franchise cost for research. For example, if the franchise is £45,000 then allocate £450 for research. This money can be used for obtaining independent advice from a commercial solicitor, an accountant and for carrying out your own research.

THE FRANCHISE COMPANY

You must verify how long the franchisor has been franchising and how many outlets they have, including franchised outlets. It is also important to know what experience they have in that field. If the franchisor is franchising for the first time you need to know how many pilot operations they have, where they are, and for how long they have been running.

Market Research

The value of market research cannot be stressed enough. It is essential that the franchisor has carried out thorough market research to ensure that there is indeed a demand or niche in the market for the product/service that he has to offer. You need to know exactly what market research the franchisor has carried out. Ask to see the results. Note who carried it out and if necessary go back to the market researcher with queries. Note over what period it was carried out and what size sample was used. Do not invest in a franchise where no or inadequate market research has been carried out.

If you are given a market research report by the franchisor as proof of research carried out but you do not understand all its implications, then approach an independent market researcher for his opinion on the worth of the report and any conclusions reached i.e. obtain an independent critical analysis.

Franchise Turnover and Failures

You need to look for a low turnover rate. Of course, change in ownership could be for reasons other than failure, for example, selling or retiring, but on the whole, a low turnover should be treated with suspicion.

The Michael Power report 'Business Format Franchises – Closing or Continuing, 1987–1992', (Prepared by Power Research Associates, Tel: 071 580 5816 Fax: 071 491 0607) states that between a quarter and a third of business-format franchise systems in the UK operating before 1987 no longer exist.

According to a report by Middlesex University Planning Centre (published in *The Times* on 5th January 1993), 42 per cent of small businesses disappeared in ten years. The figures suggest that the chances of success in a franchise are better.

The '1993 NatWest Bank/BFA Franchise Survey' (published March 1994) states that while casualties are inevitable in the current economic climate at the system level only 2 per cent of franchises closed down due to 'commercial failure'. In other cases the franchise system was taken over or it was decided not to pursue the franchise option for various reasons.

The report concludes that

... for the general health of franchising such changes do mean that opportunities continue to appear for new systems that may be better equipped to prosper in these market areas. . . . It is by no means the case that when a system fails all of the franchisees go down with it. In many cases the individual units continue to trade successfully. Even if this may now be outside a franchise system, many such businesses owe their continued success to what the franchise system originally offered them.

At the 'individual unit level' the position is much more volatile. The report reckons that 6.3 per cent of all franchised units operating a year ago have undergone some 'forced' change. The figure for 'voluntary' changes in 1993 is 4.7 per cent.

Comment: Analyzing such statistics into meaningful conclusions is very difficult. Selling could itself be a sign of failure because another person may be willing to have a go where others have failed. You should request a list of every unit in the franchise together with details of change of ownership.

You must also ask the franchisor for details of units that have closed down altogether. Also ask whether the franchisor has 'bought back' any franchises, as this could be a way of disguising a franchise failure.

Financial Disclosure Of Information

You need to look at the latest accounts of the franchisor company. Ask for them, even if they have not yet been filed with Companies House. If sufficient information is not available for you to judge the profitability of the opportunity you are considering, you should not proceed. You must obtain the advice of an accountant specializing in franchising.

Projections

Treat these with caution and do not believe in them blindly until you can verify them by your own research. Remember they are only projections – that is, a set of estimated figures for illustrative purposes only.

THE FRANCHISOR COMPANY

You need to ascertain with which company you will be signing the franchise contract. All your research should then relate to that company. There are cases where the franchisor company is a subsidiary company, i.e. a company within a group of companies. It is quite feasible for such a subsidiary to have little or no assets whilst other companies within the group have significant assets. You should ensure that the company you sign your franchise contract with is the one with the significant assets.

Directors

How long has the company been trading? The longer the better. Who are the directors and key executives? Do they have relevant experience in that trade, and in franchising? Ask the franchisors for CVs of the directors and executives.

Accounts

You should look at certified accounts for the company for at least three years. You may need to go back even further.

Court orders and settlements out of court

You need to ask the franchisor if there has been any litigation between the franchisor and its franchisees. If yes, then what was the outcome? In many cases settlements out of court are reached and you should request details. Everything must be obtained in writing.

Judging profitability

You want to go into business to make a profit. You need to ensure that the business opportunity the franchisor is offering you can indeed make a profit. Ideally you should ask to see audited accounts for at least three years of the pilot operations and satisfy yourself that they are indeed profitable. Of course, accounts may not be available for this length of time. However, do not rely on just seeing projected figures. *Real audited accounts must be seen.*

The audited accounts can be used to project your own figures with the assistance of the franchisor and you will then be reassured that the projections are realistic.

Researching the franchisor company

A company search should be carried out by you or an accountant at Companies House, 55 City Road, London EC1Y 1BB. On payment of £2 you will be given a microfiche which can be examined there or, if you have access to a microfiche reader, it can be taken away and examined at leisure. You can also take photocopies of anything on the microfiche reader at Companies House.

Currently there are no postal search facilities at Companies House but there are many agents who will undertake a search for you for a fee, e.g. Jordan & Sons Ltd, Jordan House, 47 Brunswick Place, London N1 6EE. Don't forget to ask the franchisor the name of the company as it may be different from the trading name.

The directors' report
This will contain:

* Information required by law.
* Information required by the Stock Exchange (where the company is quoted).
* Voluntary information.

Statutory requirements
Under the Companies Act 1985 a directors' report must give the following information:

1) The principal activities of the company and its subsidiaries and any significant change – Section 235.
2) A fair review of the development of the business during the year together with an indication of future developments and research and development activities – Section 235 and Schedule 7, paragraphs 6b and c. However, in practice you will find only the briefest of comments.
3) The names of the directors and details of their shareholdings – Schedule 7, paragraph 2.
4) Particulars of significant changes in fixed assets – Schedule 7, page 1.
5) Details of the company's shares acquired by the company itself during the year – Schedule 7, part 11.
6) Important events affecting the company which have occurred since the end of the year.
7) Statement of political or charitable contributions if over £200 per annum.

Stock Exchange Requirements

1) A geographical analysis of turnover of operations outside the UK and Ireland is required, and what this turnover contributes to the trading results if that contribution is abnormal in any way.

2) Details of anyone other than directors who hold 5 per cent or more shares of the class of voting capital.

3) Whether the company is 'closed' or not.

Chairman's statement

This may or may not be present. If present, it will contain comments on a number of general things, e.g. company strategy and plans for the future. Be cautious when reading it and always remember that it is the chairman's job to maintain confidence in the company and therefore he will be concentrating on the good points.

Auditor's Report

In the 1993 Autumn Budget Statement, the Chancellor of the Exchequer declared his intention to introduce simpler audit requirements to ease the regulatory burdens on small businesses. It was proposed that from 1994 companies with Sales of between £90,000 and £350,000 a year will only need an independent accountant's 'compilation report' on the validity of their accounting records and confirming that the company's statutory accounts have been compiled from the company's records and are in accordance with the relevant statutory requirements. For the large number of companies with turnovers of less than £90,000 per annum, there will be no audit requirement.

It is anticipated that these new rules will probably not be implemented before the end of 1994. Existing legislation will have to be amended, and these new measures are unlikely to affect the duty of the directors to maintain and prepare proper accounts.

The changes will mean that in practice the administrative costs of running a small company will be less because an annual audit will no longer be necessary. For potential franchisees wanting to investigate the accounts of a franchisor, it will mean that for smaller franchised businesses it will be essential to ask the franchisor for detailed financial information as their accounts filed with Companies House will be of limited value.

For companies with turnover of more than £350,000 per annum, an annual audit of the accounts will still be required.

INFORMATION FROM OTHER SOURCES

The main sources of information are of course the annual report and
accounts. However, there are a number of other sources of information which will give you a more complete picture of the company.
These are:

Quarterly or half yearly reports

Such interim statements are not audited but are useful.

Prospectuses

A prospectus must be issued by a company when it offers shares or
debentures for sale to the general public. The Third Schedule of the
Companies Act 1985 lays down the items that must be contained in
the prospectus. Furthermore, when a company goes 'public' i.e. its
shares have a listing on the Stock Exchange, the prospectus has to include information for listing. Thus, the prospectus contains a lot of
really useful information – this is usually as follows:

* Details of the offer, share capital, and how much has been borrowed.
* Details of directors, company secretary, auditors, financial advisers, solicitors, stockbrokers and bankers.
* Description of the company
  – history
  – business description
  – details on management and staff
  – company premises
  – where new shares are being issued a statement saying how pro-
    ceeds will be used
  – forecast of year's profits, details of dividends
  – future prospects and plans for the company.
* The accountant's report – profit and loss accounts, source and
  application of funds over three years and the latest balance sheets.
* General information, e.g. directors' interests, pending litigation.
* Statutory information.

Circulars

For quoted public companies which are subject to the rules of the
Stock Exchange. The Yellow Book (The Listing Rules), section 10
divides transactions into four classes. Depending on which class the

transaction falls into, rules are set down as to what the company is required to do, e.g. Class 1. Company is required to make an announcement to the Company Announcements Office and to the Press, *and* must send out a circular to shareholders (and obtain their consent if necessary) *or* publish listings particulars (if no consent is required).

The information in circulars is very useful as it will give you details of any major additions to, or realizations of the company's assets.

Newsletters and magazines
Many companies produce magazines or newsletters for their employees once a year. These can be very useful, if you can get your hands on them, as they may contain information that is not in the accounts. Some companies will make newsletters and magazines available to shareholders as well. They may even be distributed more frequently.

Sales information
Look at all the promotional literature of the company. It will give you an insight into, for example, its pricing policy and the quality of its product range.

Documents issued in a contested bid
If you are interested in a franchisor company which has successfully defended a bid then it will be useful to look at the documents which were issued in defence of the bid, because the company will have been fighting for its independence and will have been more forthcoming about its future plans.

THE PROFIT AND LOSS ACCOUNT

What it looks like
                            Example
The profit and loss account. For the year ending 31.12.93
1) Sales turnover   £150,000
   Opening stock   10,000
   Purchases   45,000
   Closing stock   15,000
2) − Cost of sales (opening stock + purchases −
   closing stock)   40,000

3) = Gross profit (sales + closing stock − opening stock + purchases)	110,000
4) − Expenses	90,000
5) = Operating profit	20,000
6) − Interest charges	5,000
7) = Profit before tax	15,000
8) − Taxation	4,000
9) = Profit after tax	11,000
10) − Dividends	4,000
11) = Profit retained	7,000

Points to note

The date – note this carefully, as it shows what time period the accounts cover.

Sales turnover – this is the total income that you receive into the business.

Cost of sales – this is obtained by adding the opening stock to the purchases and then deducting the closing stock.

Gross profit = sales turnover minus cost of sales (but before overheads). This figure will give you an indication of how efficiently the business is run.

Expenses – these are all the costs incurred in selling the product or service. For example:

+ business salaries (including own drawings)
+ rent
+ rates
+ lighting/heating
+ telephone/postage
+ insurance
+ repairs
+ advertising
+ bank interest
+ other expenses
= Total overheads

Operating profit = gross profit minus expenses.

Interest charges – these could be a major expense depending upon how much has been borrowed.

Profit before tax = operating profit minus interest charges.

Tax then deducted to give you *profit after tax*, and *dividends* are deducted to leave you with *retained profits*.

You need to work your way through the company's profit and loss accounts over at least a three year period. Certain key profitability ratios will be useful in interpretation of the accounts, and will be discussed later. Next you need to look at the company's balance sheet.

THE BALANCE SHEET

Balance Sheet as at 31.12.93

Capital £	Fixed assets
Cash introduced/loan capital	Land and buildings
	Machinery
	Motor vehicles
+ Net profit for the year	*Current assets*
Drawings	Stock
	Debtors
	Bank
	Cash
Current liabilities	
Trade creditors	
Accrued expenses	

Notes

The balance sheet is a statement of the company at a particular moment in time – so again, you need to note the date. The balance sheet is divided into two sections. The assets of the business on one side and on the other side what the business is financed by, i.e. liabilities. The two sides have to balance as a business can only have assets to the value of what it has invested in the business.

The working capital is calculated by subtracting current liabilities from current assets, i.e.

current assets − current liabilities = working capital

The working capital represents money immediately tied up in the business. The money that is needed to finance the working capital is often called net current assets in the balance sheet, although at other times the term working capital tends to be used.

Capital
This can be from three sources:

* share capital
* profit/loss from previous years
* loan capital – e.g. from a bank.

Overdraft from a bank
This would be treated as a current liability. Interest will be payable on the overdraft and will have to be repaid whether or not the business is successful.

There are two types of assets – fixed and current. They are usually listed starting with the most permanent assets, i.e. *fixed assets*, the one most difficult to turn into cash progressing to the one most easily turned into cash. These are such things as the premises, business and machinery. Basically they are assets of the company which will be assets over a long period of time. *Current assets* are assets that represent cash or are mainly used for conversion into cash and they usually have a short life. As in the example they are such things as stock, debtors, bank and cash.

It is absolutely essential for anyone going into a business not only to look at the above financial reports but to interpret the accounts using key ratios or to consult an accountant to do the same. You need to ensure that the business is financially sound and that you will make a good profit.

USE OF KEY RATIOS

Three types of ratio will be discussed:

1) Operating ratios – these show how the company is trading.
2) Financial ratios – these measure the financial structure of a company and relate to the company's trading activities.
3) Investment ratios – these relate the number of ordinary shares and their market price to the profits, dividends and assets of the company.

We shall be concentrating on the first two types of ratio.

Operating Ratios

1)

$$\frac{\text{trading profit}}{\text{turnover (sales)}} \times 100 = \text{profit margin on sales}$$

trading profit =
profit before interest
charges and tax.

In a manufacturing industry the profit margin on sales is between 8 per cent and 10 per cent, while in food retailing it is about 3 per cent because dealing in high volumes and low margins.

Note: Profit margins on sales is *not* the same as gross profit margin.

If the profit margin on sales is *low* it is a sign of poor performance. What you need to look for is better than average margins which will indicate good management within the company.

2)

$$\frac{\text{trading profit}}{\text{capital employed}} \times 100 = \text{return on capital employed (ROCE)}$$

This is one of the most important ratios as a measure of profitability. The ROCE can be calculated for the company or any of its trading activities; if it is very low for any part of the business then this suggests that activity should not be continued unless obviously an integral part of the business. When the ROCE is very low the company should also be wary of starting new activities.

3)

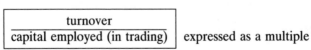

$$\frac{\text{turnover}}{\text{capital employed (in trading)}} \quad \text{expressed as a multiple}$$

An increase in this ratio indicates improvement in performance but if the ratio is increasing too rapidly watch out! It could be a sign of overtrading.

4)

$$\frac{\text{stocks}}{\text{turnover}} \times 100$$

A well-run company usually tries to carry the minimum stock needed, simply because it will not want money tied up unnecessarily. A rising stock ratio without any reason reflects lack of demand for the goods and/or poor stock control. An average manufacturing company should have a stocks/turnover ratio of around 25 to 30 per cent.

5)

$$\frac{\text{trade debtors}}{\text{turnover}}$$ expressed as a percentage or multiplied by 365, as the collection period in days

Normal terms of payment for most companies are at the end of the month following delivery. The average credit given would be about six to seven weeks, making debtors about 12 per cent of turnover. Realistically, a debtors' figure of 20 to 28 per cent is quite normal, although some companies do give longer credit to be more competitive. A decreasing collection period may at first appear to be a good sign but you need to verify that the company is not just desperate for cash and exerting undue pressure on customers or giving extra discounts for cash.

6)

$$\frac{\text{trade creditors}}{\text{sales}} \times 100$$

This ratio indicates the amount of credit the company is allowed by its suppliers. It is a very useful ratio to monitor because the suppliers are closest to the company. If you see that the company is trying to get as much credit as it can despite forfeiting on discounts it shows that it is short of cash. Be especially wary of the company changing suppliers – it is usually a good warning signal.

7)

$$\frac{\text{working capital}}{\text{sales}} \times 100$$ working capital = (stocks and trade debtors − trade creditors)

This ratio shows how much capital is needed to finance operations in addition to capital invested in fixed assets. This ratio can vary vastly but if it drops you should be wary because the company may be overtrading.

Financial Ratios

In addition to analyzing the above ratios you should be aware of the following financial ratios which can prove very informative. You need to ensure that the franchisor company is not 'over geared', i.e. that it has not borrowed so much (compared to equity) that it has an adverse effect on business. You will also need to ensure that you are not over-geared when you set up your franchise. Interest paid to service borrowings is profit forgone.

8)

$$\frac{\text{debt}}{\text{equity}} \times 100 \qquad \text{A good ratio to check on}$$

When setting up the borrowings for your franchise your gearing should be no more than 50 per cent. This will alleviate pressures on the business. In many cases banks will be prepared to lend up to 75 per cent, but be careful to ensure that the business can support the borrowings.

You will need to assess the franchisor company's liquidity. You can do this by looking at the companies within the franchisor group of companies.

9)

$$\text{current ratio} = \frac{\text{current assets}}{\text{current liabilities}}$$

This ratio can vary widely depending on the type of business but generally a current ratio of between 1.5 to 2 is regarded as normal. Any lower ratio is a warning sign.

Another ratio to consider here would be what is called the quick ratio or acid test.

10)

$$\text{acid test} = \frac{\text{current assets} - \text{stock}}{\text{current liabilities}}$$

This ratio is very important because it recognizes that a certain amount of the current assets are tied up in stock and cannot be readily converted to cash. If the company was put into a situation where it had to settle with its creditors by collecting immediately from its debtors this ratio will indicate whether the company can indeed do that. If the ratio is less than 1 then the company will not be able to settle.

Cash flow can be the biggest problem in a business. If the above ratios cause concern the company might be having cash flow problems and you will need to investigate the matter in more detail. If the company is experiencing cash flow problems it will eventually run into an overtrading situation unless it rectifies the problem – which it can do in a number of ways. You need to establish whether or not the problem exists and if it does exist that the company is dealing with it effectively. Remember that cash flow difficulties experienced by the franchisor will adversely affect its franchisees, e.g. reduced advertising, limited new stock.

It is not suggested that you should laboriously work through all the above ratios. But, you must be aware of the depth of research that is absolutely necessary before you invest your monies. It would be very useful to follow the above guidelines for example where you are interested in several franchise opportunities. Carry out your own DIY research on all of them and after you have eliminated some (which is a certainty) approach a commercial accountant for an independent, professional analysis. If the franchisor company is sound you can continue.

The franchisor will provide you with projected figures (which are based on the pilot operations and other franchises) and you will have to research all the above points in relation to what is being offered to you. Research the profit and loss account and balance sheet using the projected figures and key ratios. You need to ensure that the projected figures are realistic and that business can be profitable. You must contact all existing franchisees and ask them whether they are making a profit. Ask to see their accounts – they may oblige. Do not take anything on trust. You should calculate the following for a six month projection:

1) *Your gross profit*

Projected sales – direct costs = gross profit
(purchases,
labour costs)

e.g. £100,000 − (£20,000 + £30,000) = £50,000 GP

2) *Your gross profit margin*

$$\text{GPM} = \frac{\text{gross profit}}{\text{sales}} \times 100$$

e.g. $\text{GPM} = \dfrac{50,000 \times 100}{100,000} = 50\%$

3) *Your overheads or expenses* – (see list on page 56)
For example, take them as being £30,000 in this case and then you can calculate your breakeven point.

4) *Your breakeven*

$$\frac{\text{overheads}}{\text{gross profit margin}} \times 100 = \text{breakeven}$$

e.g. $\dfrac{30,000 \times 100}{50} = 60,000$

  i.e.   £60,000 is needed just to break even.

The monthly breakeven can be calculated by simply dividing the breakeven sales by 6 if projections are for 6 months (as here) or 12 if they are annual projections.

e.g. $\dfrac{60,000}{6} = 10,000$

So, in this example £10,000 is needed per month just to break even. Anything above this will be a profit. If the business is unable to generate a minimum of £10,000 per month it will be trading at a loss and will be unable to meet liabilities.

Before you start in business you need to ensure that the level of sales needed to break even is indeed realistic, and when you are trading you will need to monitor the sales and the breakeven continuously and regularly. Remember that your breakeven calculations will give you an average monthly or weekly breakeven target, but in practice actual sales can fluctuate due to seasonal differences.

5) *Profit*

Projected sales – breakeven sales × gross profit = profit margin

e.g. $100,000 - 60,000 \times 50\% = 20,000$
  i.e.   Profit = £20,000 or six months in this example.

The calculations above are essential, not only for analyzing the franchise opportunity but for inclusion in your business plan and presentation to your bank manager. Discuss all projections with an accountant and make sure that they are advisable for the location you are considering.

Remember: *Research is a blind date with knowledge*. You do not know what you will find. You should research with an open mind. Be prepared for anything. Your research may show that it is not worth investing in the venture – heed the facts and figures you have found and do not go ahead regardless because you have a hunch that it will work. In such a case your research will have saved you from investing in a bad business opportunity.

On the other hand your research may be very positive and you will be able to invest with confidence. Always remember, however, that no business is risk free.

7

The franchise contract

Once you have researched and assessed the franchise opportunity and satisfied yourself that the franchisor's claims are realistic and achievable you need to *research and understand* the franchise contract and the implications of the terms.

No reputable franchisor is out to score points or gain an unfair advantage over you in the agreement, *but remember* that the franchisor and his advisers have written the agreement – so it is bound to favour his interests rather than yours. The balance of doubt is *not* on your side and the scales are tipped in his favour. It is up to you to make sure you even the odds.

The franchise contract is traditionally regarded as non-negotiable. The reason being that the foundation of the franchise concept is strict uniformity between outlets. This is absolutely correct. But there is no reason why all the franchisees in a chain cannot have the same equitable and fair contract. You have to stand firm in trying to get what is best for you. Don't put up with unfair clauses. Get your solicitor to negotiate on terms that are a problem. If you get no joy from the franchisor don't proceed any further. If enough franchisees make it clear that they won't settle for the unfair contracts that can and do exist the franchisor will eventually have to play ball fairly or not play ball at all. It's up to you. *Remember* – the contract is the only formal, legally binding agreement that you will have. The terms within it are vital. It will govern every aspect of your franchise relationship. (A specimen franchise contract is given at the end of this chapter.)

THE CONTRACT TERMS

The contract begins with a statement of the parties to the agreement. Of course, contracts vary but there are a number of standard clauses

65

that you must understand and certain things to look out for. There will be a general clause stating that the franchisor operates through franchised outlets, stating trademarks and the existence of an operating manual. This will be followed by a *grant* of the franchise and the time period for which the franchise is to operate.

Time period renewal

Make sure the franchise runs for a reasonable period – usually five to ten years. This plays an important part in ensuring that you get your start-up costs back. Make sure the franchise is renewable after your period is up. Your *renewable option* should be present without any further payment; it should be renewable for a similar period to the original term and terms should be similar and not less favourable than you originally enjoyed. You need to protect yourself against unfair and unreasonable refusal to renew on the part of the franchisor.

As mentioned previously, there has been a case where a franchisor insisted on the property being revamped before renewal and then still refused to renew after considerable monies had been spent on doing just that. Don't always believe anything the franchisor says. It is essential that everything is obtained in writing and that the franchisor cannot unreasonably withhold consent to renew. GET IT ALL IN WRITING FROM DAY ONE!!!

Territory

Normally, you will be given an *exclusive territory* in which to operate the business. It is best to have details of this on an *actual* map. Find out where your neighbouring unit is, because obviously they will be competition for you. Make sure the franchisor cannot reduce your territory and find out on what basis he has allocated the territory, i.e. what market research has he carried out? Make your own enquiries about this, verify everything the franchisor says and get it stated in the contract. Be very cautious if a franchisor doesn't give you an exclusive territory or sufficient details.

As far as a franchisee is concerned it is in your interest to obtain the largest territory possible. However, this is not always ideal for the franchisor who will naturally be concerned that you may not exploit the full market potential. Some established franchisors have great market power and indeed refuse to grant territorial exclusivity. Such franchises should be considered with great care, but bear in mind that some excellent franchisors refuse to give territory on the ground that they need to be able to respond flexibly to market demand. This of course is to everyone's advantage.

A franchisor will be concerned that you may not work hard enough to make your business a success. He will expect you to achieve a certain level of performance, failing which he may take back part of the territory or remove the exclusivity from the territory. Again this would not be a satisfactory arrangement for a franchisee since other factors, e.g. insufficient franchisor support, may be responsible for the low performance of the franchise.

Property
There will be various clauses in relation to your business property.

First ownership
It is better to lease the premises yourself. At least that way the increase in property value (assuming there is one) will benefit you, or if the franchise agreement is terminated for any reason you will be able to continue another business on the same premises. However, a number of franchisors insist on leasing the premises themselves. They will then sublease or rent the premises to you, usually at a markup. It can be an advantage that you don't have to lay out a premium but you need to know exactly what the terms are to be. Enquire whether some form of scheme is operated whereby you will share in the increase in property values if any.

Reverse Premium
If the franchisor is well known (like The Body Shop or McDonald's) they may be offered a 'reverse premium' by the landlords i.e. the latter pays the franchisor a premium for leasing the premises. Such reverse premiums can be large and you should ensure that the benefit of it is passed on to you if you are taking on the site.

The franchisor will assist you in finding suitable sites. This service is usually included in the initial franchise fee. *Know* what your business requires. Do you need a high street position or will a good secondary position suffice? There will be a big price difference between the two. Do not overspend. Consider only what is within your financial limits.

There will be clauses stating that erection or conversion of the property must be at your expense and in accordance with the franchisor's plans and specifications and that you must complete works by a certain date. Make sure everything is priced carefully. Some franchisor's estimates on job costs are painfully unrealistic and outdated and franchisees find themselves in the position where costs have overrun to twice as much; they have premises they don't know what to do with and they can't raise extra funds to complete the works. Make sure that if this happens the franchisor is prepared to alter specifications to within the budget and the figures they originally provided.

The manual

You will have to undertake to comply with the operating manual which contains the know-how of the business. As the information in it is confidential a franchisor may refuse to allow you to see it before signing the contract. Insist on seeing a specimen and make sure that you will be able to comply with it. No reasonable or reputable franchisor can expect anyone to agree blindly to comply with something they have never seen. The information contained in the manual, together with the training, should impart the know-how and expertise to make your franchise unit a success. It should clearly illustrate how the business should be conducted. The franchise contract will contain clauses to restrict you from divulging the confidential information in the manual.

Advertising

In relation to advertising it is essential for you to verify

1) How money for advertising is to be utilized.
2) What percentage of your royalty fee will go towards advertising?
3) Does it get paid into a separate fund?
4) How can you check that the money is being correctly spent, e.g. for advertising the product or service as opposed to merely advertising the franchise opportunity to get more franchisees?

Where independent advertising is allowed, the franchisor's approval will usually be necessary – make sure it cannot be withheld unreasonably. A franchise chain should have a uniform image and therefore franchisees will be restricted from unauthorized advertising – both national or local. The franchisor will either undertake to spend a certain amount of the royalty on advertising on behalf of the franchisees or may set up a separate advertising fund to which every franchisee contributes an equal amount, e.g. 4 per cent of their gross income each week or month.

A franchisor may refine the system further by allowing a particular franchisee to pay extra for additional advertising should they require it. The franchisor will recommend how much advertising should be carried out. Of course this will be more in the first year when the business is unknown and will decrease with the build-up of goodwill.

Training

Training is an essential part of your franchise. You need to find out what the training involves, where it takes place, who pays for it. Does it cover training of staff? Will it be continued throughout your franchise when necessary and will that cost extra? All this must be covered in the contract.

Training and the operations manual

The franchisee should confirm:

* the minimum period of training
* the place of training
* any additional cost, e.g. travel and subsistance
* what the training will consist of, and who provides it.

It is crucial that a franchisee is trained to the highest standards in accordance with the expertise that the franchisor is offering. The franchisor should impart all the skills necessary for that particular franchise including staff selection, management and accounting procedures. The franchisor will be present when problems arise but the franchisee can only make the business a success if he also becomes an expert in the market.

Training should continue during the running of the franchise as no doubt the market will change, new systems will be developed and products improved. The franchisee should ensure that the franchisor will continue to provide necessary training.

Stock and supplies

One of the most important aspects of your contract will be the clauses dealing with *stock, supplies* and *equipment*. You need to verify mark-ups that the franchisor makes to you the franchisee. You need to know whether there is quality control on stock and goods supplied, how this is achieved and what happens if you are not happy with the quality – what will you be able to do about it? You must know how efficient supplies will be. What happens if there are delays? Will you be able to use alternative supplies? If not, will the franchisor compensate you for loss of sales due to insufficient stock? Do you have a choice of suppliers other than the franchisor? Some franchisors do allow you to purchase stock from other sources provided they approve. Make sure they cannot withhold approval unreasonably.

Exclusive supply

Some franchisors will be primarily concerned in distributing a particular product to you. You will be expected to purchase the product exclusively from the franchisor. The contract should state what will happen if the franchisor fails to provide the product. Under such conditions it should allow you to replenish from elsewhere.

Trading hours

In relation to your minimum opening hours be careful. Some franchisors very unrealistically base the profit projections *on all the hours God sends*. Convenience food stores are particularly notorious for this. You might face the problem, and it has happened, where you will be prosecuted for Sunday trading and realize that your profits are nowhere near the franchisor's projections. Make sure your contract states what trading hours are necessary to achieve your projections.

Price

A maximum/minimum price policy will normally be imposed. Make sure it gives you an adequate profit margin and that the goods are priced competitively with similar goods available in your area.

Royalty payments

Where *royalty payments* are due be cautious. If there is a low royalty fee it could mean that back-up services are poor, and if combined with a high initial fee it could mean that the franchisor will take your money and run. On the other hand, where the royalty fee is very high and because it is usually based on sales, you might find yourself in the unfortunate position of being pushed by the franchisor to increase sales at the cost of profitability. Always remember *turnover is vanity, profit is sanity*.

Nearly all franchisors rely on regular income from providing continuing services to the franchisee and obtaining a royalty payment on a weekly or monthly basis. This is usually calculated as a percentage of the gross income of the franchise unit. Sometimes a franchisor splits up the payments, e.g.

8 per cent royalty fee
1 per cent freight charge
1 per cent advertising fund
—

Total: 10 per cent

Don't be fooled by what he calls the payments. At the end of the day it is like paying a royalty of 10 per cent of the business's sales.

There is no royalty usually where the franchisor provides the franchisee with an exclusive product. In such cases the franchisor derives his income from a mark-up on the sale of the products to you. A test of reasonableness should be applied as to whether the royalty fee/mark-up is sensible depending on the services the franchisor provides. Royalty fees are seldom more than 10 per cent and mark-ups should be in accordance with the standard mark-ups for that type of business operation. Mark-ups on products and royalty fees need to be balanced and you should obtain an accountant's advice.

Sale or assignment by the franchisee
You need to have freedom and control in relation to selling or assigning your franchise at its market value. If you can only sell the business back to the franchisor, or the franchisor is unreasonable about sale to a third party, the value of business will suffer and you won't reap the benefits of your hard work.

You will usually have to give the franchisor first refusal and the franchisor's approval will be necessary for transfer to a third party. You must make sure he cannot withhold consent unreasonably, that an excessive transfer fee is not payable and that the franchisor cannot change the contract for the third party.

A franchisee may well wish to sell the franchised business for many reasons. In which case, he should consider the following:

* If the franchisor inserts a clause stating they have a first option should the franchisee wish to sell, the franchisee should ensure that the valuation is based on an open market value of the franchise.
* A franchisor will wish to control who the franchisee sells to. This is quite natural as an image needs to be preserved. However, the criteria by which a prospective purchaser will be judged by the franchisor should be clearly stated in the contract so that consent cannot be unreasonably withheld.

Sale or assignment by the franchisor

Most franchise contracts allow the franchisor to sell or assign the franchise without prior consultation with or approval by franchisees. This unilateral aspect of the franchise relationship is very undesirable and should not be tolerated by any franchisee. As previously stated, there have been cases where a franchisor has assigned the franchise contract to a new franchisor who cannot provide the support and services the franchisees contracted for. In certain cases this has been so detrimental to the franchisee's business that it has then failed. You should endeavour to have a clause in the contract by which the franchisor can only sell/assign by a majority vote of the franchisees.

Termination of the contract

It is very important that you know the reasons for which the franchisor could terminate the agreement. The obvious reason is that you fail to comply with the contract. You need to ensure that the franchisor gives you a reasonable time period to rectify any breach. Some franchisors will list breaches which they think are so serious that they merit termination without notice, for instance, failure to report sales or selling non-franchise goods. Make sure anything listed is indeed a material breach and not something trivial.

Don't sign anything which allows the franchisor to terminate if, for example, you don't purchase a minimum quantity of goods or services, or you don't reach a certain sales quota. You do not know how your business will perform so don't commit yourself.

STANDARD CLAUSES

All contracts will contain certain standard clauses which are to be expected because of the franchise relationship but you must make sure they are still reasonable. For example, a *secrecy clause* to protect know-how; an *inspection clause* to make sure that the franchisor can enter the business premises at a reasonable time to ensure you are complying with the contract. An *indemnity clause* will state that you must indemnify the franchisor against loss, damage, liability by you or your agent. This is fine, provided it only applies if the franchisor is blameless. A *restraint of trade clause* will be present to prevent ex-franchisees from engaging directly or indirectly in a business venture in competition with or in conflict with the franchisor in the territory for a given period of time – usually one year. It will probably also include a clause restraining employment of former employees in the franchise or of the franchisor.

A *choice of law clause* can be very important. It is particularly crucial where the franchisor is based abroad. Such a clause will state which law will govern the contract. For example, if the franchisor is based in France, will it be French or English law? Where the reader is thinking of taking up a 'foreign' franchise he needs to be particularly careful. Is the law that is stated as applying the most beneficial for him? If the franchisor is based say in the USA, the contract may still state that English law is to apply. However, this will not be wholly beneficial to the franchisee because the USA has franchise legislation while we don't and if the worst came to the worst the damages that could be obtained in a legal action in the USA would be greater than in England. Sometimes foreign franchisors specifically state that English law is to apply because they can get away with doing things here that legislation in their own countries makes illegal. Really, you should be able to choose which law is to govern the contract where the franchisor is based abroad.

An *arbitration clause* may also be present. This states that an 'arbitrator' (someone both the franchisor and franchisee agree upon) will decide any dispute. It has the advantage for the franchisor that the proceedings are private but there is no real advantage for the franchisee who may be stuck with an unsatisfactory decision. For the franchisee it is more beneficial to be able to resort to the usual legal remedies.

It is important to remember that whether or not such a clause exists a franchisee can approach the BFA under its arbitration scheme (see Chapter 4). The advantage of their scheme, as discussed earlier, is that franchisees only pay one third of the costs, even if they lose, and pay nothing if they win. Only the franchisee can initially elect to use the scheme. The only problem is that the franchisor can refuse to refer the dispute to arbitration. Then the franchisee has no choice but to go to court.

In case of *death or incapacity* you need to ensure that provisions are made by which the franchisor must assist to continue the business until it can be sold profitably, or the franchisor buys the business at market value or helps the franchisee's dependants take over. It is vital that you take out *life assurance*. Both the bank and your franchisor will usually insist on this anyway.

A franchisor may try to put a *decisions in writing* clause in the contract stating that the franchisor is only bound by statements or promises made in writing. You should not accept such a clause *unless* you feel comfortable that all your discussions are fairly represented in the contract.

All franchisors make a 'sales pitch' to interest you in their business but where they make oral representations to induce you to enter into the contract they must be prepared to be bound by their statements. To avoid misunderstandings all representations should be recorded in writing and added as an appendix to your contract.

Some franchisors may have the nerve to try to go even further and put a clause in the contract stating the contract is the entire agreement and that you have not relied on other oral or written representations. Obviously you have relied on information and representations by the franchisor so don't accept such a clause.

In order to protect yourself further request a *no discrimination between franchisees* clause. A reputable and fair minded franchisor should not object. There have been cases where some franchisees were given preferential discounts and company-owned shops supplied with superior stock to that of its other franchisees.

In other countries, for example the USA, Franchisee Associations are very popular and provide an invaluable function. You should have a clause in the contract allowing you to set up such an organization. Be very wary of a franchisor who will not agree to it. The chances are he will be pursuing a divide and rule policy between the franchisees and this will certainly not benefit you.

Annual meeting and franchisee association

It is extremely important that franchisees be able to meet at least once a year to discuss important issues and exchange ideas. A clause should be inserted to require the franchisor to arrange such events. It should be stated who is to bear the cost. Normally the franchisor will arrange the event with franchisees contributing to the cost. A franchisee association is extremely useful. Some people fear that it may be like a trade union. This is unlikely. It is useful for both franchisees and franchisors. For instance, if a particular franchisee is letting standards slip other franchisees within the group will soon put him right as they will not want their image tarnished. On the other hand, if for example the franchisor is not providing sufficient support, the franchisees will have more impact if they act together in approaching the franchisor with their complaints.

Depending on the nature of the franchised business there may be other clauses in the contract, and you should be aware of their implications. I will discuss some of these now.

Insurance
The franchisee will have to effect his own insurance. The franchisor will do likewise. You would be well advised to ask for the franchisor's assistance in negotiating suitable policies with an insurance company for the franchise chain. This will reduce costs. The franchisee should carry personal insurance in case of incapacity. In most cases the bank will insist on this.

Minimum wage provision
The franchisee is in control of hiring and firing employees. It is rare that wages disputes arise but there is always the possibility that a franchisee may get involved, and of course this would reflect badly on the whole chain. Thus it is not unreasonable for the franchisor to impose a minimum wage policy in the contract to avoid any problems.

Vehicles used in the franchised business
For those franchises which require specially equipped vehicles the contract will contain provisions regarding ownership of those vehicles. The franchisee may have already paid for them in the initial fee or may lease or hire them. It would be in the franchisee's interests to have a clause outlining the rate at which the vehicles should depreciate and an agreement under which the franchisor will buy back the vehicles should the franchise agreement terminate.

Liability of the franchisor to his franchisee
No doubt some franchisors will want to exempt liability in contract or in tort. In such cases the Unfair Contract Terms Act 1977 must be considered. It is not entirely clear how this Act applies to franchise agreements. Sections two and three of this Act regulate the exclusion of liability or negligence or breach of contract. As far as you are concerned liability for death or personal injury cannot be excluded and other exemptions have to satisfy the test of reasonableness.

Franchisor third party liability for defaults of franchisee
There is a real risk that the franchisor could be held liable to third parties if a franchisee goes bankrupt or into liquidation. Therefore the franchisor will wish to protect himself. It will not be unusual for him to require the franchisee to declare the franchisee relationship

on the premises, on order forms and on other stationery. This will be especially important in relation to trade creditors. Normally, amounts owing to customers will be insignificant.

The franchisor usually sets up an arrangement whereby they grant a master licence to a subsidiary which in turn franchises to the franchisee. The franchisee pays the franchise fee to the subsidiary who then pays it to the holding company:

The theory of doing it this way is that licence of a trademark is unlikely to result in liability to third parties. Thus, there is only a risk for the subsidiary company.

The situation may be varied so that the Holding Co. Ltd grants the franchisee the licence, use of intellectual property and manages the advertising, while the subsidiary enters into the franchise agreements and exercises control. The real reason for doing it this way is tax. The problem of third party liability is a bonus. Usually franchisors adopt simpler structures – but it really depends on the amount of money at stake. Either way, you will probably find that the franchisor has arranged his business in such a way as to avoid liabilities to third parties.

Severance clause
This will state that if any part of the contract is held invalid or unenforceable it will not affect the validity or enforceability of the remainder.

You will need to research and understand every clause of the contract. Do not, as discussed earlier, go to just any solicitor; go to a commercial solicitor who understands franchising. Don't be afraid to ask for amendments or additions or deletions to the contract. If the franchisor is not reasonable you should not continue. If the franchisor is honest and reputable he should welcome your comments and be prepared to make the contract equitable for all franchisees, if it isn't already. Treat the whole research process like a game of chess. You must be practical, methodical and unemotional. No matter how fantastic the franchise opportunity seems to be, the contract should represent a real picture of what has been agreed and should be equitable.

Always remember you cannot ask enough questions. There is no greater force in business than facts combined with ideas. Once armed with all the facts look at them as they are. Use them to your advantage. List all the pros and cons on a piece of paper. Think about it for a few weeks and ask your solicitor's and accountant's advice.

Remember also what the outcome of research can be. You could analyze a glass of water into its chemical components and be left with nothing to drink and, as Thomas Huxley said, 'There is no sadder sight in the world than to see a beautiful theory killed by a brutal fact.' If this happens with your franchise, and you realize that the franchise is not as marvellous as the franchisor claims, at least you will not have invested your money on a bad business opportunity.

On the other hand, your research could have positive results and you will be able to proceed with confidence. However, always remember there is no such thing as 'zero risk'.

EUROPEAN COMPETITION LAW

Unlike the USA, there is no legislation in the UK governing franchise contracts. The law of contract and competition law applies, and because franchise agreements contain restrictions on the way a franchisee trades, European competition law also applies.

Franchise contracts always favour the franchisor and contain certain restrictions and obligations on the franchisee. For example, these can include limiting the area in which the franchisee can trade within an exclusive territory and restricting the supply of goods by letting the franchisor control how the franchisee acquires stock. Such restrictions are generally contrary to competition law and would normally have to be registered with the Office of Fair Trading and may also mean that an application has to be made to the European Commission for specific clearance.

European Block Exemption

To deal with what would soon be an avalanche of applications from franchisors, the European Commission has, through a series of documents called Block Exemptions, listed clauses within franchise contracts that do not need to be disclosed to the Commission together with clauses which are not acceptable because they are too restrictive and which mean that a franchise contract requires a specific exemption.

If a clause is not exempt, it will mean that it and perhaps the entire contract is not enforceable. So it is important for both the franchisor and the franchisee to be aware of how extensive the Block Exemption is, and its implications for the franchise contract.

The European Commission's Block Exemption Regulation No. 4087/88 sets out what obligations and restrictions a franchisor can impose on a franchisee and also lists what is not allowed to be included in a franchise contract without the agreement being granted a specific exemption. So it is important to look out for those clauses which could make the franchise agreement unenforceable.

A franchisor can include various clauses in the contract to protect the know-how and commercial integrity of his franchise system and such clauses are within the Block Exemption.

Unacceptable Provisions

The unacceptable provisions where the Block Exemption does not apply (and so for the clause to be legally enforceable the agreement would have to be subject to a specific exemption from the European Commission) include:

* Where the franchisor fixes the prices at which the franchisee may sell goods/services. However, a franchisor can *recommend* prices.
* Where the franchisor prevents a franchisee from selling to a customer because of the location of the customer's address. Although the franchisor can grant an exclusive territory to a franchisee and the franchisee can be prevented from soliciting custom from outside his territory, he cannot be prevented from serving unsolicited customers from outside his territory.
* Where undertakings which produce goods or provide services which are identical and are considered by users as equivalent in view of their characteristics, price, and intended use, enter into franchise agreements in respect of such goods or services.

* Where the franchisee is prevented from obtaining alternative supplies of goods of the same quality to those supplied by the franchisor and his nominated suppliers. This does not effect the franchisor's right to prevent the franchisee from selling goods which compete with the franchisor's goods (except for spare parts or accessories).
* Where the franchisee is prevented, after the termination of the franchise agreement, from using the franchisor's know-how where it has become generally known except where the franchisee has broken the contract.
* Where the franchisor prohibits the franchisee from challenging the validity of any industrial or intellectual property rights which are franchised. However, the franchisor can reserve the right to terminate the franchise if such a challenge is made by the franchisee.

Well-known franchisors who have successfully obtained individual exemption for their franchise agreements include Pronuptia (wedding dresses), Computerland (computer equipment), ServiceMaster (contract cleaning) and Yves Rocher (perfumes). However, these notifications were made before the Block Exemption Regulation on franchising. Now the Commission is less likely to grant individual exemption to a franchise system which cannot comply with the Block Exemption Regulation.

In practical terms a franchise contract, if properly prepared by an experienced franchise lawyer, will be drafted so as not to offend these rules. As a potential franchisee you should be aware of these issues and must, before signing any agreement, obtain independent legal advice to ensure that all the terms of the contract are enforceable.

At the time of writing contracts still exist that do not comply with these provisions simply because the franchisor has not got around to updating the contract.

There follows a specimen short form contract which you should look through to familiarize yourself with what a contract looks like, plus a specimen 'PizzaExpress' contract.

Franchise agreement – short form

By John Adams and
K. V. Prichard Jones

REPRINTED FROM *FRANCHISING: PRACTICE AND PRECEDENTS IN BUSINESS FORMAT FRANCHISING* BY KIND PERMISSION OF THE PUBLISHERS, BUTTERWORTHS

Dated .... 19 ....

1 Parties
.... whose [registered office *or* principal place of business] is at (*address*) ('the Franchisor') (1)
.... whose [registered office *or* principal place of business] is at (*address*) ('the Franchisee') (2)

2 Definitions
The following terms shall have the following meanings:
2.1 'Advertising Contribution': ....% of Gross Turnover (as defined in clause [3.12] of the Conditions) of the Business
2.2 'Business': the use (for mutual benefit) of the Mark and the Know-How in the business of trading under the Permitted Name in the style and manner stipulated by the Franchisor for (*insert details of Business to be carried out*)
2.3 'Conditions': the Standard Conditions and Special Conditions (if any) annexed to this Agreement which shall be deemed to be incorporated in this Agreement in their entirety
2.4 'Continuing Fees': the franchise fees of .... % of Gross Turnover (as defined in clause [3.12] of the Conditions) of the Business
2.5 'Financial Year': each year during the Term ending on the .... (*year end date*)
2.6 'Initial Fee': the initial franchise fee of £ .... (........ pounds)
2.7 'Know-How': the operational systems and methods of the Franchisor as divulged to the Franchisee from time to time during the Term
2.8 'Location': the premises shortly described as .... or such other premises as are approved by the Franchisor during the Term
2.9 'Manual': the confidential written systems of and regulations for the operation of the Business issued and amended by the Franchisor from time to time during the Term incorporating part of the Know-How and deemed to form part of this Agreement (Serial Number ....)
2.10 'Mark': the [Legend] [and design] and the logos associated with the

same and any additional or substitute Marks which the Franchisor shall deem suitable for the Business during the Term

2.11 'Minimum Package':

    2.11:1 The equipment products literature stock of all types and

    2.11:2 The minimum staff levels [at the location] stipulated in the manual from time to time during the Term

2.12 'Payment Dates':

    2.12:1 For the Initial Fee: on the signing of this Agreement

    2.12:2 For the Advertising Contributions and the Continuing Fees: the [tenth] day of each [calendar month] during the Term in respect of the Business during the immediately preceding calendar month

2.13 'Permitted Name': the permitted business name of the Franchisee which shall be '...........'

2.14 'Term': .... years from .... 19 ..... (the Commencement Date) and expiring on .... 19 ..... (the Expiry Date) unless sooner determined as provided in the Conditions

2.15 'Territory': the geographical area of (*insert description of area*) [and shown edged red on the map annexed to this Agreement]

3 The Right

In consideration of the payment of the Initial Fee the Insurance Premium the Advertising Contribution and the Continuing Fees by the Franchisee to the Franchisor and of and subject to the agreements on the part of the Franchisee in this Agreement the Franchisor grants to the Franchisee the right of using the Mark and the Know-How only:

3.1 In the Business

3.2 At and from the Location

3.3 Within the Territory

3.4 For the Term

3.5 Under the Permitted Name

3.6 In accordance with the Manual

Dated .... day of .... 19 ......

Signed by .... (*name of director*) for and behalf of .... (*name of Franchisor*)

Signed by .... (*name of director*) for and behalf of .... (*name of Franchisee*)

STANDARD CONDITIONS

1 Title

The Franchisor warrants that it is the beneficial owner of the Mark and Know-How

2 Franchisor's obligations

The Franchisor agrees as follows:

2.1 Training

To provide training within 90 days of this date at a place chosen by the Franchisor training in the conduct of the Business for one director of the Franchisee and all the initial employees of the Franchisee the cost of which is included in the Initial Fee

2.2 Manual

To issue the Franchisee with the Manual and to update it (provided the same shall remain the property of the Franchisor)

2.3 Advertising

To undertake an advertising and promotional programme for the Mark in selected areas of the British Isles in such manner as it considers appropriate using the Advertising Contribution

2.4 Advertising bank account

To pay the Advertising Contribution (together with similar contributions from [stores *or* outlets] owned by the Franchisor) into a separate bank account of the Franchisor maintained for that purpose only

2.5 Expenses

To issue to the Franchisee an account of the total expenditure by the Franchisor on advertising and promotion in each Financial Year of the Term provided that the Franchisor shall be entitled to recoup at any time from the total of the Advertising Contribution from all its franchisees in any year any excess of such expenditure over the total of receipts of the Advertising Contributions in previous or future years

2.6 Exclusive

Not to undertake on its own behalf nor to grant any franchise to any other person or entity in respect of the Business in the Territory (subject as appears later in these Conditions)

2.7 Information

Throughout the Term to consider and respond to all reasonable requests from the Franchisee for information and assistance concerning the Business

2.8 Supply Conditions

To procure that products for the Business shall be supplied to the Franchisee by the Franchisor or its approved suppliers on the same terms as those supplies to [stores *or* outlets] operated by the Franchisor itself in the United Kingdom

[2.9 Additional sales

To permit the Franchisee to sell such equipment and similar items in addition to the Minimum Package in order to satisfy specific orders or demand subject to the prior approval by the Franchisor of such equipment and other items]

3 Franchisee's obligations
The Franchisee agrees throughout the Term:
3.1 Training first
3.1:1　Not to commence the Business until [one director of] the Franchisee and all its senior employees have received training from and have been approved as competent by the Franchisor

3.1:2　To notify the Franchisor whenever it employs new staff in the Business

3.1:3　Not to permit any person to be employed in the Business unless such person is first trained and approved as competent by the Franchisor

3.1:4　To procure that all its executives and employees attend further training during the Term when required by the Franchisor

3.2 Registered user
Where necessary to become the registered user of the Mark or to execute on demand from the Franchisor such formal licence for record purposes as may be required in the United Kingdom

3.3 Authority
To display at the Location and on all stationery and any literature used by the Franchisee the text stipulated in the Manual from time to time disclosing that the Franchisee is licensed by the Franchisor and is not a branch or agent of the Franchisor

3.4 Mark
3.4:1　Constantly to protect and promote the goodwill attached to the Mark (which the Franchisee acknowledges is of great value)

3.4:2　To hold any additional goodwill generated by the Franchisee for the Mark or the Permitted Name as bare trustee for the Franchisor

3.4:3　Not to cause or permit any damage to the Mark or the title of the Franchisor to it or assist others to do so

3.4:4　Not to use the Mark, the Know-How or the Permitted Name except directly in the Business

3.4:5　Not to use the Mark, the Know-How or the Permitted Name in any manner after the Term or other sooner determination of the Agreement

3.4:6　Not to use the Mark or any derivation of the same in the corporate name (if any) of the Franchisee

3.5 Secrecy
Not at any time during or after the Term:
3.5:1　to divulge to any third party any information concerning the Business the Franchisor the Know-How or any other systems or methods of the Franchisor used in the Business (especially that contained in the Manual)

3.5:2   to copy in any way in any part of the Manual

3.6 Disclosure

Not to employ any person in the Business until that person has signed a non-disclosure undertaking in the form approved by the Franchisor from time to time

3.7 Volume

To use its best endeavours to achieve the greatest volume of business for the Business at the Location consistent with good service to the public

3.8 No other business

Not without the prior approval of the Franchisor:

3.8:1   to permit any other business venture to operate or trade at or from the Location

3.8:2   to extend the scope or range of the Business at the Location

3.8:3   to engage directly or indirectly in any other business other than the Business

3.9 No illegal use

Not to engage in any activities in the Business which may be contrary to law or governments or other regulations

3.10 Payments

To pay the Initial Fee the Continuing Fees and the Advertising Contribution (without demand deduction or set-off) to the Franchisor (or as it directs) on each of the Payment Dates (time being of the essence)

3.11 VAT contingency

Whenever applicable pay to the Franchisor VAT or any other tax or duty replacing the same during the Term charged or calculated on the amount of the Initial Fee the Continuing Fees and the Advertising Contribution

3.12 Calculations

To calculate the Continuing Fees and the Advertising Contribution on the gross turnover of the Business arising directly or indirectly from the conduct of the Business in the Territory during each calendar week of the Term (and for any period less than a complete calendar week) and gross turnover shall include

3.12:1   all credit sales of whatever nature whether or not the Franchisee has received payment of the outstanding accounts by the Payment Date relevant to the week when such credit sales were made

3.12:2   all cash sales of whatever nature made but not invoiced by the Franchisee in each week

3.12:3   all services performed and business dealings whatsoever (other than purchases) made or conducted in the Territory by the Business during each week

But shall exclude

3.12:4   any VAT

3.12:5   any customer refunds or credits arising from the supply of defective goods or services or the like provided that such refunds or credits shall only be deducted from gross turnover in the calendar week in which they are paid or allowed to the customer

3.13 Service report

On each Monday of each week to post by first-class mail (or by electronic means if required by the Franchisor) to the Franchisor complete and accurate statements in the form approved by the Franchisor in the Manual) of the sales and services performed by the Business since the last such Payment Date

3.14 Accurate accounts

To keep accurate books and accounts in respect of the Business in accordance with good accountancy custom in the United Kingdom and the standards set out in the Manual and to:

3.14:1 Accountants

have them audited at the expense of Franchisee once a year during the Term by the firm of Chartered Accountants nominated by the Franchisor

3.14:2 Audit

submit the whole of such audited accounts to the Franchisor within three months of the end of such year

3.14:3 Custody

keep them for not less than [3] years

3.14:4 Inspection

permit the Franchisor to inspect and take copies (at the expense of the Franchisor) of any financial information or records it requires (on reasonable prior notice in the event of inspection after normal business hours)

3.14:5 Financial Year

procure that each financial year or period of the Business shall be the same as the Financial Year

3.15 Discrepancies

In the event of discrepancies (amounting in total to more than [2%] per year of gross sales) in any such books or accounts to permit accountants nominated by the Franchisor but at the expense of the Franchisee to undertake audits of the same in each year of the Term of the Franchisor (at intervals at the discretion of the Franchisor) on reasonable notice and during normal business hours

3.16 VAT report

Within 14 days of submission or receipt to supply to the Franchisor a copy of each VAT return and/or assessment in respect of the Business

3.17 Conduct of the Business

Not to conduct the Business except:

3.17:1 Standards

In respect of services to the standards and quality and in the standard style and by the methods stipulated in the Manual from time to time ·

3.17:2 Regulations
        In confirmity with all relevant government or other regulations

3.17:3 Financial systems
        Under proper and comprehensive financial systems and con-
        trols as approved or stipulated by the Franchisor

3.17:4 Venue
        At or from the Location or such other venue first approved by
        the Franchisor

3.17:5 Inside Territory
        Inside the Territory

[3.17:6 Equipment
        With the equipment part of the Minimum Package in good and
        reliable condition]

[3.17:7 Staff
        With the staff part of the minimum package at full complement
        and fully trained and approved by the Franchisor]

3.17:8 Dealerships
        In accordance with the rules and regulations of any dealership
        or distributorship arrangements for any of the equipment or
        products dealt in by the Business

3.18 Insurance policy

3.18:1 To maintain and pay all premiums in respect of a compre-
        hensive insurance policy (in terms approved by the Franchisor)
        issued by an insurer nominated by the Franchisor in respect of
        the Location for all items stored there and for the business

3.18:2 To note on such policy that:

3.18:2.1 the Franchisor shall be covered by such policy in respect of
          all claims arising from activities at the Location or in the Busi-
          ness or of the Franchisee which are risks covered by such
          policy

3.18:2.2 the insurer shall notify the Franchisor in the event of any late
          premium payment by the Franchisee

3.19 Inspection of Premises

To permit the Franchisor or its representatives to inspect the Location at
any time during the Term

3.20 Right notices

To affix such patent copyright or trade mark ownership notices to any
stationery or literature used by the Franchisee in the Business as the Franchisor may require from time to time

3.21 Infringement indemnity

To indemnify the Franchisor from:

3.21:1 any alleged unauthorised use or infringement of any patent
        trade mark copyright or other intellectual property (other than
        the Mark and Know-How) by the Franchisee

3.21:2 any claim by any third party in respect of the conduct of the
        Business or the conduct or neglect of the Franchisee

3.21:3 any infringement by the Franchisee of any relevant regulations

3.22 Infringement notice

To notify the Franchisor of any suspected infringement of the intellectual property or other rights of the Franchisor and to take such reasonable action thereupon as the Franchisor directs at the expense of the Franchisor

3.23 Payment

Not to purchase any supplies [courses] products equipment or literature for the Business except from the Franchisor or (with the consent of the Franchisor) its approved suppliers to ensure even standards of quality of products and services from all the franchisees of the Franchisor and:

3.23:1 to pay the Franchisor for any equipment stationery or other items so purchased within 21 days of dispatch by the Franchisor

3.23:2 to pay promptly any other suppliers of the Franchisee in accordance with their usual terms and conditions

3.24 No sub-franchise

Not to grant any sub-franchise in respect of the Mark the Know-How or the Business

3.25 Promotions

3.25:1 To advertise the Business in the Territory in accordance with the requirements of the Franchisor set out in the Manual from time to time

3.25:2 (As part of such obligation) to expend not less than .... % of the gross turnover of the Business in each Financial Year upon local advertising and promotional activities

3.25:3 To participate in such promotional activities for the Business in the Territory as the Franchisor requires during the Term

3.26 Assignment

Not to assign transfer or otherwise deal with the Right or this Agreement or the Business in any way without the prior approval of the Franchisor which shall not be unreasonably withheld in the following circumstances:

3.26:1 if the proposed assignee is acceptable to the Franchisor and shall agree to be bound by the terms and conditions of the standard franchise agreement used by the Franchisor at the time of such proposed assignment for the residue of the Term and

3.26:2 if the Franchisee shall pay to the Franchisor the reasonable costs and expenses incurred by the Franchisor in the assessment of each proposed assignee

3.27 Director reliance

(As the Right has been granted to the Franchisee by the Franchisor in reliance upon the quality of the directors and shareholders of the Franchisee) not to permit any change in the same without the prior approval of the Franchisor which shall not be unreasonably withheld subject to the provisions in sub-clauses [3.26:1 and 3.26:2] of these conditions

3.28 Prices

3.28:1 Not to charge any customer any prices in excess of those stipulated in the Manual from time to time

3.28:2 Not to sell any items or provide any services to any person or entity associated with the Franchisee or its shareholders except at prices usually charged by the Franchisee to its non-connected customers

3.29 No competition

And for a period of [two] years afterwards:

3.29:1 Not to engage directly or indirectly in any capacity in any business venture competitive with or likely to damage the surviving goodwill of the Business in the Territory or in any territory any business venture competitive with any business of the other franchisees of the Franchisor

3.29:2 Not to solicit the customers or former customers of the Business with the intent of taking their custom

3.29:3 Not to employ any employee or former employees who were employed in the Business by the Franchisee or by the Franchisor or any other franchisee of the Franchisor and to procure that all directors and shareholders of the Franchisee enter into direct covenants of similar content with the Franchisor

3.30 Grant back

To notify the Franchisor and provide full details of any improvements in the methods systems products or programmes described by the Franchisor in the Manual or employed in the Business and to permit the Franchisor to incorporate free of charge any such improvements in its Manual for the benefit of the Franchisor and all its franchisees.

[3.31 Premises

3.31:1 To maintain the Location in good decorative repair and condition

3.31:2 To alter the exterior and interior decoration signs and furnishings of the Location when required to do so by the Franchisor in accordance with any amendments it may make to the house style of the Business

3.31:3 To observe and perform all its obligations under any lease or tenancy of the Location]

4 Expiry procedure

On expiry or termination of this Agreement the Franchisee agrees:

4.1 Not to endeavour to surrender the telephones used in the Business nor to hinder the transfer of such telephones to such person as the Franchisor directs

4.2 To return to the Franchisor all stationery used in the Business

4.3 To return to the Franchisor all publicity promotional and advertising material

4.4 To return to the Franchisor the Manual in good condition and without having made any copy of the Manual

4.5 To sign such notification of cessation of use of the Mark as is necessary for recording at the Trade Marks Registry

4.6 To cease carrying on the Business immediately

4.7 (When the Franchisee is the tenant or lessee of the Franchisor at the Location) to surrender to the Franchisor the relevant tenancy agreement or lease immediately upon such expiry or termination and to vacate the Location immediately

5 Expiry financial procedure

The Franchisee agrees:

5.1 Four weeks prior to the expiry of the Term or three weeks after receipt of notice of termination of this Agreement to furnish to the Franchisor a complete and accurate up-to-date list of customers of the Business with estimates of turnover of the Business to such expiry of termination date and

5.2 Thereupon to pay the Continuing Fees and the Advertising Contribution on the estimated Gross Turnover to such date and

5.3 Not later than the first Friday after such date to pay to the Franchisor any additional amount of the Continuing Fees and the Advertising Contribution calculated on actual gross turnover of the Business to such date

6 Miscellaneous

It is further agreed between the parties:

6.1 Reservation of rights

6.1:1 All the rights not specifically and expressly granted to the Franchisee in this Agreement are reserved to the Franchisor

6.1:2 The Franchisor may grant a licence to any entity to manufacture any products in the Territory or elsewhere for use in connection with the Business or displaying the Mark or for other purposes (except in competition with the Franchisee in the Territory) without any liability to the Franchisee

6.2 Interest

Without prejudice to the rights of the Franchisor and the condition that the Initial Fee the Advertising Contribution and the Continuing Fees are paid on time (time being of the essence) all sums due to the Franchisor which are not paid on the due date shall bear interest from day to day at the annual rate of ...... % over the current Bank plc daily base interest rate with a minimum of ...... %

6.3 Payment not on time

In the event that the Franchisee fails to pay any money due to the Franchisor on time the Franchisor may

6.3:1 cease immediately to take orders from and to deliver goods and services to the Franchisee

6.3:2 afterwards impose whatever credit limit it considers appropriate in respect of the Business of the Franchisee

6.4 Receipt

The receipt of money by the Franchisor shall not prevent either of the parties questioning the correctness of any statement in respect of that money

6.5 Force majeure

Both parties shall be released from their respective obligations in the event of national emergency war prohibitive governmental regulations or if any other cause beyond the control of the parties shall render performance of the Agreement impossible provided that this clause shall only have effect at the discretion of the Franchisor except when such event renders performance impossible for a continuous period of [12] calendar months

6.6 Severance

In the event that any provision of this agreement or these Conditions is declared by any judicial or other competent authority to be void voidable illegal or otherwise unenforceable [or indications of the same are received by either of the parties from any relevant competent authority] [the parties shall amend that provision in such reasonable manner as achieves the intention of the parties without illegality or the Franchisor may sever the offending provision from the same at its discretion *or* the remaining provisions of this Agreement shall remain in full force and effect unless the Franchisor in the Franchisor's discretion decides that the effect of such declaration is to defeat the original intention of the parties in which event the Franchisor shall be entitled to terminate this Agreement by [30] days' notice to the Franchisee and the provisions of clause [4] shall apply accordingly]

6.7 Low sales

The Franchisor may terminate this Agreement in the event that reasonably substantial turnover (which shall be calculated by the Franchisor on the basis of demographic and socio-economic data in respect of the Territory and the performance of its other franchisees) arising from the Business at the Location is not achieved within two years of the Commencement Date of the Agreement or for a continuous period of twelve months at any time afterwards during the Term provided that the Franchisor shall have the right (but not the duty):

6.7:1 then to appoint management personnel to supervise the Business at the expense of the Business to assist the Franchisor to increase sales and/or

6.7:2 to reduce the area of the Territory in proportion to such sales

6.8 New outlets

6.8:1 In the event that the Franchisor decides that the Territory is sufficiently large geographically and has a sufficiently large population to justify one or more further outlets for the Business in the Territory it may notify the Franchisee of such decision and on receipt of such notice the Franchisee shall have the right to open such further outlet elsewhere (than at the Location in an area of the Territory nominated by the Franchisor) provided that the Franchisee informs the Franchisor within 90 days of such notice of its agreement to do so

6.8:2 In the event that the Franchisee fails to notify the Franchisor of such agreement within 90 days or fails to open such further outlet in the Territory within six months of such notice the Franchisor shall have the right to reduce the Territory to enable it to provide an exclusive area in which a new franchisee may trade using the Mark and the Know-How without liability to the Franchisee

6.9 Prior obligations

The expiration or termination of this Agreement shall not relieve either of the parties of their respective prior obligations or impair or prejudice their respective rights against the other

6.10 Discretion

No decision exercise of discretion judgement opinion or approval of any matter mentioned in this Agreement or arising from it shall be deemed to have been made by the Franchisor except if in writing and shall be at its sole discretion unless otherwise expressly provided in this Agreement or these Conditions

6.11 Notice

6.11:1 Any notice to be served on either of the parties by the other shall be sent by prepaid recorded delivery or registered post (as the case may be) or by telex or by electronic mail and shall be deemed to have been received by the addressee within 72 hours of posting or 24 hours if sent by telex or by electronic mail to the correct telex or electronic mail number of the addressee

6.11:2 Each of the parties shall notify the other of any change of address or number as soon as practicable and in any event within 48 hours of such change

6.12 No agency

The parties are not partners or joint venturers nor is the Franchisee able to act as the agent or to pledge the credit of the Franchisor in any way

6.13 Whole agreement

The Franchisee acknowledges that this Agreement and these Conditions contain the whole agreement between the parties and it has not relied upon any oral or written representations made to it by the Franchisor or its employees or agents and has made its own independent investigations into all matters relevant to the Business

6.14 Breach procedure

In the event that the Franchisee fails to observe or perform any of its obligations under this Agreement or these Conditions in any way then the Franchisor may terminate this Agreement on 30 days' written notice and

6.14:1 notwithstanding such notice period if the breach complained of is incapable of remedy this Agreement shall terminate absolutely on service of such notice

6.14:2 in every other case if the breach complained of is remedied to the satisfaction of the Franchisor within the notice period this Agreement shall not terminate

6.14:3 no waiver of any breach of those obligations shall constitute a waiver of any further or continuing breach of the same

6.15 Insolvency

If the Franchisee enters into liquidation or suffers a receiver to be appointed to it or to any of its assets or makes a composition with any of its creditors (or the equivalent in Scotland) the Franchisor may at any time afterwards terminate this Agreement on notice with immediate effect and:

6.15:1 no creditor agent representative or trustee of the Franchisee shall have the right to use the Mark or the Know-How or continue the Business without the prior consent of the Franchisor

6.15:2 until payment of all money due to the Franchisor from the Franchisee on any account the Franchisor shall have a lien on any of the stock literature or other products held by the Franchisee

6.16 Assignment

The Franchisor may assign charge or otherwise deal with this Agreement in any way

6.17 Renewal option

The Franchisee shall have the option to extend the Term for a further period of .... years commencing on the day following the Expiry Date subject to the following:

6.17:1 service of notice of extension by the Franchisee on the Franchisor not later than ...... calendar months prior to the Expiry Date and

6.17:2 payment by the Franchisee to the Franchisor not later than two calendar months prior to the Expiry Date of a renewal fee of ...... % of gross turnover of the Business during 12 calendar months prior to the first day of the calendar month in which such notice is served or the then current Initial Fee charged by the Franchisor to its franchisees (whichever is the less) and

6.17:3 proper performance and observance by the Franchisee of all its obligations under this Agreement throughout the Term and

6.17:4 execution by the Franchisee of a new franchise agreement in the standard form used by the Franchisor at the time of service of such notice in respect of the further period of ...... years without any option to review

6.18 Further extension

In the event that any regulation requires the Franchisor to extend the Term beyond the period of a further ...... years as mentioned in clause [6.17] of these Conditions then the same provisions and procedure as set out there shall apply to any such subsequent extension:

6.19 Death or incapacity

    6.19:1 In the event of the death of an individual Franchisee the personal representatives of the Franchisee shall have six calendar months from the date of death to notify the Franchisor of their decision

        6.19:1.1 to continue the Business whereupon such personal representatives shall be deemed to be proposed assignees of the Business or

        6.19:1.2 to assign the Business to any of the heirs of the Franchisee or to a third party

    whereupon the provisions set out in subclauses [3.26:1 and 3.26:2] of these Conditions shall apply

    6.19:2 In the event of the incapacity of [the Franchisee *or* .... (*the key director of the Franchise*)] at any time or after such death (but prior to any such decision by such personal representatives) the Franchisor shall have the right (but not the duty) to appoint management personnel to supervise the conduct of the Business (at the expense of the Business) to ensure that the Business shall operate in a satisfactory manner to preserve the goodwill of the Mark pending the recovery of the Franchisee or such decision

    6.19:3 If so requested by the Franchisee (or the personal representatives of the Franchisee) the Franchisor may act as a non-exclusive agent for the sale of the Business and in such event shall be paid its expenses and fees as follows:

        6.19:3.1 in the event that the assignee is found by the Franchisee [3%] of the sale price of the Business (including any lease premium and fixtures and fittings) or

        6.19:3.2 in the event that the assignee is found by the Franchisor [5%] of such sale price

6.20 Headings

Headings contained in these Conditions are for reference purposes only and shall not be incorporated in the Agreement or these Conditions and shall not be deemed to be any indication of the meaning of the clauses and sub-clauses to which they relate

6.21 Proper law

English law only shall apply to this Agreement in every particular (including formation) and the English Courts shall have sole jurisdiction to which the parties exclusively submit

SPECIMEN PIZZAEXPRESS CONTRACT

Reproduced by Kind Permission of PizzaExpress

DATED   199

PIZZAEXPRESS (FRANCHISES) LIMITED (1)

(2)

FRANCHISE AGREEMENT
RE:

PIZZAEXPRESS FRANCHISE AGREEMENT

PIZZAEXPRESS FRANCHISE AGREEMENT
CONTENTS OF THE FIRST SCHEDULE

PARTICULARS OF FRANCHISE AGREEMENT

A. DATE

B. PARTIES

    (1)   THE FRANCHISEE   of

    (2)   THE PRINCIPAL   of
                                   and
                                   of

C. THE TERM   10 years from   199

D. ADDRESS OF FRANCHISED RESTAURANT

as held by the Franchisee under the Underlease specified below ('the Premises')

UNDERLEASE DATED

BETWEEN   PIZZAEXPRESS (FRANCHISES) LIMITED   (1)
                THE FRANCHISEE   (2)
                THE PRINCIPAL (if any)   (3)

TERM   YEARS less 10 days
FROM   199

E. THE FRANCHISE FEE (Clause 6.1)

TWENTY THOUSAND POUNDS (£20,000.00) exclusive of VAT

F. MINIMUM OPENING HOURS (First Schedule paragraph 25)

The minimum opening hours prescribed by PizzaExpress at the date hereof are 11.30 a.m. to Midnight.

G. FRANCHISE PURCHASE CONTRACT

dated the   199 and made between PizzaExpress (1) the Franchisee (2) and the Principal (if any) (3)

H. LAST ACCOUNTING DATE

the   199

FRANCHISE AGREEMENT dated with the date specified in paragraph A of the Particulars

BETWEEN

(1) PIZZAEXPRESS (FRANCHISES) LIMITED of whose head office is Unit 7, McKay Trading Estate, Kensal Road, London W10 5BN ('Pizza-Express');

(2) The person persons or company whose name(s) and address(es) appear in paragraph B(1) of the Particulars (hereinafter called 'the Franchisee' which expression shall where the context so admits include his, its or their assigns); and

(3) The person or persons (if any) whose name(s) and address(es) appear in paragraph B(2) of the Particulars (hereinafter called 'the Principal')

RECITALS

(A) PizzaExpress has developed and operated a chain of Pizzeria Restaurants under the name of 'PizzaExpress' and has established an exclusive reputation and goodwill in such name and has licensed others to establish and operate Pizzeria Restaurants in the same style.

(B) Each of such restaurants is known as 'PizzaExpress' and has similar menu, decor, furnishings, facilities, services and the like more fully described and illustrated in PizzaExpress's Operating Manuals.

(C) PizzaExpress PLC (the holding company of PizzaExpress) is:
   (i) the proprietor of or has applied to register certain trade marks ('the Trade Marks') which have become associated with the products sold at its restaurants;
   (ii) the proprietor of or has applied to register service marks ('the Service Marks') which have become associated with services provided at its restaurants or by PizzaExpress.

(D) PizzaExpress PLC is the proprietor of the design and copyright in the get-up of such restaurants including colour schemes, signs, patterns of furnishings, both soft and hard, inventories, dress styles of the staff and the like being the insignia of the style of PizzaExpress restaurants (hereinafter referred to as the 'Copyright Designs').

(E) The Franchisee has requested PizzaExpress to provide instruction to the Franchisee and the Franchisee's staff in the know-how for operating the Business.

(F) PizzaExpress PLC has granted to PizzaExpress all such rights in the Trade Marks, the Service Marks and the Copyright Designs as are necessary for the purpose of this contract.

(G) PizzaExpress desires to establish PizzaExpress restaurants throughout the United Kingdom and has in consideration of the price and obligations on the part of the Franchisee set out below agreed to train the Franchisee as a PizzaExpress franchisee and to supply other services on the terms set out below.

OPERATIVE PROVISIONS:

1   INTERPRETATION

In this agreement, unless inconsistent with the context:

1.1   'Accounting Date'

means the date specified as the Last Accounting Date in paragraph H of the Particulars and the date of expiration of each consecutive period of four weeks thereafter or such other dates as PizzaExpress shall from time to time in writing prescribe

1.2   'Accounting Period'

means any period (currently a period of four consecutive Accounting Weeks) commencing on the day following an Accounting Date and ending on the next following Accounting Date

1.3   'Accounting Week'

means the period of seven whole days beginning and ending at 12 o'clock midnight between Sunday and Monday

1.4   'the Basic Ingredients'

means all dough and tomato sauce required to produce the pizzas and other dishes offered for sale at the Premises

1.5   'the Business'

means the business of a Pizzeria carried on or to be carried on at the Premises by the Franchisee in exercise of the rights hereafter granted and pursuant to and in accordance with this agreement

1.6   'Copyright Designs'

has the meaning accorded to it in Recital (D)

1.7   'the Current PizzaExpress Franchise Contract'

means the standard agreement appropriate for the circumstances herein upon the terms of which PizzaExpress is at the date when this falls to be considered offering to grant a franchise to operate premises as a PizzaExpress restaurant to a prospective franchisee

1.8   'Design'

has the meaning accorded to it in clause 4.2

1.9   'Franchisees' Association'

means any association or body for the time being recognised by PizzaExpress *for the purpose of facilitating links with PizzaExpress* as representing a substantial number of its franchisees in the United Kingdom

1.10 'Franchise Fee'
      means the sum specified as the Franchise Fee in paragraph E of
      the Particulars

1.11 'Head Office'
      means Unit 7, McKay Trading Estate, Kensal Road, London W10
      5BN

1.12 'the Know-how'
      means the package of practical information resulting from ex-
      perience and testing by PizzaExpress or any member of the group
      relating to the operation of a PizzaExpress franchised restaurant

1.13 'Particulars'
      means the Particulars annexed hereto

1.14 'the Personal Representatives'
      means the personal representatives of the Franchisee or of one of
      the persons constituting the Franchisee

1.15 'PizzaExpress'
      means PizzaExpress (Franchises) Limited and where the context
      so admits such expression shall include its successors and assigns

1.16 'PizzaExpress Group'
      means PizzaExpress and its holding and subsidiary companies
      and subsidiaries of its holding companies

1.17 'PizzaExpress's Operating Manual'
      means the collection of manuals, bulletins, memoranda and other
      documents containing the instructions, procedures, standards
      and methods for operation of the Business from time to time
      issued by PizzaExpress or any member of the group including, but
      without limitation to, the PizzaExpress Food Preparation Manual

1.18 'Pizzeria'
      means a restaurant in which pizzas are prepared and cooked to
      the order of the customer in a pizza oven

1.19 'the Premises'
      means the premises mentioned in paragraph D of the Particulars

1.20 'Promotion and Management Material'
      means point of sale advertising and display material and any
      printed matter bearing the name 'PizzaExpress' and all sales re-
      turns and other returns forms for completion by the Franchisee
      and including, but not limited to, bills, napkins, book-matches,
      mats and menus

1.21 'Service Marks'
      has the meaning accorded to it in Recital (C)

1.22 'Term'
      means the term mentioned in paragraph C of the Particulars

1.23 'Total Sales'
      means the aggregate of the price excluding value added tax of
      everything sold at, from and through the Premises calculated
      according to the menu prices in force at the Business at the date

of sale including, but not limited to, the sale price of things sold on credit and not yet paid for and without making any allowance or deduction for any commission reduction or discount allowed to a customer or a third party such as a credit card company

1.24 'Trade Marks'
has the meaning accorded to it in Recital (C)

1.25 'the Underlease'
means the Underlease mentioned in paragraph D of the Particulars and shall include any licence or other document which is supplemental to that Underlease or which is entered into pursuant to or in accordance with its terms

1.26 The expressions 'Holding Company' and 'subsidiary' shall be defined as provided by Section 736 of the Companies Act 1985 (as amended by the Companies Act 1989).

1.27 The marginal notes and headings in this agreement shall not affect the construction or interpretation thereof.

1.28 Words importing the masculine gender only shall include the feminine gender.

1.29 Words importing the singular number only shall include the plural number and vice versa and where there are two or more persons included in the expressions 'the Franchisee' or 'the Principal' covenants and agreements contained herein which are expressed to be made by the Franchisee or the Principal shall be deemed to be made by and with such persons jointly and severally.

1.30 Words importing persons include corporations and vice versa.

2 RIGHTS GRANTED

2.1 Subject to and in accordance with the terms of this agreement the Franchisee shall have:

(a) the right to operate the Premises as a PizzaExpress franchised restaurant and to use at the Premises the trade name 'Pizza-Express', the Trade Marks and the Service Marks and other symbols, insignia, distinctive designs and plans or specifications together with the benefit of the PizzaExpress Group's accumulated experience and knowledge relating to the merchandising and promotion of the sale of pizzas and related products;

(b) the right to use at the Premises PizzaExpress's methods of merchandising, promotion and packaging in or in connection with the Business;

(c) the right to the use of the Copyright Designs and Know-how at the Premises;

(d) the benefit of PizzaExpress's accounting and merchandising knowledge or experience;

(e) all other rights and benefits accruing to the Franchisee by virtue of this agreement.

2.2 The Franchisee shall display in such manner and upon such part or parts of the Premises as PizzaExpress may direct a sign or signs bearing the following words (or such other words to similar effect as may from time to time be specified by PizzaExpress) 'a Pizza-Express franchise owned and operated under Licence by' followed by the Franchisee's name.

2.3 The Franchisee shall in all such situations as PizzaExpress shall from time to time specify (and in particular upon all letter headings employed by him in connection with the Business) place in such manner and in such position as PizzaExpress may direct, the following words (or such other words to similar effect as may from time to time be specified by PizzaExpress) 'a PizzaExpress franchise owned and operated under Licence by' followed by the Franchisee's name.

3 TERM OF LICENCE

3.1 This agreement shall take effect from the commencement of the Term mentioned in part C of the Particulars and shall continue until the expiration of the Term when the rights granted to the Franchisee shall terminate.

3.2 The Franchisee shall have the right to renew such rights at the expiration of the Term upon the following terms and conditions:

3.2.1 The Franchisee may exercise such right by notice in writing to PizzaExpress given not more than six (6) months nor less than three (3) months before the expiration of the Term subject to the conditions precedent that the Franchisee shall have substantially performed and observed the terms and conditions in this agreement and the obligations on the part of the Tenant contained in the Underlease throughout the Term; that there shall be no material outstanding breach of any such terms, conditions or obligations at the date of exercise of such right or at the date of exchange of the new franchise agreement referred to below; and that the terms set out in clauses 3.2.2.1 to 3.2.2.3 shall all have been complied with by no later than [14] days following the date of submission to the Franchisee of the form of new franchise agreement referred to in clause 3.2.2.2

3.2.2 Such renewal shall be upon the following terms:

3.2.2.1 The Franchisee shall undertake to execute at his own expense within a period of not more than six (6) months from the date of renewal if and to the extent requested by PizzaExpress such works of refurbishment, renovation and modernisation and such replacement of fixtures, fittings, furniture, equipment, chattels and signs as may be necessary to bring the Premises up to the then current standards of design and decor for new PizzaExpress restaurants and to comply with all relevant statutory requirements and regulations.

3.2.2.2   The Franchisee shall execute a new franchise agreement with PizzaExpress (Franchises) Limited for a period of ten (10) years in the form of the Current PizzaExpress Franchise Contract save that the Franchisee will not be obliged to pay any sum by way of initial franchise fee but may be required to pay to PizzaExpress in respect of PizzaExpress's advice as to the works and replacements required under paragraph 3.2.2.1 a fee not exceeding one-tenth of the initial franchise fee then payable by new franchisees and save also that such new franchise agreement shall omit the obligations on the part of PizzaExpress applicable only to the establishment of a new restaurant.

3.2.2.3   The Franchisee, if so required by PizzaExpress, shall relinquish in such form as PizzaExpress may require all *such* claims against PizzaExpress or any third party associated with PizzaExpress *as PizzaExpress in its sole discretion judges to be such as to prejudice the existence of such a relationship between the parties as is required for the effective conduct of a successful franchise.*

3.2.2.4   The Franchisee, the Principal and any person employed by or concerned with the Franchisee specified by PizzaExpress shall have completed at the Franchisee's expense such retraining or refresher training at such time and at such place as PizzaExpress may require.

3.2.2.5   PizzaExpress's legal costs (if any) relating to the grant of the new franchise agreement shall be reimbursed.

4.   PIZZAEXPRESS'S OBLIGATIONS

4.1   In so far as PizzaExpress has not supplied the training assistance and advice referred to in the Franchise Purchase Contract referred to in paragraph G of the Particulars annexed hereto PizzaExpress shall supply such services to the Franchisee.

4.2   In so far as PizzaExpress has not done so prior to the date of this agreement PizzaExpress shall:

4.2.1   specify to the Franchisee the standard fixtures, fittings, equipment and other articles required to fit out the Premises as a PizzaExpress franchised restaurant and the name and address of the suppliers approved by PizzaExpress from whom the same may be purchased;

4.2.2   supply such details of the Copyright Designs as the Franchisee shall require in order to conform to the same in the decor and furnishings for the Premises; and

4.2.3   provide the services of its designer to design the layout, general appearance, decor, furniture, furnishings and fittings of and for the Premises (such design, including any part designed prior to the

103

date of this agreement, being herein called 'the Design') the Franchisee however remaining responsible for employing an architect to be approved in writing by PizzaExpress to prepare drawings and a specification in accordance with the Design and to obtain all necessary consents and supervise the works required to execute the Design.

4.3 PizzaExpress shall provide assistance at the opening of the Premises as a PizzaExpress franchised restaurant including the provision of not less than one week.

4.4 PizzaExpress shall specify to the Franchisee the Promotion and Management Material required by the Franchisee.

4.5 PizzaExpress shall make available to the Franchisee from time to time:

4.5.1 the results of its research and development into products, format, market image and equipment;

4.5.2 the result of its regular costing of products and analyses of margins;

4.5.3 its recommendations as to menu prices to be charged by the Franchisee.

4.6 PizzaExpress shall provide a free consultancy service to the Franchisee on matters affecting the operation of the Business, such service to be available to the Franchisee at the time of regular visits by PizzaExpress executives to the Premises and by correspondence or telephone to PizzaExpress Head Office or such other location as PizzaExpress shall from time to time designate for the purpose.

4.7 PizzaExpress shall provide free and reasonably sufficient instructions in the Know-how to the Franchisee's staff for operating the Business subject to the Franchisee being responsible for their salaries and expenses of travel and subsistence during the period of instruction and in the case of a change of staff shall provide free instruction at some suitable PizzaExpress restaurant or elsewhere in case the Franchisee cannot himself give the required instruction the Franchisee again to be responsible for salary, expenses and the subsistence of such new employee during such training.

4.8 Should the Franchisee require any advice, training or assistance in relation to the operation of the Business beyond that which PizzaExpress has, previously in this agreement, undertaken to provide PizzaExpress will as promptly as practicable after the Franchisee's written request to do so provide to the Franchisee such executive staff or consultants as the Franchisee (in the judgement of PizzaExpress) needs, the Franchisee being responsible for the expenses of such persons including a proportion of their salary and their travelling and subsistence together with fees to PizzaExpress in accordance with the scale in operation as published from time to time.

5 **FRANCHISEE'S COVENANT**

The Franchisee COVENANTS with PizzaExpress to perform and observe and follow throughout the Term the covenants, restrictions, conditions, agreements and procedures contained in the First Schedule and in PizzaExpress's Operating Manual together with any amendment or modification of them or any further or additional ones from time to time notified by PizzaExpress to the Franchisee (but only after PizzaExpress has invited consultation on the question with the Franchisees' Association(s) (if any) without in any way becoming legally or contractually bound by the view of such Association(s)).

6 **PAYMENTS**

In consideration of the agreements on the part of PizzaExpress and the rights granted to the Franchisee, the Franchisee shall pay to PizzaExpress without any abatement, set-off or deduction except in respect of admitted over-payments or *other quantified sums admittedly due from PizzaExpress to the Franchisee:*

6.1 the Franchise Fee payable on or before the signing hereof (the receipt of which PizzaExpress acknowledges); and

6.2 a fee of five per cent. (5%) of Total Sales ('the Continuing Fee') together with value added tax thereon at the rate from time to time in force, such Continuing Fee and value added tax to be calculated on the Total Sales during each Accounting Period, the first payment in respect of the period commencing upon commencement of the Business and ending on the first Accounting Date to occur after commencement of the Business to be paid within fourteen (14) days of such first Accounting Date and payments in respect of subsequent Accounting Periods to be paid within fourteen (14) days of the Accounting Date at the end of the Accounting Period in respect of which payment is due. Time is of the essence for the purposes of this clause.

7 **ADVERTISING**

7.1 In this clause, the following expressions shall have the following meanings:

7.1.1 'the Advertising Levy'

shall mean a levy comprising the Interim Percentage (for the relevant Financial Year) of the Franchisee's Total Sales in each Accounting Period during such Financial Year or (if an Interim Percentage shall be specified for part only of a Financial Year) a levy comprising the Interim Percentage (for each such part of the relevant Financial Year) of the Franchisee's Total Sales in each Accounting Period during each such part;

7.1.2 'the Interim Percentage'

shall mean a percentage from time to time specified by Pizza-Express as being the Interim Percentage for the purposes of the Advertising Levy for a Financial Year or for any part of a Financial Year which percentage shall not exceed the lesser of:

(a) one half of one per cent (0.5%); and

(b) the Variable Percentage for the relevant Financial Year calculated applying Estimated Total Promotion Costs and Estimated Group Sales for such Financial Year in lieu of the actual Total Promotion Costs and Group Sales respectively;

7.1.3 'the Specified Percentage'
shall mean a percentage from time to time specified by Pizza-Express as being the Specified Percentage for the purposes of the Advertising Balancing Charge for a Financial Year which percentage shall not exceed the lesser of:

(a) one half of one per cent (0.5%); and

(b) the Variable Percentage for the relevant Financial Year.

7.1.4 'the Variable Percentage'
shall mean the percentage which expresses a fraction in which Total Promotion Costs for the relevant Financial Year are the numerator and Group Sales for such Financial Year are the denominator;

7.1.5 'the Advertising Balancing Charge'
shall mean a charge comprising the difference between:

(a) the Specified Percentage for the relevant Financial Year of the Franchisee's Total Sales for such Financial Year; and

(b) the Advertising Levy for such Financial Year;

7.1.6 'Financial Year'
shall mean a financial year of PizzaExpress determined in accordance with Section 223 of the Companies Act 1985;

7.1.7 'Total Promotion Costs'
shall mean the costs incurred by the PizzaExpress Group in advertising and promoting the name 'PizzaExpress' (apart from the supply of point of sale material);

7.1.8 'Estimated Total Promotion Costs'
shall mean PizzaExpress's estimate of the Total Promotion Costs to be incurred in a Financial Year;

7.1.9 'Group Sales'
shall mean the sum of gross sales in a Financial Year of the Pizza-Express Group's owned and franchised PizzaExpress restaurants calculated on the same basis as Total Sales;

7.1.10 'Estimated Group Sales'
shall mean the PizzaExpress Group's estimate of Group Sales for a Financial Year.

7.2 PizzaExpress shall in respect of each Financial Year give notice in writing to the Franchisee of the Interim Percentage applying for that Financial Year and shall with such notice supply the Franchisee with its figures for Estimated Total Promotion Costs and Estimated Group Sales for such Financial Year.

7.3 The Franchisee shall on the due date for payment of each payment of the Continuing Fee due hereunder pay to PizzaExpress without any abatement, set-off or deduction the Advertising Levy together with value added tax thereon at the rate from time to time in force and calculated on the Total Sales during the Accounting Period in respect of which the Continuing Fee is due.

7.4 PizzaExpress shall also in respect of each Financial Year give notice in writing to the Franchisee of the Specified Percentage for such Financial Year and shall supply the Franchisee with a certified copy of a certificate by PizzaExpress's auditors that the Specified Percentage does not exceed the Variable Percentage.

7.5 If the Specified Percentage for a Financial Year of Franchisee's Total Sales for such Financial Year shall exceed the Advertising Levy for such year the Franchisee shall within twenty-eight (28) days of the notice referred to in clause 7.4 pay to PizzaExpress without any abatement, set-off or deduction the Advertising Balancing Charge together with value added tax thereon at the rate from time to time in force but if the Advertising Levy for a Financial Year shall exceed the Specified Percentage for each year of the Franchisee's Total Sales for such year PizzaExpress shall issue to the Franchisee a credit note in respect of the Advertising Balancing Charge together with value added tax thereon.

7.6 PizzaExpress shall have the right to vary from time to time the method of calculating the Advertising Levy and the Advertising Balancing Charge and the method and frequency of payment of the same and any such variation shall be effective after Pizza-Express shall give notice in writing thereof to the Franchisee. PizzaExpress shall also have the right to vary from time to time the maximum percentages specified in clauses 7.1.3 and 7.1.2 but only after obtaining the approval of a majority of PizzaExpress franchisees and any such variation shall be effective after Pizza-Express shall give notice in writing thereof to the Franchisee with evidence of the approval required for the purposes of this clause.

8 INDEMNITY AND INSURANCE

8.1 *The Franchisee and the Principal JOINTLY AND SEVERALLY COVENANT with PizzaExpress to keep PizzaExpress and its assets and effects indemnified from and against all sums which PizzaExpress may become liable to pay or which it may consider it advisable to pay in order to preserve the good name of Pizza-Express; and all losses, damages, costs and expenses which it may suffer as a direct or indirect result of:*

8.1.1   any action or omission of the Franchisee in breach of the covenants, agreements, restrictions, conditions and provisions hereof;

8.1.2   the failure or refusal of the Franchisee to pay its debts, costs and
expenses or to perform and observe its contracts;

8.1.3   accidental bodily injury, harm, pain or suffering happening to any
person on the premises or due to activities on the Premises and
accidental damage to any property on the Premises subject to the
terms of the Underlease referred to at Part D of the Particulars and
the Franchisee will keep itself, its officers and employees insured
at all times in some Insurance Office approved by PizzaExpress
(such approval not to be unreasonably withheld) in the sum of ONE
MILLION POUNDS (£1,000,000) at least against all and any such
liability as is mentioned in sub-clause 10.1.3 and all liability
normally covered under employer's liability policies and public liability policies and the Franchisee will at the request of Pizza-
Express produce the said policies to PizzaExpress with the receipt
for the last premium due.

8.2   The Franchisee covenants with PizzaExpress:

8.2.1   to insure the furniture, fixtures, fittings and equipment used in the
Business and the profits of the Business against loss or damage
by fire and the usual comprehensive risks in accordance with
recommendations made from time to time by PizzaExpress to its
Franchisees; and

8.2.2   to ensure that PizzaExpress (or any member of the PizzaExpress
Group nominated by PizzaExpress from time to time) is named on
its insurance policy as an additional insured;

8.2.3   upon demand by PizzaExpress to supply details of its insurance to
PizzaExpress including if so required the policy or policies of insurance and receipt for the last premium.

9   ASSIGNMENT CHARGING AND SALE OF BUSINESS

9.1   The Franchisee hereby covenants with PizzaExpress not to assign
charge or otherwise deal with this agreement in any way without
the consent of PizzaExpress which consent in the case of a charge
shall not be unreasonably withheld

9.2   The Franchisee grants to PizzaExpress a pre-emption right on the
terms set out in the Second Schedule

9.3   In the case of an intended assignment of the whole benefit of this
agreement by the Franchisee the consent of PizzaExpress shall
not be unreasonably withheld provided as follows:

9.3.1   that the Franchisee and the Principal have duly performed and
observed the provisions of this agreement and in particular the
foregoing provisions of this clause 9;

9.3.2   that the prospective assignee (in this clause referred to as 'the Purchaser') shall supply such information as PizzaExpress shall

reasonably require relating to himself and (if the Purchaser is a corporation) to the shareholders, directors and persons concerned in the management of the Purchaser and in all cases to their business experience, financial status and any other matters that PizzaExpress reasonably considers to be relevant to that person's suitability to be involved in the ownership, management or control of a PizzaExpress franchised restaurant;

9.3.3   that the Purchaser agrees directly with PizzaExpress to be bound by the terms of this franchise agreement so far as they relate to the Franchisee;

9.3.4   that such of the controlling shareholders, directors and persons concerned in the management of the Purchaser as PizzaExpress shall reasonably require shall enter into the Principal's agreements and covenants contained herein;

9.3.5   that the Purchaser shall pay to PizzaExpress (Franchises) Limited its current fee for the investigation to be made by it under this clause for training of the Purchaser or a director or other officer of the Purchaser together with its current fee for administration on the sale and its proper legal costs in connection with any consent given hereunder; and

9.3.6   that the Purchaser or a director or other officer authorised by the Purchaser and approved by PizzaExpress shall present himself (after payment of the fee referred to above) to PizzaExpress for training in the operation of a PizzaExpress franchised restaurant and shall successfully complete such training course.

10   DEATH OF THE FRANCHISEE OR ONE OF THE PERSONS INCLUDED IN THE EXPRESSION 'FRANCHISEE' OR A PRINCIPAL

10.1   In the event of the Franchisee or the Principal or one of the persons who are the Franchisee or the Principal dying PizzaExpress undertakes that it will at the request of the deceased Franchisee's Personal Representatives together with the surviving Franchisee (if applicable) or a director of the Franchisee (if the Franchisee is a Company) provide as soon as is reasonably practicable such staff as are necessary to replace the deceased Franchisee or Principal for a maximum period of three months subject to payment monthly in advance of PizzaExpress's charges for providing the same which charges will be at the rate of one hundred and fifty per cent (150%) of the wages and one hundred per cent (100%) of the hotel, subsistence, travelling and other expenses of the staff provided and of any other costs and expenses incurred by PizzaExpress in connection with the provision of such staff.

10.2   If the deceased Franchisee's Personal Representatives together with the surviving Franchisee (if applicable) desire to vest the Business in a beneficiary of the deceased Franchisee jointly with the surviving Franchisee (if applicable) (hereinafter together called 'the Proposed Transferee') otherwise than by way of sale and shall within twelve months from the date of the death of the deceased Franchisee give notice in writing of such desire (a 'Transfer Notice') with the name and address of the Proposed Transferee, then, subject as provided in clause 9.3 but substituting the words 'the Proposed Transferee' for 'the Purchaser':

10.2.1 PizzaExpress shall not unreasonably withhold its consent to the assignment of the whole benefit of this agreement to the Proposed Transferee without the provisions of clause 9.2 and the Second Schedule applying; and

10.2.2 PizzaExpress will train the Proposed Transferee in the operation of a PizzaExpress franchised restaurant

10.3 In the event that the Personal Representatives have not completed the sale of the Premises or assented to the vesting of the Premises within fourteen (14) months of the Franchisee's death, Pizza-Express may at any time thereafter by notice in writing to the Personal Representatives and to any surviving Franchisee (if there are two or more persons included in the expression 'Franchisee') given by posting the notice to or leaving it at the Premises addressed to the Personal Representatives and any surviving Franchisee terminate this agreement at the expiration of a further period of twenty-eight (28) days from the giving of such notice and this agreement shall upon the expiration of such notice terminate but without prejudice to any rights which may have accrued prior to such termination.

10.4

10.4.1 If within twelve months from the date of death of the Principal or one of the persons constituting the Principal the Franchisee shall not have procured that some other person acceptable to Pizza-Express shall have agreed with PizzaExpress in a form acceptable to PizzaExpress to be bound by the Principal's covenants herein or if within such period the personal representatives of the deceased Principal shall not have obtained PizzaExpress's approval to the transfer (consequent upon such death) of such shares (if any) held by the deceased in the Franchisee then PizzaExpress may termi-nate this agreement PROVIDED THAT if the transferee of such shares shall be one or more of the Principals hereunder Pizza-Express shall not require some other person to be bound by the Principal's covenants herein. Any such termination shall be by notice in writing to the Franchisee, the Personal Representatives of the deceased Principal and any surviving Principal (if there are two or more persons included in the expression 'Principal') given by posting the notice to or leaving it at the Premises addressed to the Franchisee, the Personal Representatives of the deceased

Principal and any surviving Principal. At the expiration of twenty-eight (28) days from the giving of such notice this agreement shall terminate but without prejudice to any rights which may have accrued prior to such termination.

10.4.2 PizzaExpress undertakes with the Franchisee that it will not unreasonably withhold its approval to the transfer of the deceased's shares in the Franchisee made within the above period and that it will train the transferee of the shares in the Franchisee previously held by the deceased Principal (in this clause referred to as 'the Transferee') in the operation of a PizzaExpress Franchised Restaurant, subject as follows:

10.4.2.1 to the Franchisee and the Principal having duly complied with the terms of this contract;

10.4.2.2 to the Transferee supplying such information as PizzaExpress shall reasonably require relating to himself and to the persons who will after the transfer of the shares be the shareholders, directors and persons concerned in the management of the Franchisee and to their business experience, financial status and any other matters that PizzaExpress reasonably considers to be relevant to their suitability to be involved in the ownership, management or control of a PizzaExpress franchised restaurant;

10.4.2.3 to the Transferee and such of the controlling shareholders, directors and persons concerned in the management of the Franchisee following the transfer to the Transferee as PizzaExpress shall reasonably require entering into the Principal's agreements and covenants herein contained;

10.4.2.4 to the Franchisee paying to PizzaExpress its current fee for the investigation to be made by it under this clause for training of the Transferee or some other person approved by PizzaExpress and for administration in connection with the said Transfer;

10.4.2.5 to the Transferee or some other director or other authorised officer of the Franchisee approved by PizzaExpress presenting himself (after payment of the said fee) to PizzaExpress for training in the operation of a PizzaExpress franchised restaurant and successfully completing such training course.

11 TERMINATION

11.1 Without prejudice to any other right of termination conferred on it by this agreement or at law, PizzaExpress may terminate this agreement forthwith by giving notice in writing to the Franchisee in any of the following events:

11.1.1 if the Franchisee shall at any time fail to pay any amounts due to any member of the PizzaExpress Group and such failure shall not have been remedied in full *within 14 days* after written notice to the Franchisee;

11.1.2   if the Franchisee shall fail to operate the Business in accordance with the terms of this agreement or PizzaExpress's reasonable written instructions and (if such failure shall be capable of being remedied) such failure shall not have been remedied in full within such reasonable period as shall be specified by PizzaExpress in a written notice to the Franchisee;

11.1.3   if the Franchisee shall transfer any of the rights, licences or obligations contained in this agreement other than in accordance with the terms hereof;

11.1.4   if the Franchisee discloses or allows the disclosure of any part of the confidential information relating to the Business otherwise than in accordance with the terms of this agreement;

11.1.5   if the Franchisee fails to obtain any prior written approval or consent of PizzaExpress expressly required by this agreement;

11.1.6   if the Franchisee or any officer, director or employee of the Franchisee or any of the persons comprised in the expression 'the Franchisee' gives to PizzaExpress any false or misleading information or makes any misrepresentation in connection with obtaining this agreement or at any time during the continuance of this agreement in connection with the Business;

11.1.7   in the event of the Franchisee ceasing to carry on the Business at the Premises *except for a short emergency or other temporary closure of the Premises previously approved by PizzaExpress*;

11.1.8   in the event that any of the persons comprised in the expression 'the Franchisee' or any of the persons comprised in the expression 'the Principals' shall have a bankruptcy order made against him or if a person who is qualified as an insolvency practitioner shall be appointed in relation to him pursuant to Section 273 of the Insolvency Act 1986 or if a receiver or manager (including for the avoidance of doubt an interim receiver within the meaning of Part IX of the Insolvency Act 1986) shall be appointed in respect of him or the whole or any part of his property or estate or if an interim order shall be made in relation to him pursuant to Section 252 of the Insolvency Act 1986 or if he shall enter into any arrangement or composition with his creditors (including for the avoidance of doubt any voluntary arrangement within the meaning of Part VIII of the Insolvency Act 1986);

11.1.9   in the event that any of the persons comprised in the expressions 'the Franchisee' or 'the Principal' becomes a patient as defined by the Mental Health Act 1986 or commits any criminal offence (other than a road traffic offence);

11.1.10   in the event of the Franchisee going into liquidation (other than voluntarily for the purpose of amalgamation or reconstruction) or being unable to pay its debts within the meaning of Section 123 of the Insolvency Act 1986 (or any statutory modification or re-enactment thereof) or suffering a distress or execution to be levied on or a receiver appointed over any property used in connection with the Business or if the Franchisee makes any arrangements with its creditors;

11.1.11 in the event of persistent justifiable complaints to the PizzaExpress Group as to the quality of the service given or food served by the Franchisee which complaints continue after notice of complaints being made shall be given to the Franchisee by PizzaExpress in writing;

11.1.12 in the event of a change in the beneficial ownership, de facto control, financial interest or active management of the Franchisee from that set forth in the statement of ownership annexed to this agreement unless the previous written consent of PizzaExpress has been obtained pursuant to clause 16;

11.1.13 if the Franchisee shall be in breach of any of the terms of this agreement (except as set out above or of the Underlease) and in case the breach shall be remediable PizzaExpress shall have notified the Franchisee in writing of such breach and the Franchisee shall not have rectified such breach within such reasonable period as shall be specified by PizzaExpress in such notification;

11.1.14 in the event of the termination for any cause of the Underlease.

11.2 If PizzaExpress shall commit a serious breach of any of the terms of this agreement and the Franchisee shall have notified PizzaExpress in writing of such breach and shall have called upon PizzaExpress to remedy the breach within a specified time not being less than twenty-eight (28) days and PizzaExpress shall not have rectified such breach within such period then the Franchisee may terminate this agreement forthwith by giving notice in writing to PizzaExpress.

11.3 Any termination under this clause shall be without prejudice to the rights of any party hereto against any other party hereto in respect of any antecedent breach of any of the terms and conditions of this agreement.

11.4 In the event of termination of this agreement the Franchisee shall not be entitled to recover any part of the initial fee paid to PizzaExpress.

12 CONSEQUENCES OF TERMINATION

12.1 The rights of each party hereunder existing at or immediately before the termination or expiration of this agreement shall not be prejudiced by or cease on account of the cessation of the agreement but shall survive and be enforceable.

12.2 Unless requested in writing by PizzaExpress not to do so the Franchisee shall forthwith on or before the termination or expiration of this agreement or (in case this is impossible at that time) as soon as is practical thereafter take steps to remove from the Premises and the Franchisee's vehicles, notepaper, invoices or labels, all reference to the Trade Marks and to the names 'PizzaExpress' or 'Pizza Pizza Pizza' and every form of indication by which the Premises or the aforementioned might be recognised as being connected with PizzaExpress and arrange for the cancellation of any such reference on hoardings or other advertisements and in directories or other books of reference on a reprinting and permit PizzaExpress to enter upon the Premises at any time during business hours for the purpose of removing such references or forms of indication and not hold itself out as being in any way connected with PizzaExpress whether as Franchisee or otherwise.

12.3   On termination of this agreement the Franchisee shall cease to have rights in the Know-how, the Copyright Design and the Design and shall be obliged to return all documents and drawings related thereto and all copies thereof including in particular all copies of the PizzaExpress Operating Manual in the possession, power or custody of the Franchisee and procure the return of copies in the possession of any employees of the Franchisee and thereafter the Franchisee shall not use such information.

12.4   On termination of this agreement for whatever cause PizzaExpress will have the option but shall be under no obligation to take and pay for at a valuation to be made as specified in clause 12.5 the trade fixtures, fittings, furniture, effects and other articles belonging to the Franchisee and used by the Franchisee in the Business on the Premises and all of the sound or saleable stock-in-trade of the Business on the Premises at such date the Franchisee hereby agreeing to leave the same upon the Premises (unless or until required by PizzaExpress to remove the same) provided that any sums or sum of money which may then be due or owing from the Franchisee to PizzaExpress on any account whatsoever shall be paid and deducted out of the amount of the said valuation and any balance paid by or to the Franchisee as the case may be.

12.5   The valuation referred to in clause 12.4 shall be made in the usual way by two valuers, one to be appointed by each party, or by their umpire in the event of the said valuers not agreeing, but if PizzaExpress or the Franchisee fails to appoint a valuer within seven (7) days after notice in writing so to do then the valuation shall be made by the valuer appointed by the other.

12.6   On termination or expiration of this agreement for any reason PizzaExpress shall have the right to apply for the cancellation of any entry of the Franchisee on the Register of Trade Marks or of Service Marks as a registered user of any of the Trade Marks or any of the Service Marks and the Franchisee undertakes not to oppose any such application for cancellation and agrees not to make any use of any of the Trade Marks or of any of the Service Marks following termination or expiration of this agreement.

13 TRADE MARKS SERVICE MARKS AND INTELLECTUAL PROPERTY

13.1

13.1.1 The Franchisee shall render to PizzaExpress and PizzaExpress PLC all reasonable assistance (including but not limited to evidence of user) in obtaining registration of such of the Trade Marks and Service Marks as are not yet registered.

13.1.2 In no circumstances shall the Franchisee apply for registration as proprietor of any trade mark which is identical to any trade name for the time being used by any member of the PizzaExpress Group or the Trade Marks or the Service Marks or any or part of them or which would conflict with any such Trade Marks or Service Marks or so resembles such trade names Trade Marks or Service Marks as to cause confusion or deception.

13.1.3 If at the time PizzaExpress desires to apply for registration of a trade mark and has so applied and the Franchisee is deemed in law to have rights in the trade mark so as to make it necessary for an application to be proceeded with in the name of the Franchisee the Franchisee shall at the request and expense of PizzaExpress or PizzaExpress PLC make and proceed with such application and do all acts and execute all documents necessary for obtaining registration in the name of the Franchisee and thereupon the Franchisee shall assign such registration to PizzaExpress or to PizzaExpress PLC.

13.1.4 The Franchisee shall in all representations of the Trade Marks and the Service Marks used by him append in a manner approved by PizzaExpress or PizzaExpress PLC such inscription as is usual or proper for indicating that such Mark is registered.

13.2 The Franchisee shall immediately notify PizzaExpress of all infringements or imitators of the Trade Marks and the Service Marks the said trade names or any business which appears to be passing itself off or to be attempting to pass itself off as a PizzaExpress outlet which come to his attention or any attempts to challenge the Franchisee's right to use any of the Trade Marks and the Service Marks or the said trade names or to carry on the said business as PizzaExpress so long as this Agreement shall subsist. PizzaExpress shall take such action as it in its sole discretion considers appropriate. The Franchisee agrees to provide such co-operation in the prosecution of any such action, including the provision of evidence and being named as a party to any legal proceedings as PizzaExpress may request. PizzaExpress shall have the conduct of any such action and pay all legal expenses and costs which may arise from the joining of the Franchisee as a party save such legal expenses and costs which the Franchisee may incur by taking separate legal advice. The Franchisee shall not without the prior written notice of PizzaExpress take any action of whatever nature based upon the Trade Marks the Service Marks the said trade names or any common law right which the Franchisee is licensed to use or exercise pursuant to this agreement or any registered user agreement entered into between the parties.

13.3   No warranty expressed or implied is hereby given by PizzaExpress with respect to the validity of any of the Trade Marks or Service Marks.

13.4   If and in so far as PizzaExpress PLC is advised that it is necessary or desirable so to do, PizzaExpress and the Franchisee agree to execute a separate agreement for recordal of the Franchisee as a registered user of any of the registered Trade Marks or any of the registered Service Marks subject to all the terms and conditions of this agreement and to join in any application necessary for cancellation of any entries at the Trade Marks Registry forthwith after termination of this agreement.

13.5   In no circumstances shall the Franchisee use any of the Trade Marks the Service Marks or the said trade names as part of its corporate name nor, except as expressly permitted by this agreement, as its trading style or name.

13.6   The Franchisee acknowledges and agrees that:

13.6.1   all patents, trade marks, trade names, logos, designs, symbols, emblems, insignia, fascia, slogans, copyrights, know-how, information, drawings, plans and all other intellectual or industrial property rights, whether or not registered or capable of registration, owned by or available to PizzaExpress and all goodwill and other rights in or associated with any of the foregoing vest absolutely in PizzaExpress;

13.6.2   it is the intention of the parties that all such rights will at all times hereafter and for all purposes remain vested in PizzaExpress; and

13.6.3   if any such rights at any time accrue to the Franchisee by operation of law or in any other manner, the Franchisee will at his own expense forthwith on demand do all such acts and things and execute all such documents as PizzaExpress shall consider necessary to vest such rights absolutely in PizzaExpress.

14   FAILURE TO EXERCISE RIGHTS NOT TO BE WAIVER
No relaxation, forbearance or indulgence by PizzaExpress in enforcing any of the terms and conditions of this agreement nor the granting of time by PizzaExpress to the Franchisee shall prejudice or affect the rights and powers of PizzaExpress hereunder nor shall any waiver of any breach operate as a waiver of any subsequent or continuing breach.

15   INTEREST

If any sum due to be paid to any member of the PizzaExpress Group or any of its subsidiaries by the Franchisee (whether due hereunder or in respect of the supply of goods or services to the Franchisee) shall remain unpaid after the date upon which it becomes due (whether formally demanded or not) the Franchisee shall upon demand by PizzaExpress pay interest on such sum or the balance thereof for the time being owing at the rate of Five pounds (£5,00) per centum per annum above the Midland Bank PLC Base Lending Rate from time to time in force (or in the event that such base lending rate shall cease to exist or shall in the reasonable opinion of PizzaExpress cease to fulfil the purpose for which it existed formerly then at such reasonably equivalent rate of interest as PizzaExpress in its absolute discretion shall specify) from the date upon which the same becomes due until the date of receipt of the sum due by PizzaExpress.

16   OWNERSHIP OF FRANCHISEE

16.1   The Franchisee and the Principals JOINTLY AND SEVERALLY WARRANT that details of the beneficial ownership, de facto control, financial interest and active management of the Franchisee set out in the statement of ownership and executives annexed hereto are true and correct at the date hereof AND COVENANT that no change in the beneficial ownership, de facto control, financial interest or active management of the Franchisee shall be made without the prior written consent of PizzaExpress;

16.2   PizzaExpress shall not unreasonably withhold such consent, subject as provided in clauses 10.4.2.1 to 10.4.2.5 inclusive and in the application of such clauses to this clause 16 the expression 'Transferee' shall mean any person or company to whom on such change, it is intended that shares or some other interest in the Franchisee shall be transferred;

16.3   Concurrently with any such agreed change a revised statement of ownership and executives shall be completed and forwarded to PizzaExpress by the Franchisee.

17   PRINCIPAL'S GUARANTEE

17.1   The Principal COVENANTS AND AGREES with PizzaExpress that the Franchisee will duly observe and perform all the obligations on the Franchisee's part to be performed and observed under this agreement and in particular that the Franchisee will punctually pay the Franchise Fee, the Continuing Fee, the contribution towards Total Promotion Costs pursuant to clause 7 and for all goods sold and delivered by PizzaExpress to the Franchisee and all other sums due to PizzaExpress under the terms hereof on the due dates for payment thereof and that in case of default in payment of any such sum on the due date for payment thereof the Principal shall pay the same to PizzaExpress on demand and shall pay and make good to PizzaExpress on demand all losses, damages, costs and expenses arising from such default;

17.2 The Principal also COVENANTS AND AGREES with PizzaExpress:

17.2.1 that the Principal shall not during the Term or for a period of twelve (12) months after the termination of this agreement (however terminated) carry on, engage in, be employed by or be concerned or interested, directly or indirectly, in the business of operating a Pizzeria within a radius of one (1) mile from any other restaurant operated by the PizzaExpress Group or by its Holding Company or by any subsidiary of its Holding Company or by its or their franchisees save at the Premises or under franchise from PizzaExpress.

17.2.2 that the Principal shall not during the Term or for a period of twelve (12) months after the termination of this agreement (however terminated) solicit, interfere with or endeavour to entice away or employ any employee of the PizzaExpress Group or its Holding Company or any subsidiary of its Holding Company or any of its or their franchisees.

17.2.3 that the Principal shall not during or after the termination of this agreement except as authorised or required by the terms of this agreement reveal to any person, persons or company any of the trade secrets, secret or confidential operations, processes or dealings or any information concerning the organisation, business, finances, transactions or affairs of PizzaExpress or of its Holding Company or any subsidiary of its Holding Company which may come within the Principal's knowledge during the currency of this agreement and shall keep with complete secrecy all confidential information entrusted to him and shall not use or attempt to use any such information in any manner which may injure or cause loss to PizzaExpress or its business or the business of its Holding Company or any subsidiary of its Holding Company.

17.2.4 that the Principal will procure that all directors and shareholders of the Franchisee (if a company) or of any company comprised in the expression 'the Franchisee' shall enter into valid and legally enforceable undertakings with PizzaExpress to accept equivalent obligations to those imposed by this clause 17.2 and shall submit the same to PizzaExpress within seven (7) days of the date of this agreement or in the case of any person becoming a shareholder or director during the term of this agreement within seven (7) days of such occurrence.

17.3 The liability of the Principal hereunder shall not be in any way affected or impaired by PizzaExpress giving time or showing any indulgence whatsoever to the Franchisee or by any release, discharge or variation of or any agreement to release, discharge or vary the terms of this agreement or PizzaExpress's terms and conditions of trade or any deed, document or memorandum supplemental to the foregoing.

18   NOTICES AND SERVICE

18.1   Each of the following constitutes an approved means of giving notice hereunder, namely, by pre-paid recorded delivery or registered post or (provided that delivery of the original document is not essential) by telex, by facsimile transmission or by electronic mail.

18.2   Any notice required to be given hereunder shall be deemed to have been duly given if sent by an approved means addressed in the case of a notice to PizzaExpress to the Franchise Director at the registered office address for the time being of PizzaExpress and in the case of a notice to the Franchisee or if there is more than one person constituting the Franchisee to the first named of such persons at the Premises or at the last known place of business or place of residence of the first named of such persons.

18.3   Notices of documents sent by the following means are to be considered as given or delivered at the times mentioned below:
(a) by pre-paid recorded delivery or registered post, two working days after posting;
(b) by telex or by facsimile transmission or by electronic mail, on the next working day after transmission.

18.4   Service of any legal proceedings concerning or arising out of this agreement may be effected by causing the same to be delivered (in the case of proceedings against PizzaExpress) to the Company Secretary of PizzaExpress at its registered office, or, (in the case of proceedings against the Franchisee or any of the persons constituting the Franchisee) to the Franchisee or such person at the address stated in the Particulars or such other address in the United Kingdom as may be notified by the party concerned in writing to PizzaExpress from time to time.

19   PERSONAL REPRESENTATIVES

This agreement shall be binding on and shall enure for the benefit of the Personal Representatives until terminated in accordance with the terms hereof.

20   CONFIDENTIALITY

The Franchisee shall not during or after the termination of this agreement except as authorised or required by the Franchisee's duties hereunder reveal to any person, persons or company any of the trade secrets, secret or confidential operations, processes or dealings or any information concerning the organisation, business, finances, transactions or affairs of PizzaExpress, or any member of the PizzaExpress Group which may come to the Franchisee's knowledge during the currency of this agreement and shall keep with complete secrecy all confidential information entrusted to the Franchisee and shall not use or attempt to use any such information in any manner which may injure or cause loss to PizzaExpress or its business or the business of its Holding Company or any subsidiary of its Holding Company.

21   **SEVERABILITY**
If any provision of this agreement is declared by any judicial or other competent authority to be void, voidable, illegal or otherwise unenforceable or indications of the same are received by any of the parties from any relevant competent authority the parties shall amend that provision in such a reasonable manner as achieves the original intention of the parties without illegality or at the discretion of PizzaExpress it may be severed from this agreement PROVIDED THAT if in the reasonable opinion of *either* PizzaExpress *or the Franchisee*:
(a) the effect of such declaration and severance would be to defeat the original intention of the parties; and
(b) the provision cannot be amended so as to achieve the original intention of the parties without illegality;
PizzaExpress *or the Franchisee* shall be entitled to terminate this contract by thirty (3) days' notice to the *other* and clauses 11.3, 11.4 and 12 shall apply.

22   **PROPER LAW**
English law shall apply to this agreement and the English courts shall have exclusive jurisdiction

23   **RESTRICTIVE TRADE PRACTICES ACT**
If this is an agreement to which the Restrictive Trade Practices Act 1976 ('RTPA') applies the restrictions (as such term is defined in the RTPA) in this agreement shall not come into force until twenty-four (24) hours after particulars of this agreement have been furnished to the Office of Fair Trading in accordance with the provisions of the RTPA.

24   **ACKNOWLEDGEMENT**
The Franchisee and the Principal acknowledge that in giving advice to the Franchisee, assisting the Franchisee to establish the Business, specifying the fixtures, fittings, equipment and other articles required to fit out the Premises and in providing recommendations as to the layout of the Premises and in providing the

services of its designer and in assessing the suitability of the Franchisee and the Premises, PizzaExpress has based its advice, assistance and other said action on experience actually obtained in practice but that PizzaExpress does not give any guarantee or warranty with regard to such matters or generally in connection with the cost of establishing the Business, the sales volume profitability or any other aspect of the Business. The Franchisee and the Principal acknowledge that they have been advised by PizzaExpress to discuss their intention to enter into this agreement with other Franchisees of PizzaExpress and to seek other appropriate independent advice and that the decision to enter into this agreement has been taken solely on the basis of the personal judgement and experience of the Franchisee and the Principal having taken such independent advice. Accordingly the Franchisee and the Principal acknowledge that no representation, warranty, inducement or promise, express or implied, has been made by PizzaExpress or relied upon by the Franchisee or the Principal in entering into this agreement save for such of PizzaExpress's solicitors' written replies to the enquiries before contract of the Franchisee as the Franchisee has in writing notified PizzaExpress that it is relying upon.

25   **FORCE MAJEURE**
None of the parties to this agreement shall be responsible to any other party for any delay in performance or non-performance due to any causes beyond the reasonable control of the parties hereto but the affected party shall promptly upon the occurrence of such cause so inform the other parties in writing stating that such cause has delayed or prevented its performance hereunder and thereafter such party shall take all action within its power to comply with the terms of this agreement as fully and promptly as possible.

THE FIRST SCHEDULE
THE FRANCHISEE'S OBLIGATIONS

Fitting Out

1   To employ an architect approved by PizzaExpress to prepare drawings and a specification of the works required to convert the Premises into and fit them out as a PizzaExpress restaurant in accordance with the Design and to submit such drawings and specification to PizzaExpress for its approval (such approval not to be unreasonably withheld) and at its own cost and expense to convert the Premises to and fit them out as a PizzaExpress restaurant in accordance with the Design and the drawings and specification approved in writing by PizzaExpress and under the supervision of such architect and not to depart from the Design and the said drawings and specification in carrying out the said conversion and fitting out of the Premises or thereafter without the consent in writing of PizzaExpress such consent not to be unreasonably withheld.

Apply Copyright Designs

2   To conform in regard to the decor, furnishings and the like to Pizza-Express's Copyright Designs and to apply the same in all the relevant detail in the conversion and decoration of the Premises and not to depart from or alter the same without the approval in writing of Pizza-Express and not to erect or alter any signs, (including illuminated signs, free standing signs, notices and the like) except with the consent in writing of PizzaExpress (complying with all local laws and regulations and, subject thereto, so as to be in accordance with the practices established by PizzaExpress).

Equipment

3   To install in the Premises the type of oven and other equipment specified by PizzaExpress.

4   Promptly to apply for and diligently prosecute the obtaining of all necessary permits for the conversion of the Premises according to the said designs and specifications including permits for signs, the shopfront and use of the Premises as a restaurant and the like as approved by PizzaExpress including Police and Fire Authorities' approval and the obtaining of a Justices Licence in respect of the Premises in the name of the Franchisee and/or the Principals.

Staff and Training

5

5.1   The Franchisee shall engage all necessary staff for operating the Premises as a PizzaExpress restaurant and shall continue to employ sufficient staff to meet all likely demand from th customers of the Business.

5.1 The Franchisee shall engage all necessary staff for operating the Premises as a PizzaExpress restaurant and shall continue to employ sufficient staff to meet all likely demand from the customers of the Business.

5.2 The Franchisee shall ensure that all staff shall receive such training as shall from time to time be prescribed by PizzaExpress.

5.3 The Franchisee undertakes that he will procure that the persons responsible for managing the Business and all senior employees specified by PizzaExpress shall enter into valid and legally enforceable undertakings with PizzaExpress in a form from time to time specified by PizzaExpress not to reveal or disclose or use for his own benefit or for the benefit of any third party any trade secret or confidential information of PizzaExpress or any other confidential information or knowledge concerning the Business, the Know-how, the Trade Marks, the Service Marks or the PizzaExpress Group.

5.4 That at least three (3) weeks prior to opening of the Premises as a restaurant the Franchisee shall have engaged all necessary Piazzaiolos for operating the Premises as a PizzaExpress restaurant and shall arrange for their attendance at the Head Office of PizzaExpress or such other location as PizzaExpress shall notify to the Franchisee for instruction in the Know-how during such period as PizzaExpress shall deem appropriate the Franchisee to be responsible for their salaries and expenses of travel and subsistence.

5.5 At least two (2) days prior to such opening the Franchisee shall have engaged all other necessary staff for operating the Premises as a PizzaExpress restaurant and shall ensure that they receive such training as shall from time to time be prescribed by PizzaExpress.

Furnishings

6 Fully and properly to furnish the restaurant in accordance with the Copyright Designs including soft and hard furnishings, tables, chairs, linen, towels, table cloths, table napkins, stationery, cutlery, china, glasses and the like, each of such items being of a type and quality specified by PizzaExpress.

7 To operate the restaurant and maintain the Premises in accordance with the practice to the standards and upon the general conditions laid down by PizzaExpress from time to time for the operation of PizzaExpress restaurants as more particularly described in PizzaExpress's Operating Manual and to the intent that the good reputation and name of PizzaExpress and its products shall be enhanced and promoted.

Adhere to PizzaExpress Menu

8   To sell only those dishes, foods and drinks listed on the menu cur-
     rently prescribed by PizzaExpress for use at its restaurants and those
     optional extras for the time being approved by PizzaExpress and to
     operate the Premises as a PizzaExpress restaurant only and not to
     use the Premises or to permit them to be used for any other purposes
     whatsoever PROVIDED THAT the Franchisee may in addition to the
     dishes on the current menu sell each day one house speciality dish,
     the recipe, ingredients and prices of which have been previously
     approved in writing by PizzaExpress.

Recipes

9   To prepare all dishes with ingredients, mixture and products of a type
     and quality specified by PizzaExpress and in accordance with the
     recipe or cooking directions from time to time provided by Pizza-
     Express and to serve such dishes in the manner specified and in the
     quantity determined by PizzaExpress.

Supplies

10

10.1 (For the purpose of maintaining a consistently high quality and uni-
      formity for the pizzas and other dishes sold in all PizzaExpress owned
      and franchised restaurants as the Franchisee hereby admits) to pur-
      chase from PizzaExpress or its subsidiaries upon PizzaExpress's
      standard terms and conditions of trade with franchisees for the time
      being in force and at PizzaExpress's current prices to franchisees
      applying to the circumstances (a copy of which terms and conditions
      and price list current at the date hereof has been supplied to the Fran-
      chisee prior to signing hereof, the receipt of which the Franchisee
      hereby acknowledges) all of the Franchisee's requirements for the
      basic ingredients.

10.2 To purchase from PizzaExpress upon PizzaExpress's standard terms
      and conditions of trade with franchisees for the time being in force
      and at PizzaExpress's current prices to franchisees applying to the
      circumstances all of the Franchisee's requirements for Promotion and
      Management Material.

10.3 To pay for all goods purchased from PizzaExpress or any of its sub-
      sidiaries without any abatement, set-off or deduction in accordance
      with PizzaExpress's said terms and conditions and in particular within
      the credit period (if any) for the time being allowed by PizzaExpress
      and to pay interest in accordance herewith or with the said terms and
      conditions in case payment is not made within the period of grace (if
      any) allowed by the said terms and conditions.

10.4 In case any item of the basic ingredients is not for the time being available to be purchased from PizzaExpress to purchase the same from the suppliers for the time being approved or nominated by PizzaExpress as the suppliers of such item.

Choice of Drinks/Records

11 To comply with all instructions made by PizzaExpress from time to time regarding the choice of wines, beers and other drinks to be offered for sale to customers at the Premises and the choice of records to be made available in any jukebox or other recorded sound system installed at the Premises.

No other sales

12 Not to sell any dishes or drinks which have been prepared otherwise than in accordance with the terms hereof or which contain ingredients, mixture or products of a type or quality different from that specified by PizzaExpress and in the case of dishes or other items of food or drinks requiring no preparation not to sell any that do not conform to any current specification as to their type and quality made by PizzaExpress.

13 Not to permit the sale of or the traffic in any dangerous drugs on the Premises.

Records of Sales

14 To record all sales by the Business both on bills to be obtained from PizzaExpress and on a cash register of a type approved by PizzaExpress and to enter such sales in a book-keeping system approved by PizzaExpress and not to use or permit to be used any bills other than those obtained from PizzaExpress.

Sales Return

15 Not later than 3 p.m. on each Monday to notify PizzaExpress of the sales of the Business on each day of the Accounting Week ending on the previous day and within seven (7) days of the end of each Accounting Period to post or deliver to PizzaExpress's administrative offices a copy of PizzaExpress's current confirmation of sales return form signed by the Franchisee or a duly authorised officer of the Franchisee and containing all required particulars of the sales of the Business on each day of such Accounting Period and if demanded by PizzaExpress copies of the till rolls, bill pads and the daily sales analysis sheets and to give to PizzaExpress by telephone on each such Monday such of the information contained in the confirmation of sales return form as PizzaExpress shall require.

Book-Keeping System

16

16.1 To maintain at the Premises in a form from time to time approved by PizzaExpress accurate books of accounts and records including all invoices, credit notes, statements and delivery notes and to permit PizzaExpress or its duly authorised Agents and Officers at any time during normal business hours to inspect all such accounts and records and to take copies hereof.

16.2 In the case of the Franchisee being a limited company in each calendar year at the expense of the Franchisee to provide a copy of its *unaudited and, subsequently, its* audited profit and less account and balance sheet to PizzaExpress within three (3) months *and six (6) months respectively* after the end of the year or period in respect of which they are prepared and in the case of the Franchisee being an individual or partnership in each calendar year at the expense of the Franchisee to provide to PizzaExpress a copy of the profit and loss account and balance sheet relating to the Business prepared for taxation purposes within three (3) months of the date as at which the balance sheet is prepared and to certify that such profit and loss account and balance sheet are a true and complete copy of the accounts submitted to H.M. Inspector of Taxes and in each of the above cases the Franchisee shall warrant that the said balance sheet gives a true and fair view of the state of affairs of the Business or of the company which is the Franchisee as the case may be at the date as at which it is prepared and that the said profit and loss account gives a true and fair view of the profit or loss of the Business or of the company which is the Franchisee as the case may be in the period covered by the said profit and loss account.

16.3 To preserve all such accounts and records for not less than three (3) years notwithstanding the expiry or termination of this agreement.

16.4 To permit accountants nominated by PizzaExpress (Franchises) Limited (including an accountant in PizzaExpress's employ) at the expense of PizzaExpress to undertake such audits and checks as PizzaExpress may consider appropriate during normal business hours.

Stock

17 To maintain sufficient stocks to meet all likely demand from the customers of the Business and to control the stock of the Business in accordance with the stock control system from time to time specified or approved by PizzaExpress.

Staff Uniform

18 To comply with PizzaExpress's recommendations for the time being in force regarding uniform or dress for staff.

Advertising

19   Not to carry out any advertising of the Business nor exhibit any signs on the Premises without the written consent of PizzaExpress.

Compliance with statutory requirements

20   To manage and control the Premises and the Business so that nothing shall be done, permitted or omitted contrary to any statutory provision or regulation, Bye-Laws or Planning or Local Authority consent or Licence for the time being in force relating to or affecting the Premises or the Business or the terms and conditions of employment of staff or to any direction made in pursuance thereof of whereby the Franchisee or its Manager shall become liable to conviction for any criminal offence or whereby any licence in respect of the Premises may become liable for forfeiture, suspension or non-renewal or otherwise imperilled or whereby any notice or complaint shall be given or made by a justice or superintendent or acting superintendent of police with regard to the Premises or the Business or whereby any nuisance, annoyance or disturbance be thereby caused to any of the adjoining or neighbouring residents but to conduct the Business in a lawful and orderly manner so as to maintain and extend the Business and to preserve the character of the Premises with the licensing authorities and the public.

Renewal of Licence

21   To apply at all proper times to the licensing authorities and to use its best endeavours to obtain a grant or renewal of any certificate and licenses necessary for using and keeping open the Premises as a fully licensed restaurant.

Cleaning and Repair

22   To keep each and every part of the Premises and all fixtures, fittings and articles therein scrupulously clean and in good and substantial repair, decorative order and condition and to re-decorate the same both externally and internally at such intervals as PizzaExpress shall from time to time specify.

Permit entry for inspection

23   To permit PizzaExpress and its authorised agents and officers at all times to enter upon and examine the condition of the Premises and the conduct of the Business and to take any steps that PizzaExpress considers necessary in order to ascertain whether the terms and conditions hereof are being observed and performed and to make available for such examination all parts of the Premises and all books and records of the Business.

Use of Trade Marks and Service Marks

24

24.1 Not to use the Trade Marks, the Service Marks, the name "Pizza-Express" or any name comprising a multiple use of the word "Pizza" followed by the word "Express" except on the signs exhibited at the Premises and approved by PizzaExpress and on the menu, bills and point of sale and other material used at the Premises and approved or specified by PizzaExpress; and

24.2 In all such situations as PizzaExpress shall from time to time specify (and in particular on a sign exhibited at the Premises and on any letterheading approved by PizzaExpress for use by the Business) to state in conjunction with the said names that the Franchisee is proprietor of the Business and is carrying on business in the name of PizzaExpress under licence from PizzaExpress; and

24.3 Not to use the said names in any manner at any time or any place except as mentioned above and in particular not at any time to hold itself out in contracting with suppliers of the Franchisee or other persons or bodies with whom the Franchisee deals in the course of the Business as being agent of PizzaExpress but to use its own name in all such dealings.

Minimum Opening Hours

25 To observe the minimum opening hours prescribed from time to time by PizzaExpress and not to close the business during such business hours except with the prior written approval of PizzaExpress.

Similar Business

26 That the Franchisee shall not during the Term or for a period of twelve (12) months after the termination of this agreement (however terminated) carry on, engage in, be employed by or be concerned or interested, directly or indirectly, in the business of operating a Pizzeria within a radius of one (1) mile from any other restaurant operated by PizzaExpress or by its Holding Company or by any subsidary of its Holding Company or by its or their franchisees save at the Premises or under franchise from PizzaExpress.

Enticing Staff

27 Not during the Term or for a period of twelve (12) months after the termination of this agreement (however terminated) solicit, interfere with or endeavour to entice away or employ any employee of Pizza-Express or its Holding Company or any subsidiary of its Holding Company or any of its or their franchisees.

Value Added Tax

28

28.1 To supply PizzaExpress with a copy of every value added tax return made by the Franchisee relating to the Business within fourteen (14) days of submitting the same to H. M. Customs & Excise.

28.2 Wherever applicable to pay to PizzaExpress value added tax or any tax or duty additional to or replacing the same during the Term charged or calculated on the amount of the Franchise Fee, the Continuing Fee, the contribution to the Total Promotion Costs under clause 7 or other payment made by the Franchisee to PizzaExpress under the provisions of this agreement.

Liaison with Pizza Express

29 To nominate a person having responsibility for the operation of the Business and authority to take necessary action to liaise with Pizza-Express on all matters relating to the operation of the Business and the Franchisee's performance and observance of the terms of this agreement and a person to act as his deputy in case of such nominee's absence (for whatever reason) and in case such nominee or his deputy ceases to have such responsibility and authority or to be associated with the Business then promptly to nominate a substitute.

Notice of Assignment death etc

30 Within twenty-eight (28) days of any assignment, charge or other devolution of the benefit of this contract or of the sale of the Business or of the death, liquidation or bankruptcy of the Franchisee or of any person comprised in the expressions "Franchisee" or "the Principal" to give notice thereof to PizzaExpress or its solicitors and to produce to and leave with them a copy certified by the Franchisee's solicitors of every deed or document effecting or evidencing any such transaction or event.

Direct Debit

31

31.1 If so requested by PizzaExpress to pay for all goods purchased from PizzaExpress and to pay all fees and other sums due hereunder by direct debit and for that purpose to give a valid and binding instruction to his bankers (which shall be bankers willing to accept and comply with direct debit instructions) to pay direct debits from his bank account (which must be an account in respect of which his bankers agree to accept direct debit instructions) at the request of PizzaExpress or any of its subsidiaries and not to cancel such instruction without the prior express approval in writing of PizzaExpress which shall be given in the case of a change of bankers or bank account subject to the Franchisee having first given (which he agrees to do) an instruction as aforesaid (to replace that cancelled) to his new bankers or as the case may be for payment from such new bank account and subject to those bankers or, as the case may be, that new bank account, meeting the above-mentioned requirements.

31.2 To maintain sufficient balances in his bank account or sufficient facilities with his bankers so as to ensure that all *sums properly due and payable under* direct debits *under this agreement* made at the request of PizzaExpress for the purpose aforesaid are paid from the bank account in question.

SECOND SCHEDULE

Part 1

PRE-EMPTION RIGHT

1 **Interpretation**

1.1 In this Schedule, if the context so allows:

Disposal
has the meaning given to it in clause 4 of this Schedule and *Dispose* has a corresponding meaning

Disposal Period
means the period referred to in clause 9.2 of this Schedule during which the Franchisee may make a Disposal on Requisite Terms

Franchisee
means the Franchisee and the Personal Representatives

Offer
means an Offer made by the Franchisee to PizzaExpress under clause 5.2 of this Schedule

Offer Price
means the price for the Sale Property contained in the Offer or the Open Market Value of the Sale Property

Open Market Value
has the meaning given to it in clause 6 of this Schedule

Pre-emption Right
means the right granted by Pizza Express to the Franchisee in clause 2 of this schedule

Prescribed Time Limits
means the time for acceptance of an Offer

Qualifying Event
has the meaning given to it by clause 3.1 of this Schedule

Requisite Terms
has the meaning, given to it in clause 9.3 of this Schedule

Sale Conditions
means the terms of the sale and purchase of the Sale Property set out in clause 13 of this Schedule

Sale Property
means the Premises and the assets of the Business belonging to the Franchisee (excluding motor vehicles)

2   Grant of Pre-Emption Right
2.1   The Franchisee grants to PizzaExpress the Pre-emption Right
2.2   The Pre-emption Right confers on PizzaExpress the right to pur-
        chase the Sale Property and is exerciseable by PizzaExpress
        following the occurrence of a Qualifying Event

3   Qualifying Event
3.1   A Qualifying Event occurs at the time that the Franchisee makes a
        decision to Dispose (save as mentioned in Clause 10.1 of this
        Agreement)
3.2   The Franchisee may not make a Disposal of the Premises or the
        Business without first carrying out the procedure in clause 5 of this
        Schedule, unless it is made on Requisite Terms within the Disposal
        Period under clause 9.2 of this Schedule

4   Disposal
4.1   A Disposal is a sale of the Premises and/or the assets of the Busi-
        ness to a party other than PizzaExpress whether or not the
        Disposal is for money or money's worth, and a Disposal includes
        any colourable arrangement to the same or similar effect as one
        specified in this clause 4.1
4.2   A Disposal is to be treated as taking place when a binding contract
        for the Disposal is entered into unless the contract is never com-
        pleted

5   Pre-emption procedure
5.1   One the occurrence of a Qualifying Event, the procedure set out in
        this clause is to take place
5.2   The Franchisee is to give notice to PizzaExpress of the occurrence
        of the Qualifying Event and the notice is to contain:
5.2.1   the Offer Price;
5.2.2   the Offer to sell the Sale Property to PizzaExpress at the Offer
        Price, and otherwise subject to the Sale Conditions and is to be in
        the form prescribed in Part 2 of this Schedule and duly signed by,
        or by the duly authorised agent of, the Franchisee
5.3   The Franchisee shall permit PizzaExpress and its duly authorised
        agents and representatives and if applicable the expert appointed
        under clause 6 of this Schedule to inspect and examine all the
        books records papers and accounts relating to the Business and
        the Premises and will answer as fully and truthfully as possible all
        reasonable enquiries of PizzaExpress or the expert concerning the
        Business and the Premises

6   Determination of Open Market Value
6.1   PizzaExpress may give notice in writing within 20 working days
        after receipt of the Offer requiring the Franchisee to agree the Open

Market Value of the Sale Property and to which the following criteria is to apply:

6.2 the Open Market Value is to be equal to the best value of the Sale Property at which it might reasonably be expected to be sold by private treaty on the Sale Conditions at the date of the Offer assuming:

6.2.1 a willing buyer and a willing seller of the Sale Property as a going concern;

6.2.2 this Franchisee Agreement is assigned to the buyer with the consent of PizzaExpress

6.2.3 the Sale Property will be freely exposed to the market; but

6.2.4 no account is to be taken of any additional bid by a purchaser with a special interest

6.3.1 If the parties do not agree the Open Market Value within 20 working days of the date of the notice referred to in clause 6.1 of this Schedule it is to be determined by an independent valuer appointed by the parties jointly or if they do not agree on an appointment, appointed by the President (or other acting senior officer) for the time being of the Institution of Chartered Surveyors at the request of either party

6.3.2 The person so appointed is to act as an expert and not an arbitrator

6.3.3 The expert is required to afford each party the opportunity within reasonable time limits to make representations to him, inform each party of the representations of the other, and allow each party to make submissions to him on the representations of the other

6.3.4 In his determination the expert shall determine the apportionment of the Open Market Value between the property and assets included in the Sale Property

6.3.5 Subject to clause 7.2 of this Schedule the fees and expenses of the expert, including the cost of his nomination are to be borne equally by the parties

6.3.6 The determination of the Open Market Value by an expert is to be conclusive and to bind the parties

6.4 The Open Market Value agreed or determined in accordance with this clause 6 shall constitute the Offer Price and the Franchisee shall be deemed to have made the Offer on the basis of the Open Market Value

7 Withdrawal of Offer

7.1 If the Franchisee is not satisfied with the Open Market Value of the Sale Property as determined by the expert in accordance with clause 6 of this Schedule the Franchisee may within 10 working days of the experts determination by notice in writing to PizzaExpress withdraw the offer

7.2   In the event of notice being given by the Franchisee in accordance with clause 7.1 of this Schedule the Franchisee shall pay the fees and expenses of the expert and all the costs incurred by Pizza-Express in relation to the proposed sale of the Sale Property and the Pre-emption Right will resume full operation

8   Exercise of the Pre-Emption Right

8.1   PizzaExpress may (Provided the Franchisee has not withdrawn the Offer in accordance with clause 7.1 of this Schedule) accept the Offer by giving written notice to that effect to the Franchisee within whichever is the later of:

8.1.1   20 working days of the Offer; or

8.1.2   20 working days of the agreement or determination of the Open Market Value; or

8.1.3   5 working days of the Franchisee answering all the enquiries raised by PizzaExpress pursuant to clause 5.4 of this Schedule

8.2   Following the exercise of the Pre-emption Right, the Franchisee will sell and PizzaExpress will buy the Sale Property at the Offer Price on the terms of the Sale Conditions

9   Effect of the rejection of the Offer

9.1   If PizzaExpress rejects the Offer, or fails to accept the Offer within the prescribed time limits specified to in clauses 8.1 of this Schedule, the following provisions of this clause are to operate

9.2   The Franchisee may make a Disposal on Requisite Terms at any time within a period of 6 months after the rejection or lapse of the Offer, and, on the making of such a Disposal, the Pre-Emption Right will be extinguished, but:

9.2.1   until such a Disposal is made, the Pre-emption Right is to remain in operation against a Disposal which would not be on Requisite Terms; and

9.2.2   if the Franchisee does not make a Disposal on Requisite Terms within the Disposal Period, the Pre-emption Right will resume full operation

9.3   A Disposal will be on Requisite Terms only if:

9.3.1   the price or value of the consideration for the Disposal, is no less than the Offer Price; and

9.3.2   it is to a person approved by PizzaExpress as the new franchisee for the Business who together with all persons required by Pizza-Express to act as principals for the approved persons have respectively agreed with PizzaExpress to be bound by the terms of this Agreement applicable to the franchisee and principals respectively upon the same terms in all material respects as were offered to PizzaExpress; and

9.3.3   the other terms of the Disposal are not such as to reduce the value or the price or consideration in a manner which could be regarded as an exercise principally to defeat the operation of the Pre-emption Right and a Disposal is to be treated as incorporating the terms of any collateral document or transaction on which the Disposal depends or which otherwise materially affects it

9.4   A Disposal to a connected party may be treated as a Disposal on Requisite Terms only if it cannot be regarded as an exercise principally to defeat the operation of the Pre-emption Right, and, in relation to a Disposal, a party is to be treated as connected if he would be so connected for the purposes under section 839 of the Income and Corporation Taxes Act 1988

10   Notification of the terms of a Disposal

10.1   The Franchisee is to notify PizzaExpress of the details of a Disposal that it intends to make before entering into commitment to make it, and to allow reasonable time before doing so for PizzaExpress to verify that the Disposal qualifies as being on Requisite Terms; but

10.1.1   for this purpose, a contract for a Disposal, subject to a condition of agreement with PizzaExpress or the determination of an independent expert that it would be on Requisite Terms, is not to be treated as a commitment to make the Disposal until the condition is discharged; and

10.1.2   if the condition is discharged, clause 4.2 of this Schedule is then to apply

10.2   The Franchisee is required to notify PizzaExpress of all relevant information to enable PizzaExpress to ascertain whether the Disposal would be on Requisite Terms, and in the case of a Disposal for a consideration which is not wholly for money or money's worth, a valuation of the consideration for the Sale Property by reference to the Disposal;

and to give such other information as may reasonably be required for the purpose

11   PizzaExpress's right to object to a Disposal

11.1   This clause applies to the rights of PizzaExpress to object to a Disposal as not being on Requisite Terms

11.2   In order to make objection to the Disposal, PizzaExpress is required to give notice to the Franchisee setting out the grounds of objection within 20 working days after receipt of the notification and relevant information under clause 10, but, if PizzaExpress does not so object, then , in relation to the Disposal, his right of objection to the Disposal and to submit the issue to the determination of an independent expert under clause 12 will lapse

11.3   Following the giving of notice of objection by PizzaExpress, either party may submit the objection for independent expert determination under clause 12

11.4   The Franchisee may not make the Disposal while the objection remains undetermined unless PizzaExpress waives the objection

11.5   PizzaExpress may add to or change the grounds of objection as further relevant information or explanation is given to it

11.6   Where it is determined that the Disposal would be on Requisite Terms, or PizzaExpress concedes the issue before the determination is made;

11.6.1   the Franchisee may require the expert to determine whether there had at any time been reasonable cause for PizzaExpress to object, or to continue to object, to the Disposal; but

11.6.2   PizzaExpress is to be treated as having reasonable cause to object for so long as it is kept without sufficient information to enable it to assess whether the Disposal would be on Requisite Terms

11.7   Nothing in this clause 11 deprives a party of any right or remedy against the other to which it may be entitled for a breach of this Agreement, but the determination of issues by the independent expert under clause 12 acting in accordance with this Agreement may not be challenged

12   Disputes over Disposals on Requisite Terms

12.1   In case of dispute over or incidental to whether a Disposal would be on Requisite Terms, the issue in dispute is to be dealt with by submission to an independent expert

12.2   The expert is to be appointed by the parties jointly, but, if they do not agree on an appointment, appointed by the President (or other acting senior officer) for the time being of the Institution of Chartered Surveyors at the request of either party

12.3   The person so appointed is to act as an expert and not an arbitrator

12.4   The expert is to be a person who has at least 10 years experience of valuing property and business assets of the same type and in the same location as the Property

12.5   The expert is required to afford each party the opportunity within reasonable time limits to make representations to him, inform each party of the representations of the other, and allow each party to make submissions to him on the representations of the other

12.6   The fees and expenses of the expert, including the cost of his nomination are to be borne equally by the parties, who, unless they otherwise agree, are to bear their own costs relating to the determination of the issue by the expert

12.7   The determination of the issue in dispute by the expert is to be conclusive and to bind the parties

13   Sale Conditions

13.1   Completion is to take place 20 working days after the acceptance by PizzaExpress of the offer in accordance with clause 8.1 of this Schedule

13.2   The interest to be sold is leasehold under the Underlease

13.3   The sale includes all properties assets rights and goodwill used in or arising from the Business

13.4   The Franchisee sells as beneficial owner

13.5   The sale is with vacant possession of the Premises

13.6   The Premises are effected by and sold subject to the Underlease

13.7   The Premises are sold subject to;

13.8   all local land charges whether or not registered before the date of this Agreement, and all matters capable of registration as local land charges whether or not actually registered;

13.9   all notices served and orders, demands, proposals or requirements made by any local or any public authority after the date of this Agreement;

13.10   all actual or proposed orders, directions, notices, charges, restrictions, conditions, agreements and other matters arising under any statute affecting the Premises;

13.11   all rights of way, drainage, watercourses, light or other easements, or quasi or reputed easements, and rights of adjoining owners affecting the Premises, and all liability to repair or covenants to repair roads, pavements, paths, ways, passages, sewers, drains, gutters, fences and other like matters, without obligation on the Franchisee to provide evidence of the creation of or to define or apportion any such liability; and

13.12   overriding interests as defined in the Land Registration Act 1925

13.13.1 The Conditions of Sale (Second Edition) apply to this Agreement with the variations set out in this clause but the terms of this Agreement are to prevail in case and to the extent of inconsistency

13.13.2 The standard conditions 2.2 3.1.3 6.1 6.7(a) and 8.3 do not apply

13.13.3 The Contract rate means an interest rate equal to 4% over the Base Rate of Barclays Bank plc from time to time

Part 2

PRESCRIBED FORM OF NOTICE

Clause 5.2

To PizzaExpress
and to whomsoever it may concern

In the matter of a Pre-emption Right contained in the Second Schedule of a Franchise Agreement ('the Franchise Agreement') dated [   ] made between the Franchisee (1) and PizzaExpress (2) relating to 'the Sale Property'

TAKE NOTICE that a Qualifying Event has now occurred entitling you to exercise the Pre-emption Right

An Offer is now made to you under clause 5.2 of the Second Schedule of the Franchise Agreement on the following terms:

1   The Offer Price is £[   ].

2   This notice constitutes an Offer to you to sell the Sale Property to you at the Offer Price, on the terms of the Sale Conditions.

3   The Sale Conditions and terms of the Second Schedule of the Franchise Agreement are incorporated by reference in this Offer.

4   The words and expressions designated by initial capital letters which are not defined in this notice are defined in the Second Schedule of the Franchise Agreement and have the same meanings in this Offer.

You may accept this Offer by signing the duplicate of this letter, or another copy of it, in a manner indicating acceptance and giving or sending it to us.

You are referred to the Second Schedule of the Franchise Agreement as to your rights, and the consequences of failure to accept the Offer in time or at all.

Dated [   ]

....
[The Franchisee]

I acknowledge receipt of the notice of which this is the duplicate [a copy], and accept the Offer

....
PizzaExpress

IN WITNESS whereof the parties hereto have hereunto set their hands the day and year first before written.

Signed by

_____

Director for and on behalf of
PIZZAEXPRESS (FRANCHISES) LIMITED

Signed by

_____

Director for and on behalf of

SIGNED by the said   }

in the presence of: }

Witness:
Address:

Occupation

SIGNED by the said   }

in the presence of: }

Witness:
Address:

Occupation:

STATEMENT OF OWNERSHIP

(partnership or sole trader)

PizzaExpress Franchise at

Name of Franchisee/s	State which will work full time in the business	Share in Capital of Partnership	Share in Profits of Partnership
1	Yes/No		
2	Yes/No		
3	Yes/No		

Executives/Managers of the business

Name	Address	Job Title	Full time part time

Nominated person to act as liaison (para 29 – the First Schedule)

Source & Amount of Finance (and security therefor) for Establishment of Business and Working Capital.

£   from   Bank plc secured by

Charge of Underlease fixtures and fittings
Otherwise finance to be approved from Franchisee's own resources or by personal loans by partners named above from their own resources.

We certify that the above particulars are true and correct at the date hereof and that no-one apart from the above named has any interest (legal, beneficial or otherwise) in the franchised business.

Signed _____

Dated _____

STATEMENT OF OWNERSHIP AND EXECUTIVES
(Limited Company)

PizzaExpress Franchise at

Franchisee   LIMITED (Co. Reg. No   )

Total Issued Share Capital   £
divided into   shares of £   each

Principal Shareholders (viz holding at least 10% of total issued share capital)

Name	Address	No of shares held
1.		
2.		
3.		

Principal Shareholders of any holding company of Franchisee (as defined in s.376 Companies Act 1985)

1.
2.
3.

Directors	Name	Address	No of Shares held as Trustee/Benefi-ciary
Managing			
Others			

Executive/Managers of Business

Name	Address	Job Title	Full time/part time

Nominated person to act as liaison (para 29 – the First Schedule)

Source & Amount of Finance (and security therefor) for Establishment of Business and Working Capital.

£   from   Bank plc secured by

otherwise finance to be provided from Franchisee's own resources or by personal loans by shareholders named above from their own resources.

We certify that the above particulars are true and correct at the date hereof and that no-one apart from the above named has any interest (legal, beneficial or otherwise) in the franchised business.

Signed _____

Dated _____

8

Methods of trading

The franchisor is practically always a limited company. Your research will show you whether the company is sound and whether the franchisor has the resources to carry out the services promised.

You will have to decide in what capacity to sign the agreement and trade; you could sign the agreement personally as a sole trader or as a partnership or as a limited liability company. If you sign as a limited liability company the franchisor will almost definitely require you (and your partners, if any) to sign the agreement personally to guarantee the performance of the company. This chapter deals with the following methods of trading and the tax implications:

* Sole trader.
* Setting up a partnership – advantages and disadvantages.
* Setting up a company – advantages and disadvantages.

SOLE TRADER

As a sole trader you alone will be responsible for the business. You will be able to employ other people under the PAYE system. Most small businesses start trading as a sole trader and later become a limited company.

Caution: You will be entitled to all the profits, but should the business fail you alone will be responsible personally for all the debts and may well risk losing all your personal possessions including your house. As a sole trader you will need to do the following:

Keep proper records
Your franchisor will usually have a rigid system of monitoring your sales and will oblige you to use a particular system of accounting.

Good housekeeping is essential to the success of any business. In addition it will be very important for VAT and tax reasons: the Customs and Excise and the Inland Revenue may wish to inspect your records at any time. A tax inspector will have a field day if your records are bad.

VAT
Initially you should contact your local VAT office and arrange an appointment with the VAT officer who will be able to advise you fully as to which rules apply to your business. Depending on your projected turnover figures you may have to register for VAT. It is very important that you consider the VAT implications on your cash flow and profit figures – they make a significant difference but most franchisors do not take them into account.

Employees
If you are going to employ staff, whether full-time or part-time, you will need to acquaint yourself with the PAYE returns and various forms of legislation, e.g. sick pay, maternity leave, sex discrimination. Don't panic. Everyone is extremely helpful. The PAYE returns office will assist you in how to calculate wages and National Insurance contributions and tax for your employees. Once you have got the hang of using the tables and filling in the forms you will realize how easy it is, providing you keep up-to-date. The DSS is very helpful in advising about legislation and various leaflets on the subject are also available.

SETTING UP A PARTNERSHIP

You may want to set up a partnership for a number of reasons, e.g. division of labour or injection of money. The most successful partnerships tend to be between husband and wife or family members. It is normally said that the best way to lose a good friend is to go into partnership with them. There is a lot of truth in this but if that is what you want to do for whatever reason then you should carefully consider the implications of a partnership.

A business partnership is an association of two or more people (up to twenty) trading together as one firm and sharing the profits. A tax assessment is made on the profits of the partnership. The partners are responsible for the obligations of each other, so if one partner fails to pay tax the others will have to pay it. It is very important that you have a partnership agreement drawn up by a solicitor stating exactly what you and your partner have agreed, e.g. the share of profits, what happens if a partner wishes to leave or dies or a new partner comes in, conditions of termination, voting rights, holiday leave and who are signatories on cheques. Partnerships that go wrong are a nightmare and every situation should be covered by the agreement.

Sleeping partner
This is a partner who just puts in money, but takes no part in the day to day running of the business.

Ordinary partnership and the limited partnership
Two types of partnership exist. The ordinary partnership and the rare limited partnership. A limited partner cannot participate in the day to day running of the business and is only liable up to the amount of capital he contributes. A limited partnership must have at least one unlimited or general partner who has unlimited joint and several liability. He may be held responsible for all the firm's debts.

Trading name
Sole traders and partnerships can trade under their own name or names or under another name or title. If the trading name is not their own surname(s) then the name(s) of the owners must be stated on stationery and displayed at the office, shop or place of work.

Public inspection
A partnership's financial affairs are not available for public inspection.

Income tax: Sole Traders and Partnerships
All the business profits are treated as sole trader's or partner's income and taxed accordingly under Schedule D.

REMEMBER, THE MAJOR DISADVANTAGE OF TRADING AS A SOLE TRADER OR AS A PARTNERSHIP IS THAT YOUR LIABILITY IS UNLIMITED, YOU WILL BE PERSONALLY LIABLE FOR ALL THE DEBTS OF THE BUSINESS.

Your accounting year
Accounts are made up annually. However, the first trading period may be longer for a sole trader or partnership. It is up to you to

decide which day is to be your year's end. Some people use the end of the Tax Year. i.e. 5th April. Discuss the matter with your accountant. He will suggest a date which will give you the longer period for paying your taxes which will normally mean a year from 30th April.

Claiming allowances

It is in your interests that these are quickly and correctly claimed. The Inspector of taxes will want to see the firm's trading account, profit and loss account and perhaps the balance sheet. He may also ask for invoices, receipts, bank records etc., and it is strongly advised that you have an accountant to deal with the matter. He is an expert and will know exactly what the inspector wants.

Allowances on capital expenditure

Money spent on plant, buildings, machinery, vehicles and other things that benefit the business and do not have to be renewed every year are called capital expenditure. Allowances are given for this type of expenditure. For a sole trader these allowances are set off against income for tax purposes. Before making any expenditure it is wise to check with your accountant to find out whether it will qualify for the annual writing down allowance.

Deductible expenses

Those expenses which are incurred wholly and exclusively in the performance of the duties of your business can be set off against tax. Some of these are:
– expenses of business travel, but not travelling expenses from home to work. Travelling expenses on business journeys are allowed together with the cost of subsistence when away from home.
– an allowance for the upkeep of tools and special clothing is allowed, but not normal clothing even if you would not wear it outside work.
– if you have to work from home then you will be able to claim a proportion of the cost of lighting, heating, telephone etc.
– wages of wife employed in the business; however she will have to be included in the husband's tax return unless they are separately assessed.
– interest on business loans.
– interest charges on hire-purchase of capital equipment.
– hire or leasing equipment.

- insurance premiums.
- bad debts.
- entertainment for *overseas* customers.
- subscriptions to trade and professional associations.
- cost of self-employed retirement annuity.

If you have a business car you will be able to claim the running costs as a deductible expense so make sure you keep a record of the business mileage as well as the total mileage.

Tax deductible losses

A sole trader's or partnership's losses may be offset against any income that the trader or his wife may receive from other sources in that year or the next. In addition one of the biggest benefits of trading as a sole trader or partnership is that any losses in the first four years can be offset against wages or other income received in the three years *before* the trading started. So in effect you will be getting back a part of the tax you had previously paid.

If you were in the position where you hadn't previously paid much tax then you could carry the losses forward to future business years and offset against future profits.

Assessment of income tax

Special rules are applied to the first three years.

First tax year – Tax is assessed on profits from the first day of trading up to 5th April. Where the accounting year ends at a later date a proportion is calculated on a time basis.

Second tax year – Income tax is assessed on the profits of the first twelve months of trading. Again, apportionment may be necessary.

Third tax year – Income tax is assessed on the accounting year ending in the previous tax year.

Optional assessment

In the second and third year of trading you could elect to be assessed on the *actual* profits made in those years. Obviously only do that if the profits for whatever reason are lower in these years than in your first trading period.

The tax assessment situation in a sole trader or partnership is extremely beneficial to you because you can end up paying little or no tax – simply because the first twelve months' profits which you should keep low are the basis for two or even three years' tax bills.

When is the tax payable?

Income tax is payable in two instalments – due on 1st January and 1st July. This is why it is extremely important that you choose a good accounting date, e.g. if you choose a day in May as the end of your trading period then that is one month after the end of the tax year, so you won't be assessed for tax for about a year after your annual accounts are made up and you won't actually have to pay tax until the following January and July. This is great because you will not be paying anything to the Inland Revenue for about two years!

SETTING UP A LIMITED COMPANY

A limited company is treated like an individual person – a legal entity in its own right. Therefore you and the company are totally separate. Rules of company law apply and these are contained in the Companies Acts.

Shareholders

There have to be at least two shareholders and they will be responsible for the company's debts to the value of the shares they hold. Thus, their liability is said to be limited. This is the protection that a limited company gives you but you must be careful when signing the franchise contract or any agreement because you will only have limited liability if you sign in the name of the company. If you sign in your own capacity or give an additional personal guarantee then you will be held responsible for all the debts.

Public or private

A limited company can be public (plc) or private. When a company is public, shares can be bought by members of the public and the company may be quoted on the Stock Exchange. Private companies, on the other hand, do not offer shares to the public and they state limited after their name.

Registering a company

In England and Wales you will have to register a limited company with the Registrar of Companies. A number of formalities must be complied with and the following submitted:

Memorandum of association

This details the name of the company, the country in which it is registered, the company's objects, statement of the limited liability of its members, the amount of share capital and the way in which it is divided into shares. It must be signed and witnessed.

Articles of association

These cover the internal matters of the company. For example, the powers of the directors. There are other forms that will have to be filled in on registration and a fee will be payable.

Off the shelf company

You can buy a company 'off the shelf' through a company registration agent. Basically, this is a non-operating company which has been registered by the agent. After you have bought it your names will be substituted for the original names. The name of the company can be kept or changed depending on you. The cost of buying an off the shelf company is around £150.

Accounting records

Minimum accounting requirements for limited companies are laid down by the Companies Act 1976. The accounting records must:
– Disclose with reasonable accuracy the financial position of the company.
– Enable the directors to ensure that the balance sheet and profit and loss account they have prepared give a true and fair view of the company's state of affairs.
Limited companies must prepare audited annual accounts. Therefore you will have to employ the services of an accountancy firm. You will note that the accounts of sole traders or partnerships do not have to be audited.

Tax considerations

Companies pay corporation tax and usually make up accounts for a twelve month period to an accounting reference date which you can select. If you do not select a date then you are assigned the standard accounting reference date of 31 March. The twelve month period is called the corporation tax accounting period and the tax due on taxable trading income of this period is due nine months after the end of the corporation tax accounting period.

Directors
As a director of a limited company you are treated as an employee and therefore you will pay income tax on your salary under the PAYE system. Under the PAYE system you will pay the salary to yourself having deducted National Insurance and tax which you send to the Inland Revenue. You can choose to do this weekly, monthly or once a year if the Inland Revenue agree. If at the end of the year there is a profit this can be divided between the directors as additional salary and tax will be deducted. If the profit is not taken out as salary it will be liable for corporation tax.

Professional advice
It is very important that you consult an accountant for advice on whether to take out profits as salary or dividends or to leave them in the company and pay corporation tax.

Corporation Tax – Limited companies
As explained previously this is the tax that companies pay on their profits, gains and income over an accounting period which is usually the accounting period for which accounts are made up annually.

CORPORATION TAX RATES 1992 – 1993
Main rate 33 per cent
Lower rate 25 per cent
Lower-rate ceiling £250,000
Main-rate floor £1,000,000
The application of the small companies' rate is governed by the amounts of profits and not by the size of the company. In practice two-thirds of all companies pay at the lower rate. If profits are below the lower-rate ceiling in total, then the company pays the lower rate.

If the company's profits total more than the main-rate floor it pays the main rate on *all* profits.

If like most companies the total profits are between the ceiling and the floor then the company pays the lower rate on profits up to the lower-rate ceiling and the transitional rate on profits above that ceiling.

Deductions

In arriving at assessable profits a deduction may be claimed for capital allowances where expenditure is incurred on the acquisition of plant, machinery, industrial buildings and other assets.

SOLE TRADER/PARTNERSHIP OR COMPANY?

Having carefully digested this chapter you may still be unsure as to how to trade. To help you further here is a summary of the important considerations.

Sole trader/Partnership	*Company*
1) May not have to pay tax for up to two years.	Tax payable – 9 months after the profits.
2) Money may be drawn from the business without a tax cost.	Income tax is payable on any money drawn out.
3) Tax losses can be offset against the proprietor's other income.	A company tax loss *cannot* be offset against the proprietor's other income.
4) Assessment rules are very beneficial and the commencement and cessation provisions can result in certain income escaping tax.	There are no special assessment provisions.
5) Profits can be attributed to a partner's spouse if that spouse is in the partnership, and this means their personal allowances can be used.	Usually a spouse of the director/shareholder has to work full-time in the business before a deduction can be secured.
6) Expenses incurred 'wholly and exclusively' are deductible.	Expenses incurred 'wholly and exclusively' for the company's trade are deductible but if they benefit the director a taxable benefit in kind arises and the director will have to pay income

tax *unless* he can show that the expense was incurred 'wholly, exclusively and necessarily' for the purposes of his employment as a director.

7) Losses in the first four years of trading can be carried back three years against other income.	A loss attributable to first year allowances can be carried back three years. Other losses can only be carried back one year against the company's income only.
8) Capital Gains Tax is payable by the partners.	A double charge to CGT could arise – when an asset is sold by the company and when the shares are sold or the company is liquidated.
9) Relief is available on the sale of the partnership business and assets including goodwill.	No relief is available on the sale of shares in a company.
10) The partners are completely liable for the debts of the business.	Limited liability unless the Insolvency Act 1986 applies.
11) A partner may bind all the other partners. A partnership is not a separate entity.	A company is a separate legal entity.
12) Maximum of twenty partners except for solicitors, accountants and stockbrokers.	Minimum of two shareholders.
13) Partners can withdraw capital as they have agreed.	Withdrawal of capital restricted by company law.
14) Auditing of accounts not required by law.	Audited accounts required except for small companies with a turnover of less than £90,000 from 1994.

15) Accounts do not have to be filed.

Accounts have to be filed with the Registrar of Companies together with an Annual Return.

Chapter 9
Closing Down

The 1990–1993 economic recession has driven many small (and large) businesses to the wall, frequently for reasons beyond the control of the owners. If you go into business and everything goes wrong, what can you expect to happen? Having devoted the previous chapter to 'setting up the business', it is essential that the reader should be aware of what happens if all does not go according to plan.

Everybody goes into business to succeed. But unfortunately no business is risk-free. Every business-person should know what to do if things start going wrong. Most people panic. This is one time when you must stay calm. It helps to know what is going on and to remember that there is no shame in 'failing'. Some of the most successful people are where they are today because they learnt from their experiences and persevered. Deal with the situation as efficiently as possible and then carry on with your life positively. Never regard the incident as a 'personal failure'. It is an experience and you should seek a consultation with a Licensed Insolvency Practitioner. If you do not know one, your solicitor or accountant should be able to recommend one, otherwise contact The Society of Practitioners of Insolvency (Tel: 071-600-3375).

If an individual has been in business either as a sole trader or in partnership and is unsuccessful and therefore unable to pay his debts, it is usually referred to as having gone 'bankrupt'. If a limited company gets into difficulties and cannot pay its debts, it goes into 'liquidation'. In reality, bankruptcy/liquidation means the same thing. When a company goes into liquidation, its liquidator will start selling all its assets in order to convert everything into cash and satisfy, as far as possible, outstanding debts to the company's creditors. If you as an individual are in the position where even if you sell all of your assets you cannot cover your debts, then you are insolvent and you may be declared bankrupt. In effect, you or your company have died a financial death.

As a half-way house, if you or your company cannot pay all of your debts as and when they fall due, but you do think that if you were given time you would be able to pay all or a significant part of your debts, then it is possible as an individual to enter into an 'Individual Voluntary Arrangement' with your creditors to pay them off over a period of time rather than go bankrupt. There is a similar procedure for limited companies called a 'Corporate Voluntary Arrangement' where the creditors of the company agree to accept something over a period of time and let it survive long-term rather than put the company into liquidation when they might receive little or nothing of what they are owed.

If you cannot pay your debts, you can either make yourself bankrupt by doing what is known as presenting your own petition in bankruptcy, or you can wait for a creditor to put you into bankruptcy. Similarly with a company, you can either take steps to place it into liquidation, or again a creditor can petition for the liquidation of the company. However, most creditors will want you to continue trading because then they are more likely to recover their debts. However, if you are declared bankrupt, or your company goes into liquidation, all the liabilities and assets will be passed on to a Trustee in Bankruptcy, or a Liquidator, who will sell everything off and then pay off all the creditors that he can.

CREDITORS

Your creditors fall into one of four categories:

1. Fully secured creditors

A secured creditor holds security over a specific asset e.g. a 'fixed charge' over a property or a fixed asset like machinery and equipment used in the business. The most obvious example is the bank holding a mortgage over your home as security for a business loan. If you fail to meet the loan repayments as and when they fall due, the bank can demand immediate repayment of the loan and will be able to sell your house and recover the outstanding monies due. If they recover more than is owed to them they have to hand over any balance to the Official Receiver. With negative equity a common problem today, if the sale proceeds are insufficient to settle the outstanding amounts owed, then the bank becomes an unsecured creditor for the balance owed. There have been many repossessions in the last few years, and the golden rule is to keep your bank informed of your financial problems. Don't leave it too late to tell them. They will try and renegotiate the terms of your loan (e.g. by extending the term of the loan) before taking the extreme measure of repossessing your home. That said, there have been all too many dramatic and sad cases in the 1990–93 recession where families have lost their homes because business loans were secured against their house.

2. Partly secured creditors

Here the creditor is aware of what amount is fully secured and what amount is unsecured right from the start. Example:
- You borrow £5,000 for working capital.
- You provide security in the form of stock and machinery to the value of £4,600.
- The creditor is unsecured for £400.

If he manages to sell the stock and machinery for more than what is owed the balance goes to the Official Receiver. If he doesn't even manage to recover his own secured monies then the unsecured amount of the debt increases.

3. Preferential Creditors

After all the secured loans are paid, if there is any remaining money it is paid to the preferential creditors. These are the inland revenue in respect of PAYE, VAT, National Insurance and staff wages and holiday pay. (The trustee in bankruptcy fees and the Official Receiver's fees are a charge on the assets of the estate and are paid in priority to preferential creditors.) If there is enough money they are all paid. However, if there are insufficient funds they all get a percentage of their own debt. Staff wages will be paid by the government who then become a creditor for the money.

4. Unsecured Creditors

Everybody else to whom you owe money is an unsecured creditor. If any money is available after the secured and preferential creditors have been paid, it will be paid to the unsecured creditors, again as a percentage of their debt.
Note: it is illegal for you to favour a particular creditor in preference to another.

WHEN THINGS START GOING WRONG

All too many businesses, both large and small, have experienced cash-flow difficulties in this recession. If your attempts to delay paying or 'buying time to pay' have all failed and when a creditor's patience is finally exhausted, they will start legal proceedings to recover the debt due to them. This will involve the following:

The County Court
Except for very large debts, most legal proceedings to recover a debt will be in the County Court. A formal notice called a summons will be sent to you setting out the claims against you. The summons will give you one of three alternatives and fourteen days to reply. If you don't answer, judgement may be entered against you without further notice.

The three alternatives:

1) Acknowledge the debt – pay in full or offer to pay in fourteen days.
2) Acknowledge the debt and agree to pay in instalments on the basis that you do not have sufficient funds to pay immediately. The creditor can accept your proposals and then you will be notified of when to start paying the instalments. If the creditor rejects your proposals, you will be notified of the date of the court hearing.
3) Deny the whole or part of the debt.

The hearing is held in private and you may come to an agreement with the creditor before the actual hearing. Assuming you do not have a defence or a counter-claim and you accept that the debt is owed, if you haven't come to an agreement on how to settle it the registrar will make an order for you to pay by instalments. If you can't meet the payments you will be able to apply for a reduction in the amount of each instalment. This application could be granted or refused. You will be required to pay the instalments direct to the court unless you have a special arrangement allowing payment to the creditor. If you don't pay, the court won't do anything until the creditor applies for a bailiff's warrant for non-payment.

The High Court

For very substantial sums a High Court writ will be served on you. You or your solicitor will need to acknowledge it. Even if you agree that you will pay by instalments the creditor can at any time decide to have your goods seized by the sheriff.

ENFORCEMENT PROCEEDINGS TO RECOVER A DEBT

Once the creditor has judgment against you, unless you can make proposals for payment or settle the judgement debt, enforcement proceedings will start.

The bailiff and the warrant

A court bailiff will deliver the warrant to you. The order will require you to pay the outstanding amount. He will tell you to contact your solicitor immediately and meet the debt or your goods will be seized. Remember the bailiff is only doing his job so don't get irate with him. They don't particularly want to take your goods – they would rather you eventually paid and will usually be prepared to wait a few extra days for you to do just that.

The bailiff cannot take anything belonging to someone else, for instance goods belonging to a supplier, but the owner has to sign a statement saying that the goods belong to him. If he isn't around to sign, the goods may be taken away and you will have to inform the supplier that his goods have been taken by the bailiff and give him the bailiff's phone number and a reference number. The supplier can then reclaim his goods before they are auctioned. A list of the goods taken will be made and you will be asked to sign a copy. Any goods that are not reclaimed by other people, e.g. suppliers, will be auctioned. The bailiff will deduct the costs of the warrant and the collection of the goods and the remainder will go towards paying your debt.

INDIVIDUALS: SOLE TRADERS OR PARTNERS – BANKRUPTCY PETITION

Where there is a judgement debt against you and you have still not settled the debt or your proposals for paying in instalments have been rejected by the creditor and the court, the creditor or you personally can petition for your bankruptcy.

Bankruptcy
If you are declared bankrupt you cannot:

– be a director of a company.
– carry on a business under any other name.
– incur credit of £250 or more without disclosing your bankruptcy.

Ordinary bankruptcy
Where you as a sole trader or as a partner in a firm get into debt as a result of genuine difficulties the Official Receiver will deal with everything quickly and quietly.

Criminal bankruptcy
A Criminal Bankruptcy Order is only normally made where the debtor has been convicted of some form of fraud or theft and the idea is to make restitution from the bankrupt's assets.

Time with the Official Receiver
You will spend about a day with the Official Receiver, who has a duty to investigate the bankrupt's affairs and prepare a report for the creditors. You will have to list your debts and assets and compile a short life story of your business. An inspector (assistant to the receiver) will take all your accounting books, bank statements, invoices and receipts etc. He will also fill in official forms on your behalf. Co-operate with him as much as possible – he is trying to help you. Everything is being done so that the Official Receiver knows that you are not hiding anything. His job is to establish the cause of your bankruptcy and to prepare a statement of your financial affairs. It's going to feel like forever. But don't despair. Get the formalities out of the way quickly.

The Statement of Affairs
You will be asked to sign this statement and the receiver's inspector will sign as your witness. A shortened version of the statement will be drafted by the inspector and sent to your creditors with a formal notice of your bankruptcy. They will be asked to inform the receiver of the amount of money owing to them and they will be notified of the creditors' meeting and the public hearing dated (which is within four months of the bankruptcy order) and invited to attend.

Notices
One notice is placed in the *London Gazette* and another notice is placed in a local newspaper.

The Creditors' Meeting
Every creditor is entitled to attend in person or send a representative or to appoint the Official Receiver as a proxy. The objective is to enable the creditors to get together and raise any questions. While the meeting is taking place you will have to be present in the building but you don't actually have to be at the meeting. Try to attend the meeting because then you can answer questions that creditors may raise.

The Vote
The creditors will be asked whether they wish to nominate an independent insolvency practitioner as the trustee in bankruptcy. If not the Official Receiver will remain as the trustee in bankruptcy. The trustee will be responsible for overseeing the sale of your assets and the distribution to creditors.

Fees
Whoever is appointed as your trustee in bankruptcy becomes a preferred creditor and his fees and expenses will be paid first together with other statutory expenses. Any balance will then be distributed to the various classes of creditors.

The Public Hearing
Except for large and complicated cases there is no longer any public hearing.

Discharge from Bankruptcy
Bankrupts are usually automatically discharged after three years, or two years in some smaller cases. After you have been discharged you are released from your bankruptcy debts, but any property held by the trustee in bankruptcy remains under his control.

On the day you are adjudged bankrupt or shortly thereafter you have to visit the Official Receiver to provide him with details of your assets and liabilities. Once it's all over, have a rest and try to forget about it. Above all be positive and don't blame yourself. The experience, although often traumatic, could prove to be invaluable to you in the future. You will have inevitably learned a great deal from the experience. Remember those lessons for the future.

In franchising your business may have failed for circumstances beyond your control and you may well need to seek advice from a solicitor in relation to any legal claims against your franchisor and possibly other parties. Your trustee in bankruptcy can, in appropriate circumstances, pursue any legal claims on your behalf in the hope that any damages awarded to you can reduce your debts.

COMPANIES – ADMINISTRATIVE RECEIVERSHIP AND LIQUIDATION

As a franchisee you may have traded via your own limited company. When a company runs out of cash one talks of liquidation rather than bankruptcy. Often when a company is experiencing cash-flow problems a receiver is appointed where the company has granted a debenture. If a receiver cannot be appointed the company will eventually go into liquidation. To avoid a liquidation, where the company can continue trading to pay off its debts or be sold as a going concern, it is possible under the Insolvency Act 1986 for a creditor to apply to the court for an order to appoint an administrator who will run the company.

Legislation
Most of the relevant legislation is contained in the Companies Act 1985 to 1989 and the Insolvency Act 1986.

Receivership
When an Administrative Receiver is appointed under a debenture he takes control of the company's assets. The company still exists, but the directors and shareholders have no powers and all other creditors have limited rights. However, an Administrative Receiver must summon a meeting of all the company's creditors within three months of his appointment and present to that meeting of creditors a report explaining the circumstances leading up to his appointment as Administrative Receiver.

Who can put the company into receivership?
In order for an Administrative Receiver to be appointed, a debenture must exist. Sometimes the company itself recognizes that it is in difficulty and requests the debenture holder to appoint an Administrative

Receiver, or alternatively, the debenture holder becomes concerned about the recoverability of its money and decides to appoint an Administrative Receiver after having made a formal demand upon the company for repayment of the sums due to it.

Receiver's powers

The extent of a receiver's powers are as follows:

1) To collect in and sell the assets.
2) Manage the business.
3) Arrange insurances.
4) Negotiate commercial settlements.
5) Deal with the affairs of subsidiary companies.
6) Employ staff.
7) To grant leases.
8) To borrow money.
9) To exercise powers of attorney.
10) To bring and defend legal proceedings in the name of the company.

The receiver has no duty to unsecured creditors. He acts for he benefit of the debenture holder.

Types of receiver

A receiver can be appointed by the Court or by the holder of a fixed or floating charge. An Official Receiver is appointed by the Department of Trade and Industry and is an officer of the court.

Liquidations

If a company is insolvent, there are two types of liquidation. If the company decides to go into liquidation, it is known as a Creditor's Voluntary Liquidation. However, if a creditor has put the company into liquidation, it is known as a Creditors' Compulsory Liquidation.

Where a company is solvent, but the shareholders do not wish to carry on in business, the company can also be wound up. This is known as a Members' Voluntary Liquidation where all the creditors are paid in full and then surplus funds are returned to the shareholders.

Voluntary Liquidation

A liquidator is appointed by the shareholders of a company and its creditors. The liquidator's powers are set out in S165 of the Insolvency Act 1986.

Procedure

* Company becomes insolvent.
* Extraordinary resolution is passed by the shareholders to appoint and nominate a liquidator.
* Creditors' meeting arranged almost immediately. The creditors can replace the liquidator chosen by the shareholders by obtaining the support of the majority of the creditors present in person or by proxy in terms of value of their claims.

Format of meeting

The directors explain the reasons for the company failing and then the creditors can ask questions. Votes will be taken as to which liquidator is to be appointed. This can be a very noisy and frantic period as there may be serious arguments as to the choice of liquidator.

Compulsory Liquidation

Here the company or a creditor presents a petition to the court to make a compulsory winding up order. The petition gives a descriptions of the company and states the reasons why it should be wound up. Petitions can be presented in the High Court or County Court. In cases of public interest the Department of Trade and Industry can present a petition.

The petition is heard by a judge a few weeks later and he can make a compulsory winding up order. If such an order is made it is effective retrospectively from the date of presentation of the petition. When the order is made the Official Receiver becomes a provisional liquidator. He arranges for a report of the company and a statement of its affairs and convenes a creditors' meeting.

The Official Receiver does have the discretion to dispense with the convening of a meeting of creditors, if he thinks that no useful purpose will be served by the meeting. However, if a sufficient majority of creditors disagree with the decision of the Official Receiver, he can be compelled to convene a meeting.

The Creditors' meeting

Votes are cast for a Liquidator and a Liquidation Committee. The Official Receiver reports on the results of the voting to the Court and the creditors then appoint a liquidator to replace the Official Receiver and appoint a liquidation committee. Where no decision can be reached the Official Receiver continues as liquidator without a committee.

Comparison of receivership and liquidation

A receivership may not be as traumatic as a liquidation. A receiver will not usually close down the business and indeed may be active in negotiating a sale. Once liquidation starts the company will cease to exist.

Powers of receivers and liquidators differ. A company can be in receivership and liquidation at the same time and if this is the case the receiver's powers are lessened but he can still realize assets falling within the floating charge and he can still account to the debenture holder.

Directors' responsibilities during insolvency

Once the directors realize that their company is insolvent (i.e. they are unable to pay their creditors as and when their obligations fall due) they must consider receivership or liquidation. If they don't they might be subjecting themselves to civil and criminal penalties.

If you know your company is insolvent you *must* stop trading. The courts will take a sympathetic view where you continue to trade in the genuine belief that you can improve the situation – but you need to be very careful.

What is manifestly wrong is if directors allow a company to incur credit at a time when the business is being carried out in such circumstances that it is clear that the company will never be able to satisfy its creditors. However, there is nothing to say that directors who genuinely believe that they can trade out of a temporary financial difficulty are not entitled to incur credit in the normal course of business. It has been called the 'sunshine test' – directors who genuinely believe that the clouds will roll away and the sunshine of prosperity will shine upon them again and disperse the fog of their depression. But remember, you must act with the greatest of caution when continuing to trade and you must obtain independent professional advice. If you are advised to cease trading, stop at once or you could be personally liable for the company's debts.

FRAUDULENT PREFERENCE

If your business is experiencing difficulties and you are being pressur-
ised by some creditors to pay them in preference to others – *don't!*
Where your unsecured creditors are concerned you must treat them
all the same. Any payment to one creditor in preference to another
(even if you think that eventually they will all be paid) is a 'fraudulent
preference' and the liquidator may want to recover such sums in the
liquidation.

What you need to do

Above all, stay cool. Do not pay off one creditor in preference to all
the others. If your trading stock can be returned to suppliers (and
there is a 'reservation of title' clause in their conditions of sale – so
that title to the goods remains with the supplier until they have been
paid) then write to them explaining the situation and arrange for
them to collect their stock; this will at least reduce your debt to them.
Insist that they collect their own stock. You haven't the funds to
arrange deliveries if you are going insolvent!

Some creditors may threaten to wind your company up but if you
are going into liquidation anyway – don't worry about it! There is
nothing more you can do. Put the entire matter into the hands of a
solicitor or licensed insolvency practitioner. Remember the golden
rule is to keep all your creditors, especially your bank, informed of
everything that is going on.

10

Problems of unfair and fraudulent trading

WARNINGS

Franchising can be an extremely good way of doing business for everyone concerned. However, unfortunately, it is very easy for unfair and fraudulent practices to develop within it. For example, fictitious data may be provided to induce potential franchisees to sign the contract. The reader should be aware that this can go on and should be on his guard. LOOK OUT for the following:

1) Fictitious data – e.g. market research.
2) Fictitious accounting information.
3) Non-existent pilot schemes.

It is not just the cowboys who have done this. Sometimes reputable international names have been involved.

In some cases royalty payments have been presented as low and the franchisor has made extortionate mark-ups on tied products. In other cases, franchisees have been told there would be no mark-ups when in fact there were.

Sales projections may be distorted and should be carefully analysed. Remember that projections comprise estimated figures for illustrative purposes only. They are *not* the same as forecasts.

A franchisor is supposed to provide the franchisee with expertise and training. In some cases the training is quite inadequate or even abysmal, and the operating manual worthless – yet another reason why the franchisor should be asked detailed questions as outlined previously, and the franchisee should ensure that he is indeed dealing with experienced experts.

You should also ensure that the franchisor spends advertising money correctly. In some cases the franchisor's only interest has been to raise more capital by advertising for more franchisees. Thus, they have been collecting 'franchise fees' rather than making money by trading. This is simply Pyramid Selling and is illegal. Be wary of the franchisor who glowingly tells you how many units they intend to have by the end of the year – maybe he is just more interested in opening other units than ensuring that each outlet is successful. Franchisors who pursue such a policy will only wish to retain the profitable units and you will find that they then pursue a policy of getting rid of other franchisees. This can be quite easily achieved by making life very difficult for the franchisee. The franchisor can withhold sufficient services and support and supply the franchisee with inferior products or stock while supplying company-owned shops with good stock. This will inevitably affect the franchisee's sales and may lead to a situation whereby the franchisee wants to leave the franchise voluntarily.

If the franchisee does not leave voluntarily the franchisor may terminate the contract. This can be done quite easily as a termination clause will be present. Often they seize upon some trivial breach of the contract as an excuse to terminate.

Another ruse used is to withhold supplies. Obviously a franchisee cannot flourish without stock. If the franchisor is acting wrongly in doing this the franchisee will be able to bring an action.

At the present time there is no specific franchise legislation, although there is a growing body of people who feel that the time has come for such legislation in our system. Thus the usual principles of general law apply plus the regulations of the British Code of Advertising Practice established by the Advertising Standards Association (ASA). Where the franchisor is fraudulent our criminal system can deal with it adequately. The problems arise when the franchisor uses sharp and unfair practices.

BRITISH CODE OF ADVERTISING PRACTICE.

This is a self-regulating system supervised by the ASA. The chairman is appointed from outside the advertising industry and about half its members have no connection with advertising. The committee concerned with the day to day running of the organization consists of representatives of advertising organizations, agencies and the media. Pre-publication guidance can be obtained.

Object of the Code

To ensure that all advertisements are legal, decent, honest and truthful and show responsibility to the consumer and conform to the principles of fair competition as generally accepted in business. Advertisements should not abuse the trust of consumers or exploit their lack of expertise. Descriptions and claims in advertisements should be genuine and capable of being substantiated.

Consumer complaints

These are investigated by the Code of Advertising Practice Committee (CAP) and the Advertising Standards Association Secretariat which reports to the ASA. The ASA publishes details of the complaints, whether they have been upheld and the names of advertisers involved. Any advertisement found to be a breach of the code is not published by the media adherents and neither will they accept advertisements from agencies which defy the ASA's authority. In franchising you should be aware that it is arguable that statements such as: 'Be your own boss' or a 'business of your own' are misleading and do infringe the code. Misleading statements about the true rate of royalty payments would also be a breach of the code.

Television and radio advertising

This is monitored by the Independent Broadcasting Authority (IBA) constituted under the Independent Broadcasting Authority Act 1973. Standards and practices are set out in the IBA Code and are similar to those contained in the Code of Advertising Practice. If the reader feels that any advertisement is genuinely misleading he should not hesitate to lodge a complaint.

MISREPRESENTATION AND REMEDIES

Where misrepresentations of fact are made by the franchisor, his servants or agents – and these can relate to anything, whether written or oral representations – the Misrepresentation Act 1967 applies. Damages would probably be awarded in cases of fraud. Where however, the misrepresentation is merely negligent the award would probably be based under the common law. Unfortunately, a more detailed discussion is outside the scope of this book.

Unfair Contract Terms Act (UCTA) 1977 provides:

If a contract contains a term which would exclude or restrict –

a) any liability to which a party to a contract may be subject by reason of any misrepresentation made by him before the contract was made:
   or:
b) any remedy available to another party to the contract by reason of such misrepresentation.

that term shall be of no effect except in so far as it satisfies the requirements of reasonableness and it is for those claiming that the term satisfies that requirement to show that it does.

Requirement provided by the above Act is that the term shall have been a fair and reasonable one to be included having regard to the circumstances which were, or ought reasonably to have been known to or in the contemplation of the parties, when the contract was made.

In such cases a franchise would be protected as a court would hardly be prepared to hold a term fair and reasonable if it sought to exclude liability for representations made during the negotiation of a franchise.

EQUITABLE RELIEF

It has been argued that the relationship of franchisor–franchisee is a 'fiduciary' relationship. This means that the franchisor should always act in good faith. He should not

* misrepresent or conceal information.
* put himself in a position where his duty and interests conflict.

He should account for all profits made which arise from the fiduciary relationship. Any secret profits that the franchisor does make in such a way are held on trust for the franchisees. Such a 'constructive' trust will come into being for example:

– where the franchisor has set up a misleading accounting system.
– where a franchisor is withholding supplies from a franchisee.
– where a franchisor is deliberately weakening a franchisee by unfair competition through company-owned outlets.
– where a franchisor is discriminating against particular franchisees.

As has been illustrated above, there are ways that our legal system can deal with franchising problems. However, these tend to be limited and as yet no specific franchise legislation exists. Until full disclosure requirements are obligatory and franchise legislation exists, every franchisee should be aware that only limited protection is available and they should be hyper-cautious before taking out a franchise. They should ensure all details are in writing and they should keep minutes of meetings and telephone calls with their franchisor. All complaints should be in writing and replies carefully kept. Such procedures may seem laborious but are essential should problems arise and solicitors need to be consulted.

TRADE DESCRIPTIONS ACT (TDA) 1968

This Act applies to goods and services supplied by:

* franchisor to franchisee under the agreement.
* franchisee to customer.

The Act deals with goods 'supplied' regardless of being sold, hired or leased. Even if they are 'supplied' free of charge they fall within the ambit of the Act.

Section 1 of the TDA provides that any person who in the course of a trade or business applies a false trade description to any goods, or supplies or offers to supply any goods to which a false description is applied shall be guilty of an offence. Trade description relates inter alia to quantity, size, method of manufacturing production, processing, composition, fitness for purpose, testing by any person and the results thereof and approval of any person. Oral statements are sufficient in making a 'trade description'.

False and misleading statements

Section 14 of the TDA sates that it is an offence for a person in the course of any trade or business to 'knowingly' or 'recklessly' make statements which are false. Therefore, if the franchisor deliberately makes false or misleading statements on any matter they will fall within this section, providing the franchisee has not deliberately refrained from making enquiries.

As discussed earlier, statements such as a 'business of your own' – 'be your own boss' in the franchising context are misleading and contravene Section 14. Misleading statements as to franchise failure rates would also probably infringe Section 14. It is arguable academically that if a statement is made about future services to be provided by the franchisor himself, such as training and assistance in running the business, and he has no intention in any real sense of providing those services, he could be prosecuted under Section 14 and he could also be guilty of obtaining a pecuniary advantage by deception.

PERSISTENT UNFAIR CONDUCT

Under Part III of the Fair Trading Act 1973 the Director General of Fair Trading may take action against individual traders or companies who persist in a course of conduct which is 'unfair' or 'detrimental' to the interests of *consumers* in the UK. Unfortunately the definition of 'consumer' excludes persons who receive goods or services in the course of a business and therefore these provisions cannot apply to the relationship between franchisor and franchisee.

Many professionals feel that the franchisor-franchisee relationship should be covered under 'consumer' and proposals are being put forward to create perhaps a quasi-consumer class which will cover the franchise relationship.

CONSUMER CREDIT ACT 1974

The Act may apply where the franchisee raises some or all of the capital to start the business through a loan. If the loan does not exceed £15,000 the agreement will be a 'consumer credit agreement'. It does not matter if the loan is to be used for business as long as it is to an 'individual'. Partnerships are included but *not* corporations. A Consumer Credit agreement is a regulated agreement and may be cancelled within the 'cooling off' period specified by the Act. It is possible to cancel unless the agreement is secured on land or it is signed at the business premises of the creditor, owner, party to a linked transaction or negotiator.

These provisions are very useful for small investors. Antecedent negotiations are deemed to have been conducted by the negotiator, as agent for the creditor who is therefore liable for misrepresentations.

PYRAMID SELLING

Where a franchise business is essentially a trade in the sale of franchises, rather than traders in the product of the franchise, then the franchisor is pyramid selling and not franchising. The Fair Trading

Act 1973 deals with the pyramid selling type of problem and success-fully eliminates the worst abusers in this area.

Pyramid selling has been described as follows:

> The typical multi-level distributorship plan involves the manufacture or sale by a company under its own trade name of a line of products through 'franchises' which appear to be regular franchise distributorships. These plans may include three to five levels of non-exclusive distributorships and individuals may become franchisees at any level by paying the Company an initial fee based on the level of entry. Once a member of the plan, the individual earns a commission by selling the Company's own products and attracting new members. Each distributor pays less for the product than the price he receives from the public and from those at lower levels in the distribution chain to whom he sells. Since one profits merely by being a link in the product distribution chain, the emphasis is on recruiting more investor-distributors rather than on retailing products.
>
> 61 Georgetown LJ 1257 1973

Pyramid schemes are financially beneficial for those at the top of the pyramid. Eventually, however, the market will become saturated and recruitment of further participants will not be possible and the whole system will collapse.

Prospective franchisees should be aware of the above problem and particularly avoid franchises where the franchisor is more interested in attaining a rapid increase in the number of units opening in a given time rather than ensuring that sufficient support is given to existing franchise units.

11

Other Sources of information

WHERE TO LOOK

If you're contemplating taking up a franchise opportunity it's essential for you to be aware of sources providing up-to-date information.

Books like this one are excellent for giving you an 'indepth insight' into what franchising is all about but because the industry is constantly changing, with new opportunities deciding to franchise and others ceasing, you also need to keep abreast of changes. The best way to do this is:

Read Franchise Magazines
Business Franchise magazine and *The Franchise Magazine* are both available in WH Smith's.

Attend Franchise Exhibitions
At the time of writing the main exhibitions are:

* London – Olympia. For details phone the British Franchise Association, 0491 578 050
* Birmingham NEC. For details phone The British Franchise Association, 0491 578050
* Manchester & London – Contact CIA exhibitions (Mel Stride), 071 727 7380

Read Newspapers
Many local and national newspapers now cover franchising:
Evening Standard. Monday's Business Options Feature written by myself aims to cover new developments about getting into all types of business including franchising and direct selling.

Daily Mail. Monday's Money Mail often carries small business and franchise features.

Daily Express. Monday's issue carries franchising features.

Dalton's Weekly – Thursday's issue is popular for franchise opportunity ads.

Study Surveys

Annual NatWest/BFA Survey gives you up-to-date statistics on the franchise industry.

Consult a Directory

A Franchise directory is prepared every year by Franchise World, James House, 37 Nottingham Road, London SW17 7EA, 071 767 1371.

12

The future of franchising – growth and new developments

Franchising is certainly here to stay. It is a superb way of carrying on a business providing it is done correctly and ethically. Those of us involved in the franchising industry must ensure that potential franchisees are well informed and that the franchisors adhere to the highest standards.

A number of franchisors entering the market during the last ten years are still expanding and trading successfully today. Many successful and respectable franchise companies do exist.

Unfortunately franchising still has to live down the reputation it inherits from those who exploit the concept. The only way to avoid this would appear to be tighter controls and this will be reviewed later.

THE PRESENT UK MARKET

According to the latest franchise survey by NatWest Bank/BFA 'franchising looks optimistic.' With a turnover of £5 billion and a steady growth despite the recession more and more people are looking at franchising as a means of job creation.

There are about 400 franchise systems and about 25,000 franchised units. Last year about 20,000 jobs were created by franchising, reflecting the important role the industry is assuming.

The recession has taken its toll on all businesses and franchising is no exception. However, on the basis that two heads are better than one, franchisees have benefited from the advice of their franchisors in these troubled times. According to the NatWest Report 87% of franchisors forecast an improvement in their business in the next twelve months.

The Main Franchise Areas are:

Building services
Catering and hotels
Cleaning services
Commercial & industrial services
Distribution/wholesale manufacturing
Domestic & commercial services
Employment agencies, training
Estate agents, business transfer agents
Parcel, courier, taxi
Retail
Vehicle services

Other Areas:

The Retail Motor Industry

There are about 7,000 motor distribution dealerships. In 1993 there were about 1.78 million cars registered by these distributors at an average price of £10,000 each, producing a new car sales figure of £17.8 billion.

The Public House Trade

This is increasingly moving to 'franchise-type' operations. In this sector the total turnover is at least £3 billion. Greenalls is now a full member of the BFA.

Petrol Stations

These too are moving to a franchised style of trading. Fuel sales are worth an estimated £19 billion. In addition there are sales from forecourt convenience stores. This sector has an estimated 7,500 outlets with a combined turnover of £2 billion. Esso and JET are now actively franchising.

Dairies

Franchised roundsmen are estimated at 8,000. Big names like Dairy Crest actively franchise milk rounds.

Franchise Withdrawals

According to the NatWest Report, thirty-five franchise systems have withdrawn from franchising over the last year. Some of these are attributable to commercial failure while others have been taken over or have chosen not to pursue the franchise option for whatever reason. The Report stresses that when a system fails not all the franchisees necessarily go down with it. Many continue to trade independently outside the franchise.

In my experience when a franchise chain has collapsed in most cases franchisees will cease trading in that business. This is normally due to the fact that they need the franchisor's support or because the business relies on the franchisor for stock.

Expectations for the future

Existing franchisors plan to increase by 15 per cent over the next year and hope to double the current number in five years.

Increasingly the British franchise industry is adopting an international perspective. Currently 22 per cent of UK franchises have units in Europe. By 1998 as many as 54 per cent of franchises responding to the NatWest Survey indicate that they plan to be franchising in Europe.

DETERRENTS TO FRANCHISING GROWTH IN THE UK MARKET

While there is no doubt that franchising will continue to prosper, the main deterrent to growth will continue to be 'scandal'.

Scandal

Franchising lends itself easily to sharp practice. It's a minefield for the uninformed who can easily be misled with promises of high earnings. Over the last few years there have been several well publicized 'franchise failures'. In many such cases the franchisees have lost their life savings and have been unable to recover monies from the franchisor who has gone into liquidation.

Half the battle in choosing a good franchise is to know what can go wrong and then simply to avoid it. While the author has much sympathy for those who are conned, most who choose the wrong franchise do so because they have carried out inadequate research or just been gullible. At the end of the day they have only themselves to blame. Adequate research and awareness of problems will not guarantee success but will certainly help you find it.

The Table below of 'Franchise Problems and Their Resolution' should help you identify the areas where things often go wrong.

Summary of Franchise Problems and their Resolution

1) Franchisor not advised properly before business franchised.

1) No business should be franchised without the aid of expert franchise advice.

2) None/inadequate initial market research.

2) Extensive independent market research is vital.

3) Business set up badly. Poor financial controls overgeared -overtrading.

3) There should be tight controls on how money is spent – not on extravagant cars. The franchisor should ensure there is a strong cash flow.

4) Poor/inadequate management structure.

4) CVs of staff should be excellent and there should be guards against nepotism.

5) Poor franchisee selection by the franchisor.

5) A specific procedure should be used, for example the Kall Kwik Printing franchisor uses pyschometric testing and interviewing by several managers to ensure objectivity.

6) Poor Training.

6) Intensive training of at least 2 weeks is necessary. The longer the better. Should include theory and practical training on the job.

7) Inadequate operating manual.

7) The operating manual should be more than a few photocopies – it should answer all the franchisee's questions. A franchisee should see this before signing the contract.

8) Poor advertising and promotions.

8) Know exactly what you are getting for your money.

9) Inadequate market research of areas taken by franchisees.

9) Indepth research is necessary before allowing franchisees to trade in any area to ensure they

will generate enough business to achieve the expected profits.

10) Poor site selection.

10) A report should be prepared on a site and the franchisee should be involved as he may know a local area better than the franchisor.

11) Inadequate equipment package.

11) Ensure that mark-ups are not exorbitant. The franchisor should get you a better deal than you could get by yourself.

12) Inadequate communication and ongoing advice.

12) Set up a Franchisee Association/Newsletter etc. and have regular meetings.

13) Inadequate ongoing training.

13) Ensure training is comprehensive.

CASE STUDIES

Franchisor experiments at franchisees' expense

On Friday 15th November 1985 the Young's Franchise Group went into receivership. Ten days later it was bought out of receivership by Cyril Spencer of the Burton Group for £1.5 million.

The Young's group – Pronuptia, Young's Formal Menswear, La Mama

The Young's Group went into receivership in November 1985. Prior to that date the group, which included Pronuptia (wedding dresses), Young's Formal Menswear and La Mama (maternity wear), was a full member of the BFA even though in the case of La Mama, in reality, it had failed to meet the BFA's criteria for membership. The managment of the Young's group and everybody associated with it appeared to have satisfactory franchising credentials. A major institution, the National Coal Board Pension Fund, had even made a substantial investment in the group.

In late 1985 the group's bankers, Barclays Bank, appointed a receiver and certain members of the senior management moved abroad. The group was acquired by Cyril Spencer, formerly a director of Burton's and Chairman of Waring and Gillow plc.

For many months prior to the receivership, because of the cash flow difficulties of the group, franchisees experienced increasing difficulty in obtaining stock, which had an immediate and adverse effect on their business. Advertising and publicity, which the franchisor was contractually obliged to provide, deteriorated. For reasons outside the control of each franchisee their franchisor's own financial and managerial weaknesses were adversely affecting their businesses. The franchise umbrella was leaking, and subsequently collapsed.

For La Mama franchisees the new management under Cyril Spencer failed to fulfil their initial promises that La Mama would be developed and more resources committed to it. Despite repeated statements of support to the La Mama concept made by the management, within a year a chain of over twenty franchise and company-shops had ceased trading as a chain. Belatedly, the management declared the chain non-viable while they concentrated their resources on developing the Pronuptia and Young's Formal Menswear chains.

For those La Mama franchisees who had to cease trading substantial personal losses were inevitable. For selected franchisees the company offered settlements while others were not offered any settlement. Some franchisees were left owing their bankers significant debts. At least one franchisee commenced legal proceedings against the company.

A combination of receivership together with a lack of commitment by the new management proved disastrous for the La Mama concept and its franchisees. Having been a franchisee of La Mama at the time of the collapse, I can assure the reader that such problems only arise when a franchise is not operated correctly. La Mama was a regrettable example of what can go wrong and how it is the franchisees who suffer most for the shortfalls and failures of the franchisor's management. The failure of La Mama, however, cannot be laid at the door of franchising. A franchise is only as good as its management and the concept it offers. Franchising CAN and DOES work.

The La Mama problems lay in the following areas:

1) Insufficient market research into the market for maternity wear in this country.
2) Inadequate pilot operations.
3) Poor site selection.
4) Poor quality control of goods.
5) Non-competitive prices.
6) Poor communications.
7) Over optimistic sales projections.
8) Poor back-up services.
9) Poor merchandizing.
10) Poor training of franchisees in sales.
11) Poor company management.

Franchise 'opt outs'

Franchising is no easy option. Over the last few years a number of big names have tried the franchise route only to give up.

Holland & Barrett Health Food Stores started franchising in 1982 when they already had about 150 of their company shops. After taking on about twenty-three franchisees they decided to buy back the franchised units at market value.

Why has franchising not worked for them? What problems did they experience?

Problems

1) Firstly it would appear that their major problem was the fast moving market place. So many inroads have been made into

health products by big supermarkets such as Sainsbury's that in order to keep a competitive edge they have to adapt to changes very quickly. With franchised shops there are two problems:

* The changes cannot take place as quickly as necessary because the franchisees have to be consulted and allowed time to make a decision.
* The 'changes' (e.g. refurbishment to change the image of the stores) cost money which a franchisee does not have or cannot raise. Holland & Barrett research shows that they need to re-furbish every five years.

So a situation arises where some or all franchisees decide to leave their shops as they are because they cannot afford anything else whilst others and the company-shops do adapt to the changes and refurbish. The result is that in time there will no longer be a common corporate image – the very essence of franchising, and so some franchisees lag behind. This problem has been experienced by other franchisors such as Kentucky Fried Chicken and Wimpy.

2) The second problem related to the customers' perception of their product mix. Customers are not aware of the difference between health foods and healthy foods. Holland & Barrett deal with the former while supermarkets sell the latter. Holland & Barrett's mix of products at the moment is 60 per cent food and 40 per cent non-foods, e.g. vitamins, books, herbal remedies. They have to change this in the future to 60 per cent non-foods, incorporating products for a healthy environment as well as a healthy body, e.g. air pur-ifiers, ionizers, etc. – products which a supermarket is unlikely ever to stock.

3) Originally when Holland & Barrett decided to franchise, their re-search showed that by employing franchisees who would be more motivated they would achieve higher sales to the tune of at least 10 per cent. In effect, sales increased only by a factor of about 5 per cent. (This could be because the premises had just been re-furbished and not because franchisees had started running them.)

4) The cost of franchise support was greater than they had anti-cipated.

5) The management structure was 'split' and caused great problems because buyers and marketing could not make essential snap de-cisions. Everything had to be agreed with franchisees which took time.

6) Franchisee selection: they scrutinized their franchisees over a three day period, putting them through many tests and all in all

were happy with the franchisees they had taken on. However, they felt that the franchise relationship was such that a franchisee was happy to pay royalties in the early days while they needed much support but became resentful later in the day when they had 'learned' the business. It was a very difficult task to choose franchisees who would remain happy. A balance had to be struck between the complete entrepreneur and someone who would become dissatisfied and demotivated operating within the strict parameters of a franchise. Indeed Holland & Barrett felt that franchisees should be told right at the beginning what a franchise relationship is in no uncertain terms and under no circumstances should they ever be told that they are their own boss – they are not!

7) British personality – Holland & Barrett felt tht franchisees needed to be made more aware of the 'profit motive' – something the Americans are very good at while the British are not.

What lessons can be learnt?

For the franchisor the following are essential:

1) Ensure that growth by franchising is really what you want/need.
2) Rigid selection of franchisees is crucial.
3) Adequate market research is essential.
4) If anything, overestimate the resources necessary for franchise support.
5) It is not a 'make your money quick and run' business. People's livelihoods are at stake.

For the franchisee the following are essential:

1) Self-analysis. Can you 'stay-alive' within the confines of a franchise, i.e. do you have franchise mentality? If you are too much of an entrepreneur – stay clear – do it yourself!
2) Remember you are not your own boss and never will be. Franchising is a halfway house. At best you will be a 'soft entrepreneur'.
3) Carry out *all* the research mentioned before.
4) Make sure there is adequate initial and ongoing training.

Other big names like Sketchley Cleaning have also tried to franchise.

When Sketchley decided to stop franchising their then MD Mr Gudger said franchising was not right for them because 'it needed one hell of a lot of management. It took up a lot of time and effort especially in an area where the company was not well known.'

Comment

Many companies going into franchising do not fully understand the nature of the franchisor–franchisee relationship and do not have the manpower to support their franchisees. In such cases franchisees are little more than guinea pigs.

In order to ensure that the franchisor you choose has done his homework don't be impressed by a big name. Ask to see the following:

1) Their market research
2) Financial performance of their independent pilot operations.

Also ensure they have taken advice from a specialist franchise solicitor and/or consultant and employed an accountant for the production of estimated profit and loss forecasts.

Franchise Success Stories

One only has to walk down any high street to witness the many franchise success stories: The Body Shop, McDonald's, PizzaExpress, Kentucky Fried Chicken and Kall Kwik Printing to mention a few.

You too could be a success story if you choose the right franchised business. Investing in a business is one of the most important decisions of your life – so take your time and choose with care.

The Hallmark of success – PizzaExpress plc

Founded in 1965 PizzaExpress has gone from strength to strength, living up to its motto of 'to serve the world with style'. Over the last decade there has been an explosion of fast food restaurants with pizza restaurants now a usual feature in most high streets.

The company has taken full advantage of the increase in popularity of casual eating in attractive but reasonably priced surroundings. Peter Boizot, founder of PizzaExpress and still the company chairman at the time of writing, set out some basic principles right at the beginning which the company has adhered to:

* First class ingredients.
* Authentic methods of food preparation.
* Reasonable prices.

* High standards of interior design, careful maintenance and well-trained staff.
* Good service.

In February 1993 PizzaExpress became a plc and a fully listed stock market company. Committed to excellence, the company selects secondary locations and converts them into imaginative new design restaurants.

In 1993 PizzaExpress plc announced group profits before tax of £1.4 million resulting in an earnings per share of 4.7p. The interim statement for the six months ended 31st December 1993 reported profit before tax on continuing operations for the half year at £2,225,000 on turnover of £11.6 million. The company announced that restaurant turnover increased by 17 per cent compared with an increase of only 5 per cent in the previous year.

Five company restaurants were opened and three established restaurants were taken over by franchisees. Franchise turnover was up 11 per cent. To set up a franchise you need a capital investment of between £175,000 and £292,000 which includes a £20,000 franchise licence fee. This does not include a lease premium which may also be payable.

The company aims to have seventy-eight restaurants (thirty-eight company owned) by the end of June 1994. Experience shows that new restaurants typically take two to three years to reach their full profit potential. Controlled growth with a dedication to quality control is the key to this company's success.

Comment

At first glance it is easy to see why this company is successful. But things always look easy with hindsight. It had to start off somewhere. There are many new businesses franchising for the first time who may be equally successful in twenty years. Look out for attention to detail, a commitment to excellence, solid financial backing and careful growth. The recession has also shown us that it's worth going for a business that gives 'value for money', that people will still use even when times are tough.

LEGISLATION AND DISCLOSURE

At the present time there is no franchise legislation and no disclosure requirements in the UK. Caveat emptor – let the buyer beware –

rules. However, an increasing number of professionals feel that legislation or at least disclosure is necessary for protection of franchisees (and franchisors!).

Others categorically state that legislation will not work and will only serve as a deterrent to franchising growth. Certainly it may do this as franchisors will have to satisfy given criteria which they may not be able to do unless they have traded for a specific time. On the other hand the USA has franchise legislation and there the franchise industry is flourishing.

The introduction of the EEC Block Exemptions has assisted in protecting franchisees considerably. In the opinion of the author it is only a matter of time before some form of regulation is introduced in the UK. In the meantime franchisees with problems will have to continue to rely on common law procedures.

BFA members are vetted to an extent but unfortunately potential franchisees cannot rely on this as a guarantee of success. At the end of the day there are no guarantees.

A number of things need to be reviewed within the franchise industry – one of them is whether compulsory registration of a trade association would be beneficial. Another is whether there should be disclosure of certain requirements as a matter of law. It would be useful to have a committee made up of varying backgrounds (and consisting of members and non-members of the BFA) to discuss such issues.

It is always easy to lay down standards. The problem is keeping to them yourself and making sure everybody else adheres to them as well.

When there are controls and standard contracts for purchasers buying a property (National Conditions of Sale, or Law Society Conditions) surely there is a need to look at what controls are necessary for purchasers of franchises. The decision to invest in a particular business is as important and crucial as the decision to buy a particular house. Disclosure would be like a survey, i.e. not a 100 per cent guarantee that everything is satisfactory but an indication of things to be aware of and to watch out for.

CONCLUSION

The essential ingredients for a successful franchise (whatever it is) are the same. Whether franchisors have decided eventually to give up franchising or are successfully franchising they all stipulate the need for six success factors:

1) Excellent market research.
2) Excellent training.
3) Good locations.
4) Strong control over franchisees.
5) Strong management team totally committed to franchising.
6) A foundation of a successful business which is proven.

One franchisor stated that there are only two real reasons why a company would want to franchise:

1) To use franchisee financial resources to expand.
2) To have committed and motivated individuals running their businesses.

The problems arise when the system has not really been proven. The would-be franchisor thinks it will work because his one or two shops work, and he has not the resources to expand further. He then thinks he will expand by using franchising and other people's money. But the problem is that he has not the resources to carry out the market research or give adequate training or obtain prime locations, and does not have the strong management team to support the franchisees. This type of franchisor is potentially very dangerous. If the business works – fine! If it doesn't then the franchisor will not be in a position to assist franchisees or bail them out. Thus, franchisees should be particularly careful in such cases.

There are a number of cowboys in the business and the franchisee should be warned of this. Some cowboys use the BFA as a cloak of respectability – until there are legal controls franchisees should be warned of this as well.

It would appear from all the research that franchisees should:

1) Be cautious.
2) Carry out all the research stipulated.
3) Ensure that the '6 success factors' are present in the franchise they are considering investing in.
4) Have faith in the franchise concept because it does work.

Franchisees should only invest in businesses that have proven themselves successful and then invest with confidence and be prepared to work hard and with two things always in mind:

* The profit motive.
* Faith in the franchising relationship which gave them the opportunity to run their own business – an opportunity which they may not otherwise have had.

The author hopes that she has been successful in highlighting all the good and problematic areas in franchising so as to enable the reader to make an informed decision on one of the most important things in his or her life.

Only one thing remains to be said – Good luck!

Franchise listing according to category type

Key: AOR=Available on request

Company	Type of business	Cost of total investment £	Address	Tel/Fax
BUSINESS SERVICES				
The Accounting Centre	Accounting services	7,500	Elscott House, Arcadia Avenue, Finchley Central, London N3 2JE	081 349 3191/081 346 2038
Alfred Marks (Franchise) Ltd		AOR	ADRA House, PO Box 311, Elstree Way Herts, WD6 1WD	081 207 5000/081 953 2866
Driver Hire Group	Employment agency	15,000	Castlefields Lane, Cross Flatts Bingley	0274 551166/0274 370787
Everett Mason & Furby Ltd	Business transfer	25,000	18 Walsworth Road, Hitchin, Herts, SG4 9SP	0462 432377/0462 420062
Future Training Services	Training services	4,995	The Old Mill, Northgrove Road, Hawkhurst Kent, TN18 4AP	0580 752619/0480 436632

Company	Category	Fee	Address	Telephone
Hoseman Ltd	Business management	17,500	4 Archers Court, Stukeley Road, Huntingdon Cambs. PE18 6XG	0480 436676/0480 436632
Innscribe UK Ltd	Bookkeeping services	14,999	2nd Floor Suite, Thomas Duggan House, Manor Lane, Shipley, BD13 3RB	0274 530320/0274 531909
Mister Bagman Ltd	Paper & polythene bag supplier	5,000	K2 Valley Way, Welland Industrial Estate, Market Harborough, Leics, LE16 7PS	0858 461146/0850 433361
Quality Management Systems (UK) Ltd	'Quality' audit consultancy	6,950+	Hungate Bus. Centre, 4 Hungate, Beccles Suffolk, NR34 9TL	0502 711516
Recognition Express Ltd	Promotional goods	8,000	PO Box 7, Rugby Road, Hinckley, Leics, LE10 2NE	0455 238133/0455 232482
Ribbon Revival Ltd	Recycling cartridges	5,100	Caslon Court, Pitronnerie Road, St Peter Port, Guernsey	0481 729552/0481 729554
Signs Express	Suppliers of signs	9,950	25 Kingsway, Norwich, NR2 4UE	0603 762680/0603 762681
Travail Employment Group	Recruitment services	7,000	24 Southgate Street, Gloucester, GL1 2DP	0452 307645/0452 303197

VA Signs	Signs	6,000	Hennisfield, Sutton-on-the-Hill, Ashbourne, Derbyshire, DE6 5JF	0283 733961/0283 733961
VAL-U-PAK (Valufuture plc)	Direct Mail	2,500	Clare Lodge, 41 Hollybush Lane Harpenden, Herts, AL5 4AY	0582 460977/0582 462727
Wetherby Training Services Ltd	Secretarial/computer training centres	4,950+	Flockton House, Audby Lane Wetherby, W Yorkshire LS22 7FD	0937 583940/0937 584067

MOTORING SERVICES

Autela Components Ltd	Parts distributors	50,000	Regal House, Birmingham Road Stratford-Upon-Avon, Warks, CV37 OBN	0789 414545/0789 414580
Autosheen Ltd	Mobile valeting	6,000	21-25 Sanders Road, Finedon Road Est Wellingborough, Northants. NN8 4NL	0933 272347/0933 272488
Budget Rent A Car Int Inc	Vehicle rental	75,000	41 Marlowes, Hemel Hempstead, Herts HP1 1XJ	0442 232555/0442 230750

Name	Category	Amount	Address	Telephone
Clean Car	Self service car wash	180,000-250,000	Karcher House, Beaumont Road, Banbury Oxon. OX16 7TB	0295 267511/0295 266436
Computa Tune	Mobile car tuning	9,995	9 Petre Road, Clayton Le Moors Accrington, Lancs, BB5 5JB	0254 391792/0254 390361
Hertz (UK) Ltd	Vehicle rental	AOR	Radnor House, 1272 London Road, Norbury, London SW16 4XW	081 679 1777/081 679 0181
Neilsen Direct	Valeting products	Varies	Stanhope Road, Swadlincote, Derbyshire DE11 9BE	0283 221044/0283 225731
Practical Car & Van Rental Ltd	Car and van rental	35,000+	23 Little Broom Street, Camp Hill Birmingham. B12 0EU	021 772 8599
Screen Savers (UK) Ltd	Mobile windscreen repairs	7,500	2 Rugby Close, Westlands, Newcastle Staffs, ST5 3JN	0782 615764/0782 615764
Token Car & Van Rental Ltd	Car and van rental	45,000	2 Drayton Court Chambers, Argyle Road Ealing, London W13	081 991 5090/081 991 9428
Tune Up Ltd	Mobile tuning & services	15,000	23 High Street, Bagshot, Surrey, GU19 5AF	0276 451199/0276 451198
Vendo plc	Commerical fleet cleaning	11,500	215 East Lane, Wembley, Middx, HA0 3NG	081 908 1234/081 904 2698

FOOD AND DRINK

Arby's Restaurants UK Ltd	Hot roast beef sandwich restaurant	50,000-400,000	4th Floor, 24 The Haymarket, London SW1Y 4DG	071 930 7171/071 930 6061
Ashby's	Sales and distribution of fine teas and coffees	10,000	658 The Crescent, Colchester Bus. Park Colchester, Essex CO4 2YB	0206 851500/0206 854666
Bewleys Coffeeman Ltd	Sale & distribution of Bewleys coffees	5,500	Unit 29, Trent Lane Ind Est, Castle Donnington, Derby DE74 2NP	0332 850221/0332 811501
Burger King (UK) Ltd	Hamburger restaurant	AOR	Cambridge House, Highbridge Ind Est, Uxbridge, Middx. UB8 1UN	0895 206012/081 948 1630
Canadian Muffin Co	Muffin/frozen yoghurt	60,000	19 Rotterdam Drive, London, E14 3JA	071 538 1667/071 538 5490
Chez-Fred Marketing plc	Restaurant	200,000	10 Seamoor Road, Westbourne, Bournemouth, Dorset, BH4 9AN	0202 765837/0202 764133

Franchise	Category	Investment	Address	Telephone
Delifrance	Cafe/light restaurant	120,000-150,000	166 Bute Street Mall, Arndale Centre Luton, LU1 2TL	0582 422781/0582 455810
Dominos Pizza	Delivery & takeaway pizza	95,000	Unit 10, Maryland Road, Tongwell Milton Keynes	0908 618222/0908 615434
Eismann International (UK) Ltd	Frozen foods and real dairy ice cream		Margarethe House, Eismann Way, Corby Northants, NN17 1ZB	0536 407010/0536 403481
Fatty Arbuckles	American diner	100,000-250,000	Arbuckle House, High Street, Poole Dorset, BH15 1BP	0202 668909/0202 660334
Hoggies	Meal roasters for parties	19,500	Manor Farm, Battisford, Stowmarket Suffolk, IP14 2HE	0449 722500/0449 721500
Indian Cavalry Club	Indian cavalry theme restaurant	80,000	3 Atholl Place, Edinburgh, EH3 8HP	031 228 3282
Kentucky Fried Chicken	Fast food chicken	200,000+	Colonel Sanders House, 88-97 High St, Brentford TW8 8BG	081 569 7070/081 569 8733
Kloster International	Personalised wines	15,990	Old Market House, 36 High Street Buckingham, Bucks, MK18 1NU	0280 822077/0280 822077

McDonald's	Hamburger restaurant	30,000+	11-59 High Road, East Finchley London, N2 8AW	081 883 6400/081 883 6416
Master Brew Ltd	Ground coffee	14,900	Beverages House, 7 Ember Centre Hersham, Surrey, KT12 3PT	0932 253787/0932 253250
Olivers (UK) Ltd	Bread and coffee shops	300,000	7 Melville Terrace, Stirling, FK8 2ND	0786 472760/0786 472787
Perfect Pizza	Pizza delivery	75,000	The Forum, Hanworth Lane, Chertsey Surrey, KT16 9JX	0932 56800/0932 570628
Pierre Victoire	French bistro	30,000-50,000	32 West Nicolson Street, Edinburgh, EH8 9DD	031 667 2366/031 662 4708
PizzaExpress plc	Pizza restaurant	225,000	Unit 7, McKay Trading Est, Kensal Road London W10 5BN	081 960 8238/081 960 4792
Pret A Manger (Europe) Ltd	Quality sandwich bar	AOR	Old Mitre Court, 43 Fleet Street, London EC4Y 1BT	071 827 6301/071 827 6333
Pronta Pizza (Rosefun Ltd)	Pizza delivery	70,000	Floor F, Milburn House, Dean Street Newcastle-upon-Tyne, NE1 1LF	091 233 0499/091 230 0618

Name	Category	Investment	Address	Telephone
Reds Chicken and Ribs	Fast food restaurant	160,000-200,000	248 High Road, Chiswick, London, W4 1PD	081 742 8042/081 742 8082
Spud U Like	Potato restaurant	90,000	34-38 Standard Road, London, NW10 6EU	081 965 0182/081 965 6102
Tickle Manor Tea Room	High class tea room	40,000	18 High Street, Lavenham, Sudbury Suffolk, CO10 9PT	0787 248216/0787 247264
Wimpy International	Restaurant	80,000-200,000	2 The Listons, Liston Road, Marlow, Bucks, SL7 1FD	0628 891655/0268 474025
FAST PRINT				
Kall Kwik Printing (UK) Ltd	Print/copy	115,000	Kall Kwik House, 106 Pembroke Road Ruislip, Middx, HA4 8NW	0895 632700/0895 6782267
PDC Copyprint (PDC Int plc)	Print franchise	111,000	1 Church Lane, East Grinstead W Sussex, RH19 3AZ	0342 315321/0342 327117
Presto Print	Print	126,000	43 Market Place, Henley on Thames, Oxon	0491 574062/0491 410017
Prontaprint Ltd	Print copy	110,000	Coniscliffe House, Coniscliffe Road Darlington Co Durham, DL3 7EX	0325 483333/0325 488665

WALK IN RETAIL

Name	Type	Investment	Address	Telephone
Apollo Blinds	Blinds and curtains	35,000	Fountain Crescent, Inchinnan Bus. Park Inchinnan, Renfrew, PA4 9RE	041 812 3322/041 812 5253
Athena	Card/poster retailer	75,000-90,000	PO Box 918, Edinburgh Way, Harlow Essex, CM20 2DU	0279 641125/0279 635672
Bodyshop International plc	Cosmetic/skincare retailer	AOR	Waltersmead, Little Hampton, W. Sussex BN17 6LS	0903 731500/0903 726250
Bumpsadaisy Maternity Style	Maternity Wear	20,000	1606 High Street, Knowle, Solihull W. Midlands, B93 0JU	0564 775348
Circle C Stores Ltd	Shop	120,000	24 Fitzalan Rd, Roffey, Horsham W. Sussex RM13 6AA	0403 268888/0403 257682
Clarks & K Shoes	Shoe shops	100,000	Box 106, 40 High Street, Street, Somerset, BA15 0YA	0458 43131/0458 840766
Cullens Stores plc	Foodstores	250,000	248 Chiswick High Road, London W4 1PD	081 995 4841/081 742 1822
Durham Pine	Pine furniture	40,000	137 High Street West, Gateshead, Tyne & Wear	091 477 9124/091 411 5418

Company	Category		Address	Phone
Esso	Petrol retail		Recruitment Coordinator, Admail 329, London, NW7 8AQ	0372 222766/0372 22254
Freewheel-The Bicycle Specialists	Cycle shops	80,000	Buckingham House East, The Broadway Stanmore Heath, HA7 4EA	081 954 7789/081 954 7950
Greenalls	Public house	15,000+	Greenalls Avenue, PO Box 2, Warrington, Cheshire WA4 6RH	0925 651234/0925 231489
Goodbodies UK Ltd	Natural toiletries	AOR	Wallis Street, Bradford, W. Yorkshire BD8 9RR	0274 482708/0274 488368
Harriet Webster's Ltd	Toffee and fudge	10,000	Braeburn House, Arthington Lane Pool-in-Wharf Dale, W. Yorkshire	0532 524131/0532 520154
In-Toto Kitchens	Kitchen	20,000+	Wakefield Road, Gildersome, Leeds W. Yorkshire, LS27 7JZ	0532 52131/0532 520154
Mail Boxes Etc	Post & communication shop	60,000	84 Marylebone High Street, London W1M 3DE	071 935 9411/071 224 2777

Nevada Bob (UK) Ltd	Superstores	250,000	The Rotunda Broadgate Circle, London EC2M 2QS	071 628 4999/071 628 7999
Nippers UK Franchising Ltd	Baby goods	31,000+	Mansers, Nizels Lane, Hildenborough Kent, TN11 8NX	0732 838333/0732 833658
One Stop Community Stores Ltd	Convenience stores	15,000	Raebarn House, Hulbert Road, Waterlooville Hants PO7 7JT	0705 267321/0705 256927
Paco Wholesale Ltd	Fashion retailer	73,000	Kirkshaws Road, Coatbridge, Lanarkshire ML5 4SL	0236 449066/0236 449021
Pronuptia Youngs Ltd	Bridal & formal wear	70,000-90,000	Metcalf Drive, Altham, Accrington Lancashire, BB5 5TU	0282 772577/0282 776099
Snappy Snaps	One hour developing	120,000	11/12 Glenthorne Mews,115 Glenthorne Road London W6	081 741 7474/081 748 3847
Thorntons	Specialist chocolates	AOR	Thorntons Ltd, Thornton Park, Somercotes Derby, DE55 4XJ	0773 608822/0773 540757
Vantage Chemist	Retail pharmacies	AOR	Vantage House, Osborn Way, Basingstoke, Hampshire RG27 9HX	0256 760076/0256 767768

CLEANING SERVICES

Company	Category	Investment	Address	Telephone
Chem-Dry-Carpet Cleaning	Clean carpets	20,000	Unit 4, Mercian Park, Felspar Rd, Amington Ind Est., Tamworth Staffs, B77 4DP	0827 55644/0827 54482
Clean UK Ltd	Laundry service	6,000	73 Holborn Street, Aberdeen AB1 6BR	0224 211637
Dial-A-Duster	Domestic cleaning	8,500	263a Rose Lane, Mossley Hill, Liverpool L18 5UJ	051 729 0215/051 729 0215
Duds 'N Suds UK Ltd	Launderettes	123,000	141 Strand Road, Londonderry, BT48 7PB	0504 262615/0504 264083
Jani-King	Commercial cleaning	10,000	Bridge House, 3 Heron Square, Richmond Surrey, TW9 1EN	081 332 7474/081 332 7447
Jet Cleen Limited	Mobile pressure cleaning	15,000	PO Box 44, Dunstable Beds, LU6 2QT	0582 873530/0582 873519
Minster Cleaning Services	Office cleaning	50,000	Minster House 948-952 Kingsbury Road, Erdington, Birmingham B24 9PZ	021 386 1186/021 386 1191
Molly Maid UK	Domestic cleaning	AOR	Hamilton Road, Slough, SL1 14QY	0753/523388/0753 511554

Mopps plc	Commercial cleaning	8,950	PO Box 1055, Paisley, Renfrewshire, PA3 2SH	041 887 7848/041 887 8905
Professional Carpet Systems (UK) Ltd	Carpet care	14,500	North Stage, 92 Broadway Salford Quays, Manchester, M5	061 877 8902/061 877 8905
Rainbow International Carpet Cleaning Co	Carpet dyeing and cleaning	16,500	Willow Court, Cordy Lane, Underwood, Notts, NG16 5FD	0773 715352/0773 715422
Safeclean	Curtain & carpet cleaning	AOR	10 Blacklands Way, Abingdon Bus. Pk, Abingdon, Oxon, OX14 1DY	0235 833022/0235 53058
ServiceMaster	Cleaning	18,300	ServiceMaster House, Leicester Road, Anstey, Leicester LE7 7AT	0553 364646/0533 362139
VDU Services Franchising Ltd	Computer cleaning	8,000	VDU House, Old Kiln Lane, Churt, Farnham, Surrey, GU10 3JH	0428 713713/0428 713798

DISTRIBUTION SERVICES

Company	Description	Investment	Address	Telephone
Amtrak Express Parcels Ltd	Parcel deliveries	19,000	Company House, Tower Hill, Bristol BS2 0EQ	0272 272002
Apollo Despatch	Motor cycle & van despatch	35,000	Apollo House, 28/30 Hoxton Sq, London, N1 6NN	071 739 8444/071 739 6463
Blacks Unisport Ltd	Branded sportswear	20,000	Woodleigh, Whitebrook Lane, Peasdown-St-John, Bath, Avon, BA2 8LD	0761 437567/0761 434316
Chemical Express	Supplier of cleaning and hygiene chemicals	16,900	Ninian Way, Tame Valley Ind Est. Tamworth, Staffordshire B77 5DZ	0827 251431/0827 283989
City Link Transport Holdings Ltd	Express parcels	35,000	Batvia Road, Sunbury-on-Thames, Middx TW16 5LR	0932 788799/0932 785560
Intacab Ltd	Taxi service	AOR	Service House, West Mayne, Laindon, Basildon Essex SS1W	0268 415891/0268 541154
Interlink Express Parcels Ltd	Overnight parcel delivery	75,000-250,000	Brunswick Court, Brunswick Square Bristol BS2 8PE	0272 426900/0272 249742

Mac Tools	Hand tools		10-12 Ravensway, Northampton, NN3 9UD	0604 785685/0604 785573
Motabitz (Franchising Ltd)	Maintenance items	19,500	27-37 Craven Street, Northampton, NN1 3EZ	0604 231777/0604 230229
Panic Link plc	Parcel couriers	50,000	Melbourne Road, Lount, Leics, LE65 1PL	0530 411111/0530 417575
Snap-on-Tools Ltd	Tools and equipment	AOR	Palmer House, 150-154 Cross St, Sale Cheshire, M33 1AQ	061 969 0126/061 905 1175
Trust Parts Ltd	Tools and consumables	17,500+	Unit 7, Groundwell Ind. Est, Swindon SN2 5AG	0793 723749/0793 724431
Unigate Dairies Ltd	Milk Distributor	3,500-4,500	14-40 Victoria Road, Aldershot, Hants, GU1 1TH	0252 24522

HEALTH AND BEAUTY

| House of Colour Ltd | Image consultants | 7,500 | 28 The Avenue, Watford WD1 3NS | 0923 211188 |
| The Natural Way | Weight loss | 8,500 | Leeds House, 79A High Street, Newcastle Under Lyme, Staffs | 0782 711122/0782 711717 |

Rosemary Conley Diet & Fitness Clubs Ltd	Diet & exercise	8,500	Quorn House, Meeting St, Quorn, Loughborough, Leics, LE12 8EX	0509 620222/0509 621046
Saks Hair (Holdings) Ltd	Hairdressing & beauty	AOR	2 Peel Court, St Cuthberts Way, Darlington, DL1 1GB	0325 380333
The Tanning Shop	Solarium	35,000-40,000	35 Albemarle Street, Mayfair, London, W1X 3FB	071 493 0904/071 495 0616
Toni & Guy	Ladies hairdressers	60,000-70,000	Unit 14, Brentford Bus Centre, Commerce Road, Brentford TW8 8LG	081 569 9196/081 569 9094

PROPERTY SERVICES

CICO Chimney Linings Ltd	Chimney restoration	16,000	Westleton, Saxmundham, Suffolk, IP17 3BS	072 873608/072 873428
Countrywide Garden Maintenance Services	Garden maintenance	19,950	164-200 Stockport Road, Cheadle Cheshire, SK8 2DP	061 428 4444/061 428 0637
Dyno-Locks	Locksmith	15,500	Zockoll House, 143 Maple Road, Surbiton, Surrey, KT6 4BJ	081 549 9711/081 549 3870

Company	Service	Investment	Address	Telephone
Dyno-Rod	Plumbing/drainage	30,000-70,000	Zockoll House, 143 Maple Road, Surbiton, Surrey, KT6 4BJ	081 549 9711/081 549 3870
Dyno-Services	Roofing & glazing	17,500	Zockoll House, 143 Maple Road, Surbiton, Surrey, KT6 4BJ	081 549 9711/081 549 3870
First Call Ltd	Property maintenance	15,000-20,000	Chandos Mews, 34B Chandos Road Redland, Bristol BS6 6PF	0272 232525/0272 445251
Garage Door Associates	Garage door retailers	30,000	Unit 5, Meadowbrook Ind. Centre, Maxwell Way, Crawley, W. Sussex, RH10 2SA	0293 611598/0293 611040
Gun-Point Ltd	Repointing service	15,900	Thavies Inn House, 3/4 Holborn Circus London EC1N 2PL	071 353 6167/071 583 7259
Master Thatchers Ltd	Roof thatchers	15,000	Rose Tree Farm, 29 Nine Mile Ride, Finchampstead, Wokingham, Berks	0734 734203/0734 328054
Metro Rod plc	Drain & pipe cleaning	45,000	Metro House, Churchill Way, Macclesfield Cheshire, SK11 6AY	0625 434444/0625 616687

Mixamate Concrete	Ready mixed concrete	21,000+	11 Westdown, Great Bookham, Surrey KT23 4LJ	0372 456714/0372 456714
SGO UK	Stained windows	45,000	PO Box 65, Norwich, Norfolk, NR6 6EJ	0603 485454/0603 405859
Veutrolla Ltd	Sash windows	18,000	51 Tower Street, Harrogate, North Yorkshire HG1 1HS	0423 567004/0423 520897
Worldwide Refinishing Systems	Refurbishing surfaces	17,500+	Acre Business Park, Acre Road, Reading Berks RG32 0SA	0734 462140/0734 462140

TRAVEL AND ACCOMMODATION

Holiday Inn Worldwide	Hotel chain	AOR	HO: Woluwe Office Park 1, 101 Rue Neerveld, Brussels, 1200	London Contact: 0525 876025 +32 2 773 5630/+32 2 773 5603
Gem Travel	Travel agents	20,247	56 St Johns Road, Tunbridge Wells, Kent, TN4 9NY	0892 516660/0892 517270
Spice UK	Adventure/social	15,000	13 Thorpe Street, Old Trafford Manchester M16 9PR	061 872 2213/061 848 9465
Uniglobe Travel (UK)	Business travel	50,000	Exchange Tower, Harbour Exchange Sq, London, E14 9GB	071 418 0151/071 418 0151

ESTATE SERVICES

Name	Type	Investment	Address	Phone
Agency Signs	Specialist signs	10,000	20 Prince of Wales Road, Norwich, NK1 1LB	0603 766060/0603 761087
The Confederation Property Services	Estate agency		Bank House, Primett Road, Sevenoaks, SG1 3UQ	0438 744515/0438 744556
Legal & General Franchising Ltd	Estate agency	50,000	4 Bruntcliffe Way, Morley, Leeds,LS27 0JG	0532 539166/0532 524589

HOME CARE

Name	Type	Investment	Address	Phone
Colour Counsellors Ltd	Interior design	6,000-10,000	3 Dovedale Studios, 465 Battersea Park Rd London SW11 4LR	071 978 5023
Cupboard Love (UK) Ltd	Refurbishing	7,500-20,000	Unit 8, Premier Trading Estate Dartmouth, Middleway, Birmingham	021 333 3342/021 333 3611
Decorating Den	Interior design		Bowditch, Membury, Nr Axminster, Devon EX13 7TY	0404 881789/0404 881786

SPECIALIZED

Card Connection	Greeting cards	16,000	Park House, South Street, Farnham, Surrey, GU9 7QQ	0252 733177/0252 735644
Congratulations Franchising Ltd	Wedding lists	17,900	Chapel Court, Chapel Road, Astwood Bank, Redditch, Worcs	0527 894111/0527 894080
Giltsharp Technology (UK) Ltd	Mobile blade & scissor sharpening	12,950+	Suite 44, Concourse House, Dewsbury Road, Leeds, LS11 7DF	0532 706004/0532 705937
Hunt & Co Countrywide plc	Support services for the legal profession		Challenge House, Sherwood Drive, Bletchley Milton Keynes, Mk3 6DP	0908 366669
Kwik Strip (UK) Ltd	Paint stripping	12,500+	PO Box 1087, Summerleaze, Church Road, Winsomber, Avon	0934 843100/0934 844119
Lambourn Court International plc	Stress Management	16,500+	The Manor Barn, Keysoe, Bedfordshire MK44 2HR	0234 708848/0234 708702
M & B Marquees	Hirers of marquees	30,000	Premier House, Tennyson Drive, Pitsea, Basildon, Essex, SS13 3BT	0268 558002/0268 552783

Make-A-Date-Ltd	Introduction agency	15,000-28,000	Aria House, 23 Craven Street, London, WC2N 5NT	071 928 1799
Nationwide Investigation Group	Private detective agency	Varies	86 Southwark Bridge Road, London SE1 0EX	0603 51941/0603 250682
Needlepoint Network	Needlepoint teaching programme	AOR	Kenswick Hill, Norwich, Norfolk, NR4 6TT	0902 850721/0902 850922
Somerford Claims Plc	3rd party loss of earnings recovery for taxi industry	15,000	Somersford Hall, Somerford, Stafford ST19 9DQ	
Swinton Insurance	Insurance brokers	AOR	Swinton House, 6 Gt Marlborough Street, Manchester, M1 5SW	061 236 1222/061 237 9214

British Franchise Association

FULL MEMBERS LIST

Franchisors are required to submit a completed application form, including disclosure document, franchise agreement, prospectus, accounts, etc; and provide proof of a correctly constituted pilot scheme successfully operated for at least one year, financed and managed by the applicant company. In addition, evidence of successful franchising over a subsequent two year period with at least four franchisees is required.

Amtrak Express Parcels Ltd
Company House
Tower Hill
Bristol BS2 0EQ

Mr R Baines

0272 272002

Overnight parcels,
collection & delivery

Apollo Window Blinds Ltd
Inchinnan Industrial Estate
Inchinnan
Strathclyde PA4 9RE

Mr J Robertson

041 812 3322

Manufacturers &
retailers of window
blinds to the domestic
& commercial markets

ASC Network plc
24 Red Lion Street
London WC1R 4SA

Mr H Ejdelbaum

071 831 6191

Commercial Finance
Consultants & Brokers

Autela Components Ltd
Regal House
Birmingham Road
Stratford upon Avon
Warwickshire CV37 0BN

Mr R Taylor

0789 414545

Automotive part
suppliers

Balmforth & Partners Ltd
1st Floor Richmond House
High Street
Crawley
West Sussex

Mr P Siddons

0293 565575

Residential estate
agency

**Budget Rent-a-Car
International Inc**
41 Marlowes
Hemel Hempstead
Hertfordshire HP1 1XJ

Mr N Summerville

0442 232555

National and
international self-drive
car, van & truck rental
services

Burger King (UK) Ltd
Cambridge House
Highbridge Ind Estate
Oxford Road
Uxbridge
Middx UB8 1UN

Mr N Travis

0895 206000

Fast food restaurant

Chem Dry UK
2 The Metro Centre
Ronsons Way, Sandridge
St Albans
Herts AL4 9QT

Mr R Elvidge

0727 852030

Carpet, upholstery &
curtain cleaning service
to domestic &
commercial customers

Chem Dry UK
Unit 4 Mercian Park
Felspar Road
Amington Ind Estate
Tamworth
Staffs B77 4DP

Mr R Grey

0827 55644

Carpet, upholstery &
curtain cleaning service
to domestic &
commercial customers

Chem Dry UK
Suite D Annie Reed Court
Annie Reed Road
Beverley
N Humberside HU17 0LF

Mr M Hutchinson

0482 872770

Carpet, upholstery &
curtain cleaning service
to domestic &
commercial customers

Chemical Express
Ninian Way
Tame Valley Ind Estate
Tamworth
Staffordshire B77 5DZ

Mr L J Gray

0827 251431

Sell & distribute
industrial hygiene,
cleaning & maintenance
chemicals via mobile
showrooms

Circle 'C' Stores Ltd 24 Fitzlan Road Roffey Horsham West Sussex RH13 6AA	Mr J Wormull 0403 268888	Convenience stores
Circle 'K' (UK) Ltd Fareham Point Wickham Road Fareham Hampshire PO16 7BY	Mr D Ellis-Jones 0329 825989	Convenience stores
City Link Transport **Holdings Ltd** Batavia Road Sunbury-on-Thames Middlesex TW16 5LR	Mr D Ross 0932 788799	Same day & overnight parcel service
Clarks Shoes 40 High Street Street Somerset BA16 0YA	Mr P Monaghan 0458 43131	Retail shoe shops
Colour Counsellors Ltd* 3 Dovedale Studios 465 Battersea Park Road London SW11 4LR (*Particularly suitable for ladies)	Mrs V Stourton 071 978 5023	Interior decorating. Colour catalogued samples of wallpaper, carpets & fabrics
Computa Tune 9 Petre Road Clayton Park Clayton Le Moors Accrington Lancashire BB5 5JB	Mr A Whittaker 0254 391762/ 385891	Mobile tuning & servicing of motor cars
Countrywide Garden **Maintenance Services** 16-20 Stockport Road Cheadle Cheshire SK8 2DP	Mr M Stott 061 428 4444	Ground & landscape maintenance service to private & commercial clients
Dairy Crest The Dairy High Street Fenstanton Huntingdon Cambs	Mr M Allen 0932 868322	Dairy products & food manufacturer

Dampcure Woodcure/30   Mrs C Darley   Damp proofing &
Darley House   timber treatment
41 Merton Road   0923 663322
Watford
Hertfordshire WD1 7BU

Don Millers Hot Bread   Mr M J B Ward   Hot bread kitchens
Kitchens
166 Bute Street Mall   0582 422781
Arndale Centre
Luton
Bedfordshire LU1 2TL

Driver Hire   Mr J P Bussey   Employment agency
Progress House   specialising in blue
Castlefields Lane   0274 551166   collar supply of
Bingley   temporary workers
West Yorkshire BD16 2AB

Dyno Services Ltd   Mr J Chaplin   Drain & pipe cleaning
Zockoll House   service
143 Maple Road   081 481 2200
Surbiton
Surrey KY6 4BJ

Dyno Locks   Mr J Chaplin   Emergency locks –
Dyno Rod Developments   opening & fitting
Ltd   081 481 2200
143 Maple Road
Surbiton
Surrey KY6 4BJ

Everett, Masson & Furby   Mr M Carr   Sale of businesses
Ltd
18/19 Walsworth Road   0462 432377
Hitchin
Hertfordshire SG4 9SP

Francesco Group   Mr F   Ladies' & gentlemen's
Woodings Yard   Dellicompagni   hairdressing
Bailey Street
Stafford ST17 4BG   0785 47175

Greenalls Inn Partnership   Mr D Whiteley   Public House retailing
Greenalls Avenue
PO Box No 2   0925 51234
Warrington
Cheshire WA4 6RH

Gun-Point Ltd
Thavies Inn House
3/4 Holborn Circus
London EC1N 2PL

Mr H
Chamberlain

071 353 6167

A mechanized re-
pointing service for all
brick & stone
properties

Hertz (UK) Ltd
Radnor House
1272 London Road
Norbury
London SW16 4XW

Mr R G Marks

081 679 1777

Vehicle rental

Hiretech Hire Centres
Chalk Hill House
Watford
Hertfordshire WD1 4BH

Mr N Selwood

0923 30337

Tool & equipment hire
concession within
Sainsbury's Homebase
stores

Holiday Inns (UK) Ltd
21 Chalton Heights
Chalton
Bedfordshire LU4 9UF

Mr P Bell

0525 876025

Hotels

Intacab Ltd
Service House
West Mayne
Laindon
Basildon
Essex

Mr P Dance

0268 415891

Taxi, private hire,
courier

**Interlink Express Parcels
Ltd**
Brunswick Court
Brunswick Square
Bristol BS2 8PE

Mr A P Gent

0272 426900

Express courier parcel
service

In-Toto Ltd
Wakefield Road
Gildersome
Leeds LS27 7JZ

Mr M Ecclestone

0532 524131

Retailing of kitchens &
bathroom furniture,
appliances & ancilliary

**Kall-Kwik Printing (UK)
Ltd**
Kall-Kwik House
106 Pembroke Road
Ruislip
Middlesex HA4 8NW

Mr M
Gerstenhaber

0895 632700

Quick printing centre
offering comprehensive
design, printing,
finishing &
photocopying service

213

Kentucky Fried Chicken Mr M Roberts Fast food restaurant
88/97 High Street
Brentford 081 569 7070
Middlesex TW8 8BG

Kwik Strip (UK) Ltd Mr I Chivers Service to trade & retail
PO Box 1087 markets for the
Summerleaze 0934 843100 stripping & restoration
Church Road of furniture
Winscombe
Avon BS25 1BH

The Late Late Supershop Mr D Shannon Convenience store
(UK) Ltd retailing
132-135 Powis Street 081 854 2000
Woolwich
London SE18 6NL

Master Thatchers Ltd Mr R C West Thatching in water reed
Rose Tree Farm & combed wheat reed
29 Nine Mile Ride 0734 734203 including repairs,
Finchampstead patching & re-ridging
Wokingham
Berkshire RG11 4QD

McDonald's Mr P Sullivan Quick service food
11-59 High Road restaurant
East Finchley 081 883 6400
London N2 8AW

Metro-Rod plc Mr J L B Harris Domestic & industrial
Metro House drain & pipe cleaning &
Churchill Way 0625 434444 allied work
Macclesfield
Cheshire SK11 6AY

Mixamate Holdings Ltd Mr P Slinn Specialized concrete
11 Westdown delivery service to
Great Bookham 0372 456714 builders & DIY
Surrey KT23 4LJ

Molly Maid UK Mr M Tall Domestic cleaning
Hamilton Road services
Slough 0753 523388/
Berkshire SL1 4QY 535343

Motabitz (Franchising) Ltd 27-37 Craven Street Northampton NN1 3EZ	Mr K G Oliver 0604 231777	Supply of workshop consumables & maintenance material to industrial units from fleet of custom fitted out sales vans
Nationwide Investigations 86 Southwark Bridge Road London SE1 0EX	Mr S Withers 071 928 1799	Private investigations bureau
Northern Dairies Ltd Raines House Denby Dale Road Wakefield WF1 1HR	Mr D Cafferty 0924 290808	The manufacture, processing, packaging, marketing & distribution of milk & dairy produce
Olivers (UK) Ltd 7 Melville Terrace Stirling FK8 2ND	Mr N H Allen 0786 472670	Bakery & coffee shops
Panic Link plc Control Station Centre Melbourne Road Lount Leicestershire LE65 1PL	Mr E T Norman 0530 411111	Collection and delivery of parcels nationwide on a next day economy and data basis
PDC Copyprint 1 Church Lane East Grinstead West Sussex RH19 3AZ	Mr M Marks 0342 315321	Quick printing shops
Perfect Pizza Units 5 & 6 The Forum Hanworth Lane Chertsey Surrey KT16 9JZ	Mr M Clayton 0932 568000	Restaurants & take away units
PizzaExpress Ltd Unit 7 McKay Trading Estate Kensal Road London W10 5BN	Mr L Johnson 081 960 8238	Pizzeria restaurants
Practical Car & Van **Rental** 21/23 Little Broom Street Camp Hill Birmingham B12 0EU	Mr B Agnew 021 772 8599	Used car rental

Prontaprint Ltd
Coniscliffe House
Coniscliffe Road
Darlington DL3 7EX

Mr M Spence

0325 483333

Fast print centres
incorporating artwork &
design, commercial
copying & business
communications services

Recognition Express Ltd
Sketchley Business Group
PO Box 7 Rugby Road
Hinckley
Leicestershire LE10 2NE

Mr T A Holworth

0455 238133

Manufacture & sale of
personalized name
badges, interior &
exterior signage vehicle
livery, trophies &
awards

Saks Hair (Holdings) Ltd/
Command Performance
2 Peel Court
St Cuthberts Way
Darlington
Co Durham DL1 1GB

Mr D
Cheesebrough

0325 380333

Ladies' & gentlemen's
hairdressing

Safeclean International
(D G Cook Ltd)
10 Blacklands Way
Abingdon Business Park
Marcham Road
Abingdon
Oxon OX14 1DY

Mr A M Salmon

0235 833022

Hand cleaning of
carpets & upholstery,
curtain cleaning on site

Safeway Motoring School
Ltd
14 Manilla Road
Clifton
Bristol BS8

Mr A Otten

0275 392582

Motoring school

ServiceMaster Ltd
ServiceMaster House
Leicester Road
Anstey
Leicester LE7 7AT

Mr D Rudge

0533 364646

Professional cleaning
services for commercial,
domestic & insurance
customers. Furnishing
and carpet repairs &
restoration

Snap-on-Tools
Palmer House
150-154 Cross Street
Sale
Cheshire M33 1AQ

Mr T Barcham

061 969 0126

Distribution of
automotive hand tools

Snappy Snaps Franchises Ltd 12 Glenthorne Mews Glenthorne Road London W6 0LJ	Mr T MacAndrews 081 741 7474	One hour developing & printing of films, photographic services & associated products
Spud U Like Ltd 34/38 Standard Road London NW10 6EU	Mr T Schleisinger 081 965 0182	Fast food restaurants based on baked potatoes with large variety of fillings
Swinton Insurance Swinton House 6 Gt Marlborough St Manchester M1 5SW	Mr P Lowe 061 236 1222	Insurance brokers
Thorntons J W Thornton Ltd Thornton Park Somercotes Derby DE55 4XJ	Mr R E Smith 0773 608822	Specialist chocolate & sugar confectionery
Toni & Guy 14 Brentford Business Centre Commerce Road Brentford Middlesex TW8 8LG	Mr T Bellamy 081 569 9196	Hairdressing
Travail Employment Group Ltd 24 Southgate Street Gloucester GL1 2DP	Ms P Zwar 0452 307645	Business employment agency
Trust Parts Unit 7 Groundwell Industrial Estate Crompton Road Swindon Wiltshire SN2 5AG	Mr R Bourne 0793 723749	Engineering workshop & maintenance department. Consumable materials & hand tools supplied direct to users by mobile shops
Unigate Dairies Ltd 14/40 Victoria Road Aldershot Hampshire GU1 1TH	Mr D Swainsbury 0252 24522	Distribution of milk & dairy products & soft drinks

Vantage Chemist
Vantage House
Osborn Way
Hook, Basingstoke
Hampshire RG27 9HX

Mr A C Orme

0252 760076

High quality retail
pharmacies

Vendo plc
215 East Lane
Wembley
Middlesex HA10 3NG

Mr I J Calhoun

081 908 1234

Commercial vehicle
power washing

Wetherby Training Services
Flockton House
Audby Lane
Wetherby
West Yorkshire LS22 7FD

Mr D G Button

0937 583940

Secretarial & word
processing training
centres

Wimpy International Ltd
2 The Listons
Liston Road
Marlow
Buckinghamshire SL7 1FD

M M Woolfenden

0628 891655

Family hamburger
restaurant

**Legal & General Estate
Agency**
4 Bruntcliffe Way
Morley
Leeds LS27 0JG

Ms G Hynaston

0532 539166

Residential Estate
Agency, Life &
Pensions Insurance

British Franchise Association

ASSOCIATE MEMBERS LIST

Franchisors are required to submit a completed application form, including disclosure document, franchise agreement, prospectus, accounts, etc; and provide proof of a correctly constituted pilot scheme successfully operated for at least one year, financed and managed by the applicant company (as for Full Membership) but with evidence of successful franchising for a period of one year with at least one franchisee.

In addition, substantial companies with more than 25 company-owned outlets offering a franchise concept which is a replica of the existing business, with a separate franchise division, correctly constructed agreement, pilot scheme, prospectus, and accounts but without a franchisee on station at the time of application, will also be eligible under this category.

A & B Window Centres Ltd Martin Close Blenheim Ind Estate Bulwell Nottingham NG6 8UW	Mr P Mycock 0602 794977	Sale & installation of replacement windows, doors, conservatories, patio doors, porches, leaded lights, coloured glass design.
Apollo Despatch Apollo House 28-30 Hoxton Square London N1 6NN	Mr N Grossman 071 739 8444	Urgent courier & delivery service

Card Connection
Park House
South Street
Farnham
Surrey GU9 7QQ

Mr S Hulme

0252 733177

Greeting card publisher distributing through network of franchisees

Cico Chimney Linings Ltd
Westleton
Saxmundham
Suffolk IP17 3BS

Mr R J Hadfield

0728 73608

The re-lining of domestic & industrial chimneys

Coffeeman Management Ltd
9 Cedar Park, Cobham Road
Ferndown Industrial Estate
Wimborne, Dorset BH21 7SB

Mr B Hardiman

0202 896696

Selling of fresh ground coffee, tea machinery

Duty Driver
42a Station Road
Twyford
Berkshire RG10 9NT

Mr T B Bedford

0734 320200

Chauffeur services

First Call
Chandos Mews
34B Chandos Road
Redland
Bristol BS6 6PF

Mr C N Greaves

0272 232525

Property maintenance & 24 hour emergency repair

Future Training Services
The Old Mill
Northgrove Road
Hawkhurst
Kent TN18 4AP

Mr M Meakings

0580 752619

Secretarial & business skills training centre

Garage Door Associates Ltd
Unit 5 Meadow Brook
Industrial Centre
Maxwell Way
Crawley
West Sussex RH10 2SA

Mr G Danes

0293 611598

Retail sale and installation of garage doors, electric garage door operators, gates and gate openers, ancillary equipment

Hoseman Ltd
4 Archers Court
Stukeley Road
Huntingdon
Cambridgeshire PE18 6XG

Mr R M Edwards

0480 436676

Mobile on site hydraulic hose replacement service

House of Colour
28 The Avenue
Watford
WD1 3NS

Ms L Elvey

0923 211188

Personalized colour &
style consultancy with
related product sales &
service

Jani-King
Bridge House
3 Heron Square
Richmond
Surrey TW9 1EN

Mr P Howorth

081 332 7474

Contract cleaning

Jet Cleen Ltd
PO Box 44
Dunstable
Bedfordshire LU6 2QT

Mr P H Lloyd

0582 873530

Mobile pressure cleaning
service to transport &
distribution industry

Lambourn Court
International plc
The Manor Barn
Keysoe
Bedfordshire MK44 2HR

Mr D M Hinds

0234 708848

Stress management
consultancies

Master Brew
Beverages House
7 Ember Centre
Hersham Trading Estate
Hersham
Surrey KT12 3PT

Mr P Youngman

0932 253787

Supplying ground coffees
& a complete beverage
range to offices &
caterers

M & B Marquees Ltd
Premier House
Tennyson Drive
Pitsea, Basildon
Essex S13 3BT

Mr J Mansfield

0268 558002

Hire of marquees and
ancilliary equipment

Merryweathers
109 Hersham Road
Walton-on-Thames
Surrey KT12 1RN

Mr R Taylor

0932 248205

Fish & chip restaurant
and take-away

Minster Cleaning Services
Minster House
948-952 Kingsbury Road
Erdington
Birmingham B24 9PZ

Mr A Haigh

021 386 1186

Management of contract
office cleaning services

Nevada Bob (UK) Ltd Mr K Norman Golf retailing
The Rotunda
Broadgate Circle 071 628 4999
London EC2M 2QS

One Stop Community Stores Mr M Taylor Convenience stores
Ltd
Raeburn House 0705 267321
Hulbert Road
Waterlooville
Hants PO7 7JT

Paco (Life In Colour) Ms J Flannery Retailer of colourful
Kirkshaws Road fashion, knitwear,
Coatbridge 0236 449066 casualwear and
Glasgow ML5 4SL accessories for adults and
children

Pandel Tiles Mr D J Stanton Marketing ceramic tiles
Units 37-38 Forge Lane to the trade & public
Minworth Industrial Park 021 313 1990
Sutton Coldfield
West Midlands B76 8AH

Posh Windows & Mr P Vaughan Conservatories &
Conservatories replacement windows
1184 Lincoln Road 0733 322888
Werrington
Peterborough
Cambs

Segal & Sons Mr I Segal Sale of curtain
Stockholm Road furnishings, blinds &
Suttonfields Industrial 0482 835452 ancillary items
Estate
Hull HU8 0XW

Signs Express Mr D Corbett Sign makers
25 Kingsway
Norwich NR2 4UE 0603 762680

Sinclair Collis Mr K Simcox The supply of tobacco
Lower Walsall Street products vending
Wolverhampton 0902 352515 machines
West Midlands WV1 2ES

Stained Glass Overlay
23 Hurricane Way
Norwich
Norfolk NR6 0LJ

Mr S Lawrence

0603 485454

Design, sale &
manufacture of simulated
stained glass

Tune-Up
23 High Street
Bagshot
Surrey GU19 5AF

Mr A Stevens

0276 451199

Car engine tuning service
at customer's home

Ventrolla Ltd
51 Tower Street
Harrogate
North Yorkshire HG1 1HS

Mr R W Tunnicliff

0423 567004

Renovating and
performance upgrading
of existing windows using
patented system

British Franchise Association

PROVISIONAL LISTING

Provisional Listing is available for those companies developing their franchise concept and who are taking accredited professional advice on its structure.

AIMS Partnership plc
24 Red Lion Street
London WC1R 4SA

Mr H Ejdelbaum

071 831 0775

Accountancy, bookkeeping and business advisory services

Alfonso's International Ltd
3 Yeomans Way
Camberley
Surrey GU15 2HG

Mr P J Smith

0276 684915

Ice cream parlours

Arby's (Bien Cuit Restaurants Ltd)
24 The Haymarket
London SW1Y 4DG

Mr R Aiyash

071 930 7171

Quick service restaurant

Ashby's
658 The Crescent
Colchester Business Park
Colchester
Essex CO4 2YB

Mr D Barrett

0206 851500

Sale & distribution of tea & coffee to the catering, hospitality & leisure industry

Autosheen Ltd
21/25 Sanders Road
Finedon Road Estate
Wellingborough
Northamptonshire NN8 4NL

Mr G Bullock

0933 272347

Automotive mobile valeting

Blacks Unisport Ltd
Woodleigh,
Whitebrook Lane
Peasdown St John
Nr Bath
Avon BA2 8LD

Mr M Colgan

0761 437567

Branded sportswear
distribution

Choices Video Plus
The Home Entertainment
Corporation plc
19-23 Manesty Road
Peterborough PE2 0UP

Mr J M Sealey

0733 233464

Video hire & sale

Country Style Inns
Country Trust
Ryton House
46A Park Street
Luton
Beds LU1 3ET

Mr I Glyn

0582 457552

Retail catering in
licensed premises

Decorating Den
Bowditch Industrial Estate
Longbridge
Membury
Axminster
Devon EX13 7TY

Mrs S Bell

0404 881789

Van based interior design
service

Direct Express Parcels Ltd
Unit 4 Maybrook Road
Stratford upon Avon
CV37 0BT

Mr L R Valentine

0789 296893

Parcels delivery company

Delifrance
166 Bute Street Mall
Arndale Centre
Luton
Beds LU1 2TL

Mr M J B Ward

0582 422781

Bakery & restaurant

Duds 'N Suds
141 Strand Road
Londonderry
Northern Ireland
BT48 7PB

Mr E Nicell

0504 262615

Laundromats

Eismann International Ltd
Margarethe House
Eismann Way
Phoenix Park Ind Estate
Corby
Northants NN17 1ZB

Mr K Buelles

0536 407010

Home delivery of frozen
foods

Formative Fun Ltd
33 South Street
Bridport
Dorset DT6 3NY

Mrs J P Warren

0308 421811

The marketing of
educational toys, games
& books in an advisory
capacity

Greencare Ltd
The Old Saw Mill
Sharpness
Glos GL13 9UN

Mr M Macleod

0453 511366

The collection of printer
consumables & the sale
of recycled & branded
laser printer consumables

The Indian Cavalry Club
3 Atholl Place
Edinburgh EH3 8HP

Mr S Chowdhury

031 228 3282

Restaurant

Mail Boxes Etc
84 Marylebone High Street
London W1M 3DE

Ms S Lang

071 935 9411

Business, postal &
communications services

Neilsen Direct
Stanhope Road
Swadicote
Derbyshire DE11 9BE

Mr C P Gater

0283 221044

Cleaning materials for
the car & van industry

Paverprint
The Old Coach House
Newnham Manor
The Street
Crowmarsh, Wallingford
Oxon OX10 8EH

Mr N Inwood

0491 825415

Installation of decorative
pattern inprinted
concrete paving

Pret a Manger
Old Mitre Court
43 Fleet Street
London EC4Y 1BT

Mr T A Abbott

071 827 6301

High quality sandwich
shops

Pronuptia Youngs Ltd
Metcalf Drive
Altham
Accrington
Lancashire BB5 5TU

Mr P Ford

0282 772577

Retailer of bridal wear,
hire and retail of
gentlemen's formal wear

Re-Nu
17 High Way
Broadstone
Dorset BH18 9NB

Mr J Elkins

0202 687642

Replacement kitchen &
bedroom made to
measure doors and allied
accessories

226

Ribbon Revival Caslon Court Pitronnerie Road Estate St Peter Port Guernsey	Mr C Carnachan 0481 729552	Remanufacturing & recycling of office & computer printing consumables
Salisbury Consulting Group 15-17 The Broadway Old Hatfield Herts AL9 5HZ	Mr R J Unger 0707 264311	Training
Screen Savers The Thatched House Hollybank Road West Byfleet Surrey KT14 6JD	Mr C Bechgaard 0932 355177	Repair of windscreens on motor vehicles
Securicor Pony Express 2 & 3 Alexander Terrace Liverpool Gardens Worthing West Sussex BN11 1YH	Mr A J Mundella 0903 821111	Same day and overnight express parcels courier
Tele-Pages Directories Ltd Tele-Pages House 8A High Street Marlborough Wiltshire SN8 1AA	Ms D McCarthy 0672 515551	Directory Publishing
The Oscar Business Bannister Hall Mill Higher Walton Preston Lancashire PR5 4DB	Mr M Dancy 0772 626789	Pet food home delivery
The Tanning Shop 35 Albermarle Street Mayfair London W1X 3FB	Mr D Jennings 071 493 0904	Solarium

Useful Contacts

SOLICITORS SPECIALIZING IN FRANCHISING

Addleshaw Sons & Latham   Mr G Lindrup   061 832 5994
Dennis House
Marsden Street
Manchester M2 1KD

Bristows Cooke & Carpmael   Mr M Anderson   071 242 0462
10 Lincoln Inn Fields
London WC2A 3BP

Brodies   Mr J C A Voge   031 228 3777
15 Atholl Crescent
Edinburgh EH3 8HA

Burstows   Mrs C Armitage   0293 534734
8 Ifield Road
Crawley
West Sussex RH11 7YY

Church Adams Tatham & Co   Mr B J Haynes   0737 240111
Chatham Court
Lesbourne Road
Reigate
Surrey RH2 7FN

Church Adams Tatham & Co   Mr D Houlton   071 242 0841
Fulwood House
Fulwood Place
London WC1V 6HR

David Bigmore & Co Glade House 52/54 Carter Lane London EC4V 5EA	Mr D Bigmore Member BFA Legal Committee	071 329 6656
Dibb Lupton Broomhead 117 The Headrow Leeds LS1 5JX	Mrs W A Harrison Patent & Trade Mark: Dr M R Harrison	0532 439301
Dibb Lupton Broomhead Alban Gate 125 London Wall London EC2Y 5AE	Mr M R Swindell	071 600 0202
Dibb Lupton Broomhead (formerly Needham & James) Windsor House Temple Row Birmingham B2 5LF	Mr P Heatherington	021 200 1188
Dibb Lupton Broomhead Carlton House 18 Albert Square Manchester M2 5PG	Mr M S Serfozo	061 839 2266
Dibb Lupton Broomhead Fountain Precinct Balm Green Sheffield S1 1RZ	Mr N L Thompson	0742 760351
Donne Mileham & Haddock 42/46 Frederick Place Brighton East Sussex BN1 1AT	Mr A J Trotter	0273 329833
Eversheds Holland Court The Close Norwich NR1 4DX	Mr J Chambers	0603 272727
Eversheds London Scottish House 24 Mount Street Manchester M2 3DB	Mr J Boardman	061 832 6666

Field Fisher Waterhouse   Mr M Abell   071 481 4841
41 Vine Street   Member BFA Legal
London EC4N 2AA   Committee

Hopkins & Wood   Mr K O'Connor   071 404 0475
203 Cursitor Street
London EC4A 1NE

Howard Jones & Company   Mr G Howard Jones   051 632 3411
32 Market Street
Hoylake
Wirral
Merseyside

Jaques & Lewis   Mr M Mendelsohn   071 919 4500
Senator House   Legal Consultant
85 Queen Victoria Street   to the British
London EC4V 4JL   Franchising
Association
Member BFA Legal
Committee

Steven Kenton & Co   Steve Kenton   081 343 1300
Euro House
131-133 Ballards Lane
Finchley
London N3 1LJ

Lawrence Tucketts   Mr R M Staunton   0272 295295
Bush House
72 Prince Street
Bristol BS99 7JZ

Leathes Prior   Mr R J Chadd   0603 610911
74 The Close
Norwich
Norfolk NR1 4DR

Levy & Macrae   Mr A Caplan   041 307 2311
266 St Vincent Street
Glasgow G2 5RL

Mundays   Mr M Ishani   0372 467272
Crown House   Member BFA Legal
Church Road   Committee
Claygate
Esher
Surrey KT10 0LP

Owen White Senate House 62-70 Bath Road Slough Berkshire SL1 3SR	Mr A Bates Legal Adviser to the British Franchise Association Member BFA Legal Committee	0753 536846 Fax: 0753 691360
Paisner & Co Bouverie House 154 Fleet Street London EC4A 2DQ	Mr J S Schwarz	071 353 0299
Payne Marsh Stillwell 6 Carlton Crescent Southampton Hampshire S01 2EY	Mr G H Sturgess	0703 223957
Peters & Peters 2 Harewood Place Hanover Square London W1R 9HB	Mr R Cannon Member BFA Legal Committee	071 629 7991
Pinsent & Co 3 Colmore Circus Birmingham B4 6BH	Mr J Pratt Member BFA Legal Committee	021 200 1050
Pinsent & Co Royex House Aldermanbury Square London EC2V 7HR	Mr A Farkas	071 600 4999
Ross & Craig Swift House 12A Upper Berkeley Street London W1H 7PE	Mr J Horne	071 262 3077
Wragge & Co 55 Colmore Row Birmingham B2 5JY	Mr G D Harris	021 233 1000

PATENT & TRADE MARK AGENTS

Ladas & Parry 52-54 High Holborn London WC1V 6RR	Mr I C Baillie	071 242 5566

Member New York Bar and UK Chartered Patent and Trademark Agent.

International franchise law and intellectual property (eg trademarks, copyright) law.

CHARTERED ACCOUNTANTS

BDO Binder Hamlyn   Mr N Craig   041 248 3761
Ballantine House
168 West George Street
Glasgow G2 2PT

Fraser & Russell   Mr R J Mitchell   0737 765451
Albany House
128 Station Road
Redhill
Surrey RH1 1ET

Rees Pollock   Mr W A J Pollock   071 329 6404
7 Pilgrim Street
London EC4V 6DR

Kidsons Impey   Mr D V Collins   0245 269595
Carlton House
31-34 Railway Street
Chelmsford
Essex CM1 1NJ

Menzies   Mr T M Gale   0932 247611
Ashby House
64 High Street
Walton on Thames
Surrey KT12 1BW

EXHIBITION ORGANIZERS

Blenheim Events   Mr S. Thomas   081 742 2828
Blenheim House
630 Chiswick High Road
London W4 5BG

CII Exhibitions   Mr Mel Stride   071 727 7380
105 Lancaster Road
London W11 1QF

MEDIA & COMMUNICATIONS

Business Franchise Magazine Newspaper House Tannery Lane Penketh Cheshire WA5 2UD	Mrs L Lister	0925 724326
Evening Standard Business Options	Danielle Baillieu	081 445 7161/ 071 937 9244
Daily Mail	Margaret Stone/ Wayne Asher	071 938 6000
The Daily Express	Mr I Murray Ms M Nugent	071 928 8000

FRAUD INVESTIGATION

Robert Child LL.B 342 Upper Richmond Road West London SW14 7JR	Mr R Child	081 878 1498

BANKERS

Barclays Bank plc Business Sector Marketing Dept PO Box 120 Longwood Close Westwood Business Park Coventry CV4 8JN	Mr N J Wright	0203 694242
Lloyds Bank plc Retail Banking UKRB PO Box 112 Canon's Way Bristol BS99 7LB	Mr R W Hinds	0272 433138
Midland Bank plc Franchise Unit Midland Enterprise 41 Silver Street Head Sheffield S1 3GG	Mrs C Hayes	0742 529037

**National Westminster Bank
plc**
Commercial Banking
Services
Franchise Section
Level 10 Drapers Gardens
12 Throgmorton Avenue
London EC2N 2DL

Mr P Stern

071 920 5966

**The Royal Bank of
Scotland plc**
Franchise and Licensing
Department
PO Box 31
42 St Andrew Square
Edinburgh EH2 2YE

Mr G Rose

031 556 8555

FRANCHISE CONSULTANTS

David Acheson Partnership
7 Pilgrim Street
London EC4V 6DR

Mr D Acheson

071 329 6404

Danielle Baillieu
Lincoln House
661 High Road
London N12 0DZ

Danielle Baillieu

081 445 7161

Ernst & Young
Rolls House
7 Rolls Buildings
Fetter Lane
London EC4A 1NH

Dr B Smith

071 931 1952

**FMM Consultants
International Limited**
46/48 Thornhill Road
Streetly
Sutton Coldfield
West Midlands B74 3EH

Mr M Matthews

021 353 0031/2

**FMM Consultants
International Limited**
24 Cairnmuir Road
Edinburgh EH12 6LP

Mr A H James

031 334 8040

FMM Consultants   Mr J Gooderham   0293 535453
International Limited
27 Brighton Road
Crawley
RH10 3NW

Stoy Hayward Franchising   Mr I Harvey   071 486 5888
Services
8 Baker Street
London W1M 1DA

The Hambleden Group   Mr B Duckett   071 930 6446
39 Pall Mall
London SW1Y 5JG

Peter Williams   Mr P Williams   0203 329260
22 Norfolk Crescent
Nuneaton
Warwickshire CV10 8BY

BRITISH FRANCHISE ASSOCIATION

British Franchise   0491 578049/50
Association (BFA)
Thames View,
Newtown Road,
Henley-on-Thames,
Oxon RG9 1HG

Business information and organizations

Association of British Chambers of Commerce	4 Westwood House Westwood Business Park Coventry CV4 8HS	0203 694484
Business Statistics Office	Cardiff Road Newport Gwent NP1 1XG	0633 815696
Chartered Association of Certified Accountants	29 Lincoln's Inn Fields, London WC2A 3EE	071 242 6855
Companies House	Crown Way Maindy Cardiff CF4 3UZ	0222 380801
Consumers' Association	2 Marylebone Road London NW1 4DF	071 486 5544
Data Protection Registrar	Wycliffe House Water Lane Wilmslow Cheshire SK9 5AF	0625 535777
The Marketing Guild Ltd	Unit 1, Houghton Court Houghton Regis Beds LU5 5DY	0582 861556
Department of Trade and Industry	123 Victoria Street London SW1E 6RB	071 215 5000
Federation of Small Businesses	140 Lower Marsh Westminster Bridge London SE1 7AE	071 928 9272

HMSO Publications Centre	PO Box 276 London SW8 5DT	071 873 9090
Inland Revenue	Somerset House The Strand London WC2 1LB	071 438 6622

*A free video and booklet is available for people about to start in business,
from any of the Inland Revenue's 400 tax enquiry offices*

Institute of Chartered Accountants of England and Wales	PO Box 433 Chartered Accountants Hall Moorgate Place London EC2P 2BJ	071 920 8100
Institute of Chartered Accountants of Scotland	27 Queen Street Edinburgh EH2 1LA	031 225 5673
National Federation of the Self-Employed and Small Businesses	32 St Anne's Road West Lytham St Anne's Lancashire FY8 1NY	0253 720911
National Market Traders' Federation	Hampton House Hawshaw Lane Hoyland Barnsley S74 0HA	0226 749021
Office of Fair Trading	Field House Breams Buildings London EC4A 1PR	071 242 2858
Small Business Bureau	Suite 46 Westminster Palace Gardens Artillery Row London SW1P 1RR	0276 452010
Association of Independent Businesses	26 Addison Place London W11 4RJ	071 371 1299
Rural Development Commission	141 Castle Street Salisbury Wiltshire SP1 3TP	0722 336255
DTI Loan Guarantee Section	Level 2, St Mary's House c/o Moorfoot Sheffield S1 4PQ	0742 597308/9

HM Customs & Excise	New King's Beam House	071 626 1515
	22 Upper Ground	
	London SE1 9PJ	

Department of Social	Richmond House	071 210 5983
Security	79 Whitehall	
	London SW1A 2NS	

Forms FB30, NP18 and N127A all relate to self-employment

Index